THE INVISIBLE HOOK

THE INVISIBLE HOOK

The Hidden Economics of Pirates

PETER T. LEESON

PRINCETON UNIVERSITY PRESS
Princeton & Oxford

Published by Princeton University Press,
41 William Street, Princeton, New Jersey 08540
In the United Kingdom: Princeton University Press,
6 Oxford Street, Woodstock, Oxfordshire OX20 1TW

Library of Congress Cataloging-in-Publication Data

Leeson, Peter T., 1979–
    The invisible hook : the hidden economics of pirates / Peter T. Leeson.
        p.   cm.
    Includes bibliographical references and index.
    ISBN 978-0-691-13747-6 (hardcover : alk. paper)   1. Pirates—
History—Economic aspects.   2. Economics.   I. Title.
    G535.L44 2009
    330—dc22   2008049639

British Library Cataloging-in-Publication Data is available

This book has been composed in Gotham and Arno Pro

Printed on acid-free paper. ∞

press.princeton.edu

Printed in the United States of America

10 9 8 7 6 5 4 3 2 1

Ania, I love you; will you marry me?

Little Villains oft' submit to Fate,
That Great Ones may enjoy the World in State.
—Sir Samuel Garth, *The Dispensary*, 1699

Let not his mode of raising cash seem strange,
    Although he fleeced the flags of every nation,
For into a prime minister but change
    His title, and 'tis nothing but taxation.
—Lord Byron, *Don Juan*, canto III, stanza 14, 1821

CONTENTS

ILLUSTRATIONS

'm not a historian. Nor am I a pirate. I'm an economist with a long-standing interest in privately created law and order who happened to wonder one day how pirates cooperated since they had no government. Like many others, my interest in pirates goes back many years. I went to Disney World when I was eight; *Pirates of the Caribbean* was my favorite ride. My parents bought me a "silver" skull ring with "ruby" eyes from the *Pirates of the Caribbean* gift shop. I think I still have it, and I'd probably wear it if it still fit. A few years later my parents went on vacation in the Caribbean. They brought me back a carved pirate "coconut head." I loved it and used the pirate head as a still life for drawings with colored pencils. Some of these drawings are still in existence. They're not highly sought after, but I believe they should be.

My academic interest in pirates didn't emerge until much later. Several years ago I read Captain Johnson's *General History of the Pyrates* and was enthralled. Soon after, I read everything else on the history of pirates I could find. It was all fantastic but seemed to be missing something crucial. That something was economics.

My interest in economics is nearly as old as my interest in pirates and runs even deeper. I have a supply and demand tattoo on my right bicep. I got it when I was seventeen. This book is the marriage between these two great passions of mine, economics

and pirates. I hope you enjoy the result. I certainly enjoyed producing it. I think writing this book was the most "academic fun"
I've ever had and I only work on projects I find fun in the first
place.

As I mentioned above, I'm not a historian. This has undoubtedly impaired my study of pirates in one way or another. I hope
historians will forgive me if I've gotten some piece of the history wrong. I've done my best to avoid this. Working on pirates,
of course, means working with historical records. I wasn't
"trained" to do this. My comparative advantage isn't historical
method but rather bringing economics to the table. I hope this
skill—the ability to "filter" the historical record through the
"lens" of economics—makes up for my lack of historical training. I've tried to be as careful as possible throughout this book
in indicating where this "filtering" process provides only specu-
lative results. Importantly, this speculation emerges because of
the incompleteness of the historical record (or my understanding of it), not from a deficiency of economics. Despite the in-
conclusiveness in certain cases, I'm convinced economics brings
us much closer to the "correct answers" than the history does
alone, or than the history would if filtered through some non-
economic lens.

Several people besides me were critical to writing this book.
First and most important is my girlfriend, Ania Bulska. She's
been a constant source of encouragement, a superb sounding
board for ideas, and a tireless research assistant helping me re-
trieve historical documents and surrendering hours of her free
time photographing records from the Manuscript Reading
Room in the Madison Building at the Library of Congress. She
even helped gather the images in this book. I can't thank her
enough and, as with everything, I don't know where I'd be without her. In this book's dedication I ask her to marry me. If I've
succeeded in hiding my plans from her since writing this, she

should be very surprised. I hope she says "yes." If she doesn't, I might have to turn to sea banditry, which would be tough since I don't know how to sail (though I've tried to learn).

I also owe inestimable thanks to Seth Ditchik, my superlative editor. Seth's editorial assistance, comments, suggestions, and guidance throughout the process of writing and putting this manuscript together have been invaluable, and this book is incalculably better because of him. Another individual to whom I'm extremely grateful is Tim Sullivan, formerly an economics editor at Princeton University Press who recently moved to Penguin Books. Tim is the person who originally approached me about writing this book. If not for him, it wouldn't have been written. I wasn't planning on turning my research on the economics of pirates into something longer until he suggested this and gave me the opportunity to do so. I'm also very grateful to the others at PUP who assisted with this project.

I owe special thanks to my mom, Anne Leeson, who read and offered comments on every chapter of this book. I improved the readability of more than a few sections because of her remarks. My close friends and colleagues, Pete Boettke and Chris Coyne, as always, provided extremely helpful comments and advice throughout the preparation of this book, making fun of me along the way where appropriate. They always improve my work and this project was no exception.

Several others also deserve special thanks. Early on, Edward Glaeser encouraged me to write a book on the economics of pirates, which helped me decide to pursue this project. Steven Levitt published my first paper on the economics of pirates in the *Journal of Political Economy*, which was a risky move since I have no established name and the article doesn't contain a single equation or regression. I'm extremely grateful to Professor Levitt for his willingness to take this risk and for giving my paper a shot even though it doesn't fit the stylistic mold staked out by our profession. This paper, entitled, "An-*arrgh*-chy: The Law and Economics of Pirate Organization" (University of Chicago Press, 2007), formed the basis of many of the discussions in chapters 2 and 3. I thank University of Chicago Press for allowing me to reuse parts of it. Similarly, I thank the *New York University Journal of Law and Liberty* for allowing me to reuse portions of my paper "The Invisible Hook: The Law and Economics of Pirate Racial Tolerance" (*NYU Journal of Law and Liberty*, 2009) in chapter 7.

Andrei Shleifer, on this project as on many of my others, has been a source of superb suggestions and encouragement, and I'm extremely thankful for his support. A number of others have also offered helpful comments and criticisms along the way. Three anonymous referees provided useful and thorough comments on an earlier draft of this book. Others deserving special thanks include Tyler Cowen, James Hohman, Ben Powell, Bill Reece, Russ Sobel, Virgil Storr, Werner Troesken, Bill Trumbull, and especially David Friedman. I also thank Kate Huleatt, Chris Werner, and Robert Wille for helping me gain access to difficult-to-find historical records crucial to this project. Doug Rogers provided particularly helpful research assistance in combing through eighteenth-century newspaper articles and helping me negotiate other obstacles I confronted. Finally, I thank the Earhart Foundation and Mercatus Center at George Mason University for their generous financial support without which I couldn't have afforded to write this book.

It's common to tell the reader that while the acknowledged individuals and organizations are responsible for the "good" parts of the work they're about to consume, these individuals and organizations aren't responsible for any of the work's mistakes. That's also true for this book. Though, I'd like to suggest to the reader that if he or she wanted to apply the reverse standard, I wouldn't at all object.

1 THE INVISIBLE HOOK

Charybdis herself must have spat them into the sea. They committed "a Crime so odious and horrid in all its Circumstances, that those who have treated on that Subject have been at a loss for Words and Terms to stamp a sufficient Ignominy upon it." Their contemporaries called them "*Sea-monsters*," "Hell-Hounds," and "Robbers, Opposers and Violators of all Laws, Humane and Divine." Some believed they were "*Devils* incarnate." Others suspected they were "*Children of the Wicked One*" himself. "Danger lurked in their very Smiles."

For decades they terrorized the briny deep, inspiring fear in the world's most powerful governments. The law branded them *hostes humani generis*—"a sort of People who may be truly called Enemies to Mankind"—and accused them of aiming to "Subvert and Extinguish the Natural and Civil Rights" of humanity. They "declared War against all the World" and waged it in earnest. Motley, murderous, and seemingly maniacal, their mystique is matched only by our fascination with their fantastic way of life. "These Men, whom we term, and not without Reason, the Scandal of human Nature, who were abandoned to all Vice, and lived by Rapine" left a mark on the world that remains nearly three centuries after they left it. They are the pirates, history's most notorious criminals, and this is the story of the hidden force that propelled them—the invisible hook.

Adam Smith, Meet "Captain Hook"

In 1776 Scottish moral philosopher Adam Smith published a landmark treatise that launched the study of modern economics. Smith titled his book, *An Inquiry into the Nature and Causes of the Wealth of Nations*. In it, he described the most central idea to economics, which he called the "invisible hand." The invisible hand is the hidden force that guides economic cooperation. According to Smith, people are self-interested; they're interested in doing what's best for them. However, often times, to do what's best for them, people must also do what's best for others. The reason for this is straightforward. Most of us can only serve our self-interests by cooperating with others. We can achieve very few of our self-interested goals, from securing our next meal to acquiring our next pair of shoes, in isolation. Just think about how many skills you'd need to master and how much time you'd require if you had to produce your own milk or fashion your own coat, let alone manufacture your own car.

Because of this, Smith observed, in seeking to satisfy our own interests, we're led, "as if by an invisible hand," to serve others' interests too. Serving others' interests gets them to cooperate with us, serving our own. The milk producer, for example, must offer the best milk at the lowest price possible to serve his self-interest, which is making money. Indirectly he serves his customers' self-interest, which is acquiring cheap, high-quality milk. And on the other side of this, the milk producers' customers, in their capacity as producers of whatever they sell, must offer the lowest price and highest quality to their customers, and so on. The result is a group of self-interest seekers, each narrowly focused on themselves but also unwittingly focused on assisting others.

Smith's invisible hand is as true for criminals as it is for anyone else. Although criminals direct their cooperation at someone

FIGURE 1.1. Adam Smith: Father of modern economics and the "invisible hand." From Charles Coquelin, *Dictionnaire de l'économie politique*, 1854.

else's loss, if they desire to move beyond one-man mug jobs, they must also cooperate with others to satisfy their self-interests. A one-man pirate "crew," for example, wouldn't have gotten far. To take the massive hauls they aimed at, pirates had to cooperate with many other sea dogs. The mystery is how such a shifty "parcel of rogues" managed to pull this off. And the key to unlocking this mystery is the *invisible hook*—the piratical analog to Smith's invisible hand that describes how pirate self-interest seeking led to cooperation among sea bandits, which this book explores.

The invisible hook differs from the invisible hand in several respects. First, the invisible hook considers criminal self-interest's effect on cooperation in pirate society. It's concerned with how criminal social groups work. The invisible hand, in contrast, considers traditional consumer and producer self-interests' effects on cooperation in the marketplace. It's concerned with how legitimate markets work. If the invisible hand examines the hidden order behind the metaphorical "anarchy of the market," the invisible hook examines the hidden order behind the literal anarchy of pirates.

Second, unlike traditional economic actors guided by the invisible hand, pirates weren't primarily in the business of selling anything. They therefore didn't have customers they needed to satisfy. Further, piratical self-interest seeking didn't benefit wider society, as traditional economic actors' self-interest seeking does. In their pursuit of profits, businessmen, for example, improve our standards of living—they make products that make our lives better. Pirates, in contrast, thrived parasitically off others' production. Thus pirates didn't benefit society by creating wealth; they harmed society by siphoning existing wealth off for themselves.

Despite these differences, pirates, like everyone else, had to cooperate to make their ventures successful. And it was self-interest seeking that led them to do so. This critical feature, common to pirates and the members of "legitimate" society, is what fastens the invisible hook to the invisible hand.

The Invisible Hook applies the "economic way of thinking" to pirates. This way of thinking is grounded in a few straightforward assumptions. First, individuals are self-interested. This doesn't mean they never care about anyone other than themselves. It just means most of us, most of the time, are more interested in benefiting ourselves and those closest to us than we're interested in benefiting others. Second, individuals are rational. This doesn't mean they're robots or infallible. It just means individuals try to achieve their self-interested goals in the best ways they know how. Third, individuals respond to incentives. When the cost of an activity rises, individuals do less of it. When the cost of an activity falls, they do more of it. The reverse is true for the benefit of an activity. When the benefit of an activity rises, we do more it. When the benefit falls, we do less of it. In short, people try to avoid costs and capture benefits.

Economists call this model of individual decision making "rational choice." The rational choice framework not only applies to "normal" individuals engaged in "regular" behavior. It also applies to abnormal individuals engaged in unusual behavior. In particular, it applies to pirates. Pirates satisfied each of the assumptions of the economic way of thinking described above. Pirates, for instance, were self-interested. Material concerns gave birth to pirates and profit strongly motivated them. Contrary to pop-culture depictions, pirates were also highly rational. As we'll examine later in this book, pirates devised ingenious practices—some they're infamous for—to circumvent costs that threatened to eat into their profits and increase the revenue of their plundering expeditions. Pirates also responded to incentives. When the law made it riskier (and thus costlier) to be a pirate, pirates devised clever ways to offset this risk.

When pirates offered crew members rewards for superlative pirating, crew members worked harder to keep a lookout for the next big prize, and so on.

It's not just that economics *can* be applied to pirates. Rational choice is the *only* way to truly understand flamboyant, bizarre, and downright shocking pirate practices. Why, for example, did pirates fly flags with skulls and crossbones? Why did they brutally torture some captives? How were pirates successful? And why did they create "pirate codes"? The answers to these questions lie in the hidden economics of pirates, which only the rational choice framework can reveal. History supplies the "raw material" that poses these questions. Economics supplies the analytical "lens" for finding the answers.

When we view pirates through this lens, their seemingly unusual behavior becomes quite usual. Strange pirate behavior resulted from pirates rationally responding to the unusual economic context they operated in—which generated unusual costs and benefits—not from some inherent strangeness of pirates themselves. As remaining chapters of this book illustrate, a pirate ship more closely resembled a Fortune 500 company than the society of savage schoolchildren depicted in William Golding's *Lord of the Flies*. Peglegs and parrots aside, in the end, piracy was a business. It was a criminal business, but a business nonetheless, and deserves to be examined in this light.

Avast, Ye Scurvy Dogs

Many discussions of pirates use the terms *pirates, buccaneers, privateers,* and *corsairs* interchangeably. There's a reason for this; all were kinds of sea bandits. But each variety of sea bandit was different. Pure pirates were total outlaws. They attacked merchant ships indiscriminately for their own gain. Richard Allein, attorney general of South Carolina, described them this way: "Pirates prey upon all Mankind, and their own Species and Fellow-Creatures, without Distinction of Nations or Religions." Eighteenth-century sea bandits were predominantly this ilk.

Privateers, in contrast, were state-sanctioned sea robbers. Governments commissioned them to attack and seize enemy nations' merchant ships during war. Privateers, then, weren't pirates at all; they had government backing. Similarly, governments sanctioned corsairs' plunder. The difference is corsairs targeted shipping on the basis of religion. The Barbary corsairs of the North African coast, for instance, attacked ships from Christendom. However, there were Christian corsairs as well, such as the Knights of Malta. This book's discussion primarily excludes privateers and corsairs since they typically weren't outlaws.

Buccaneers, in contrast, typically were. The original buccaneers were French hunters living on Hispaniola, modern-day Haiti, in the early seventeenth century. Although they mostly hunted wild game, they weren't opposed to the occasional act of piracy either. In 1630 the buccaneers migrated to Tortuga, a tiny, turtle-shaped island off Hispaniola, which soon attracted English and Dutch rabble as well. Spain officially possessed Hispaniola and Tortuga and wasn't fond of the outlaw settlers. In an effort to drive them away, the Spanish government wiped out the wild animals the hunters thrived on. Instead of leaving, however, the buccaneers began hunting a different sort of game: Spanish shipping.

In 1655 England wrested Jamaica from the Spaniards and encouraged the buccaneers to settle there as a defense against the island's recapture. Buccaneers spent much of their time preying on Spanish ships laden with gold and other cargo sailing between the mother country and Spain's possessions in the Americas. Many of these attacks were outright piracy. But many others were not. Eager to break Spain's monopoly on the New World under the Treaty of Tordesillas (1494), England and France commissioned these sea rovers as privateers to harass Spain. "Buccaneering," then, "was a peculiar blend of piracy and privateering in which the two elements were often indistinguishable." However, since "the aims and means of [buccaneering] operations were clearly piratical," it's standard to treat the buccaneers as pirates, or at least protopirates, which I do in this book.

Although buccaneers weren't pure pirates, they anticipated and influenced pure pirates' organization in the early eighteenth century. Because of this, it's important to draw on them at various points, as I do, throughout my discussion. The same is true of the Indian Ocean pirates operating from about 1690 to 1700. These sea rovers represent a bridge between the more privateerlike buccaneers and the total-outlaw pirates active from 1716 to 1726. In the late seventeenth century, the Indian Ocean pirates, or "Red Sea Men" as their contemporaries sometimes called them, settled on Madagascar and its surrounding islands where they were well situated to prey on Moorish treasure fleets. For the most part, Indian Ocean pirates were pirates plain and simple. But some of them sailed under a veneer of legitimacy, which their successors abandoned completely. While this book covers pirates from about 1670 to 1730, it focuses on the final stage of the great age of piracy (1716–26) when men like Blackbeard, Bartholomew Roberts, and "Calico" Jack Rackam prowled the sea.

Jamaican governor Sir Nicholas Lawes described these sea scoundrels as "banditti of all nations." A sample of seven hundred pirates active in the Caribbean between 1715 and 1725, for example, reveals that 35 percent were English, 25 percent were American, 20 percent were West Indian, 10 percent were Scottish, 8 percent were Welsh, and 2 percent were Swedish,

Dutch, French, and Spanish. Others came from Portugal, Scandinavia, Greece, and East India.

The pirate population is hard to precisely measure but by all accounts was considerable. In 1717 the governor of Bermuda estimated "by a modest computation" that 1,000 pirates plied the seas. In 1718 a different official estimated the pirate population to be 2,000. In 1720 Jeremiah Dummer reported 3,000 active pirates to the Council of Trade and Plantations. And in 1721 Captain Charles Johnson suggested that 1,500 pirates haunted the Indian Ocean alone. Based on these reports and pirate historians' estimates, in any one year between 1716 and 1722 roughly 1,000 to 2,000 sea bandits prowled the pirate-infested waters of the Caribbean, Atlantic Ocean, and Indian Ocean. This may not seem especially impressive. But when you put the pirate population in historical perspective it is. The Royal Navy, for example, employed an average of only 13,000 men in any one year between 1716 and 1726. In a good year, then, the pirate population was more than 15 percent of the navy's. In 1680 the entire population of the North American colonies was less than 152,000. In fact, as late as 1790, when the first national census was taken, only twenty-four places in the United States had populations larger than 2,500.

Many pirates lived together on land bases, such as the one Woodes Rogers went to squelch at New Providence in the Bahamas in 1718. However, the most important unit of pirate society, and the strongest sense in which this society existed, was the polity aboard the pirate ship. Contrary to most people's images of pirate crews, this polity was large. Based on figures from thirty-seven pirate ships between 1716 and 1726, the average crew had about 80 members. Several pirate crews were closer to 120, and crews of 150 to 200 weren't uncommon. Captain Samuel Bellamy's pirate crew, for example, consisted of "200 brisk Men of several Nations." Other crews were even bigger than this. Blackbeard's crew aboard *Queen Anne's Revenge* was 300-men strong. In contrast, the average two-hundred-ton merchant ship in the early eighteenth century carried only 13 to 17 men.

Furthermore, some pirate crews were too large to fit in one ship. In this case they formed pirate squadrons. Captain Bartholomew Roberts, for example, commanded a squadron of four ships that carried 508 men. In addition, pirate crews sometimes joined for concerted plundering expeditions. The most impressive fleets of sea bandits belong to the buccaneers. Buccaneer Alexander Exquemelin, for example, records that Captain Morgan commanded a fleet of thirty-seven ships and 2,000 men, enough to attack communities on the Spanish Main. Elsewhere he refers to a group of buccaneers who "had a force of at least twenty vessels in quest of plunder." Similarly, William Dampier records a pirating expedition that boasted ten ships and 960 men. Though their fleets weren't as massive, eighteenth-century pirates also "cheerfully joined their Brethren in Iniquity" to engage in multicrew pirating expeditions.

Nearly all pirates had maritime backgrounds. Most had sailed on merchant ships, many were former privateers, and some had previously served—though not always willingly—in His or Her Majesty's employ as navy seamen. Based on a sample of 169 early-eighteenth-century pirates Marcus Rediker compiled, the average pirate was 28.2 years old. The youngest pirate in this sample was only 14 and the oldest 50—ancient by eighteenth-century seafaring standards. Most pirates, however, were in their mid-twenties; 57 percent of those in Rediker's sample were between 20 and 30. These data suggest a youthful pirate society with a few older, hopefully wiser, members and a few barely more than children. In addition to being very young, pirate society was also very male. We know of only four women active among eighteenth-century pirates. Pirate society was therefore energetic and testosterone filled, probably similar to a college fraternity only with peglegs, fewer teeth, and pistol dueling instead of wrestling to resolve disputes.

Yo Ho, Yo Ho, a Lucrative Life for Me

Pirate fiction portrays seamen as choosing piracy out of romantic, if misled, ideals about freedom, equality, and fraternity. While greater liberty, power sharing, and unity did prevail aboard pirate ships, as this book describes, these were piratical *means*, used to secure cooperation within pirates' criminal organization, rather than piratical *ends*, as they're often depicted.

This isn't to say idyllic notions never motivated pirates. In his book, *Between the Devil and the Deep Blue Sea*, historian Marcus Rediker considers pirates in the larger context of eighteenth-century life at sea. Rediker persuasively argues that, in part, pirates acted as social revolutionaries in rebellion against the authoritative, exploitative, and rigidly hierarchical organization of pre–Industrial Revolution "state capitalism." Others have suggested pirates may have acted partially out of concerns for greater racial and sexual equality.

Despite this, most sailors who became pirates did so for a more familiar reason: money. In this sense, though its popular treatment is riddled with myths, the traditional emphasis on "pirate treasure" is appropriate. Sea marauding could be a lucrative business. When, during war, would-be pirates could work as legalized sea bandits on privateers, they often did. During the War of the Spanish Succession (1701–14), for instance, English sailors happily cruised on private men-of-war. Shipowners and government took a cut of privateers' booty; but a successful voyage could still earn sailors a substantial sum. Britain's Prize Act of 1708 sweetened the pot for these sailors by granting them and their shipowners the full value of their captures, government generously foregoing its share. Privateering was thus a desirable option when war was raging. But when it wasn't, privateering commissions dried up. What was a sea dog to do?

One possibility was to seek employment in the Royal Navy. But at conflicts' end the Royal Navy let sailors go. It wasn't interested in hiring them. The year before the War of the Spanish Succession concluded, for instance, the British Navy employed nearly 50,000 sailors. Just two years later it employed fewer than 13,500 men. Most sailors' only other legitimate maritime option was the merchant marine. This was fine for those who no longer had a taste for sea banditry and didn't mind taking a pay cut. But it posed a problem for those who did. Between 1689 and 1740 the average able seaman's monthly wage varied from 25 to 55 shillings; that's £15 to £33 a year, or about $4,000 to $8,800 in current U.S. dollars. The high end of this range was during war years when privateers and the navy bid sailor wages up. The low end was during peace years when hordes of ex-privateer and navy seamen flooded the labor market searching for jobs. A privateer, or even a merchant seaman, who had become accustomed to higher wages during war couldn't have been pleased about his pay falling by half when war ended.

Then there was piracy. Piracy had several advantages over working on a merchant ship. For one, it allowed ex-privateers to continue in the trade they knew best—sea banditry. Several pirate contemporaries understood this draw and feared an explosion of piracy following peace precisely because privateers provided a sort of pirate training ground during war. As Captain Johnson put it, "Privateers in Time of War are a Nursery for Pyrates against a Peace." Another man close to pirates, the venerable Reverend Cotton Mather, noted this as well. As Mather put it, "The Privateering Stroke, so easily degenerates into the Piratical." Other pirate contemporaries identified the increase in sailor unemployment after government recalled privateers when war ended as the root problem. Jamaican governor Sir Nicholas Lawes pointed to this trouble when the short-lived War of the Quadruple Alliance finished in 1720. "Since the calling in of our privateers," Lawes complained, "I find already a considerable number of seafaring men . . . that can't find employment, who I am very apprehensive, for want of occupation in their way, may in a short time desert us and turn pyrates." Lawes was right. Many ex-privateers did, "for want of encouragement" in their former trade, decide to "go a roveing about."

The downside of piratical employment was that, unlike privateer work, piracy was illegal. But the prospect of sufficient gain could compensate for this inconvenience. And piracy could pay extremely well—even better than privateering. Unlike privateers, pirates didn't have pesky shipowners who took a cut of their hard-earned loot. A pirate crew enjoyed every penny of its ship's ill-gotten booty. Although there aren't data to compute the average pirate's wage, the available evidence suggests that, at the very least, piracy offered sailors the opportunity to become incredibly wealthy. "At a time when Anglo-American seamen on a trading voyage to Madagascar were collecting less than twelve pounds sterling a year . . . the deep-water pirates could realize a hundred or even a thousand times more." In 1695, for example, Henry Every's pirate fleet captured a prize carrying more than £600,000 in precious metals and jewels. The resulting share out earned each crew member £1,000, the equivalent of nearly forty years' income for a contemporary able merchant seaman. In the early eighteenth century, Captain John Bowen's pirate crew plundered a prize "which yielded them 500 l. [i.e., pounds] per Man." Several years later, Captain Thomas White's crew retired to Madagascar after a marauding expedition, each pirate £1,200 richer from the cruise. In 1720 Captain Christopher Condent's crew seized a prize that earned each pirate £3,000. Similarly, in 1721, Captain John Taylor's and Oliver La Bouche's pirate consort earned an astonishing £4,000 for each crew member from a single attack. Even the small pirate crew captained by John Evans in 1722 took enough booty to split "nine thousand Pounds among thirty Persons"— or £300 a pirate—in a matter of months "on the account." Not bad considering the alternative, which was toiling on a merchantman for £25 a year.

This evidence must be interpreted with caution, of course. More modest prizes were certainly more common. And many pirates nearly starved searching for the score that would make them rich. Still, unlike employment as a merchant sailor, which guaranteed a low, if regular, income, a single successful pirating expedition could make a sailor wealthy enough to retire. And at least a few pirates did just that. Richard Moore, for example, who a crew of pirates captured and brought to their destination at Réunion, overheard some of Condent's men say "they had got Riches enough (by pirating) to maintain them handsomely as long as they lived & that therefore . . . they had left off pirating." Bartholomew Roberts suggested that sailors who chose legitimate employment over piracy were schlubs. "*In an honest Service*, says he, *there is thin Commons, low Wages, and hard Labour; in this, Plenty and Satiety, Pleasure and Ease, Liberty and Power; and who would not ballance Creditor on this Side, when all the Hazard that is run for it, at worst, is only a sower Look or two at choacking. No, a merry Life and a short one, shall be my Motto.*"

The prospect for substantial booty wasn't the only material concern driving some sailors' choice for piracy over the merchant marine. Ships' working environments played an important role in this decision too. Merchant ships engaged in long-distance trade spent months at sea. An important part of the overall "compensation package" to consider when making employment decisions was therefore what life was like aboard these vessels. Unfortunately for sailors whose timidity or scruples prevented them from entering piracy, sometimes unpleasant, even miserable, working conditions attended merchant ships' relatively low monetary pay.

Merchant ships were organized hierarchically. On top was the captain, below him were his officers, and far below these were ordinary seamen. This hierarchy empowered captains with autocratic authority over their crews. Captains' authority extended to all aspects of life aboard their ships, including labor assignment, victual provision, wage payment, and of course, crew member discipline. The law permitted captains to dock sailors' wages for damaging freight, insolence, or shirking in their duties. It also supported the captain's right to administer "reasonable" corporal punishment to "correct" his sailors. Chapter 2 discusses the reasons for this autocratic organization. Here, I want only to point to its consequence, which was to create significant potential for captain abuse. As British marine commander William Betagh characterized the problem, "unlimited power, bad views, ill nature and ill principles all concurring" "in a ship's commander," "he is past all restraint." The trouble was that merchant captains were tempted to turn their authority against their seamen, preying on them for personal benefit.

Predatory captains cut sailors' victual rations to keep costs down or to leave more for them and their fellow officers to consume. As one sailor testified, for example, although the members of his crew "were att short allowance and wanted bread," the officers "were allowed . . . their full allowance of provisions and liquors as if there had been no want of scarcity of any thing on board." They fraudulently docked sailors' wages or paid in debased colonial currency, and voyaged to locations where their crews hadn't contracted to sail.

To keep their hungry and uncomfortable men in check, abusive captains used all manner of objects aboard their ships as weapons to punish insolent crew members. They hit sailors in the head with tackle or other hard objects, crushing their faces. In some cases captain abuse was so severe it killed sailors. In 1724 one merchant ship captain dealt two of his sailors "above a hundred Blows with a Cane upon & about their Heads, Necks & Shoulders with great force and violence in a very cruel and barbarous manner." A few days later the sailors died. Another abusive captain, "without any provocation, came ... and knock'd" one of his men "down and then stamped upon him twice with all the violence he could." Apparently it was violence enough. Shortly thereafter the sailor expired. Cruelty like this makes Captain Nathaniel Uring's treatment of a "seditious Fellow" on his ship seem downright charitable: "I gave him two or three such Strokes with a Stick I had prepared for that purpose ... the Blood running about his Ears, he pray'd for God's sake that I not kill him."

Some captains used their authority to settle personal scores with crew members. Since Admiralty law considered interfering with punishment mutinous, captains defined when discipline was legitimate. They could therefore abuse targeted seamen at will. Other predatory captains abused their authority in more heinous ways. Captain Samuel Norman ordered one of his ship's boys "to fetch a Pail of Water ... to wash his Leggs, Thighs, & privy Parts." The boy resisted, but Norman compelled him "& whilst he was washing the same, he the said Samuel let down the [boy's] Trousers ... & had the carnal use of him." This wasn't an isolated incident. Captain Norman used the boy "in the same manner" later. Outrageous treatment like this led some sailors to conclude "they had better be dead than live in Misery" under a predatory merchant ship captain.

While the historical record contains plenty of charges of captain predation, it's important to avoid overstating this abuse. Although merchant officers had ample latitude to prey on their crews, this wasn't without limit. Economic and legal factors constrained captain predation to some extent. But none was able to prevent it entirely. English law, for example, created several legal protections designed to insulate sailors from captain predation. To a certain extent these protections were successful. Merchant seamen could and did take predatory captains to court for their actions, many times successfully.

However, as is often the case with the law, many other times it failed. Part of the difficulty stemmed from the uncertainties of the sea. Once afloat in the briny deep, there were rarely impartial spectators to verify a sailor's word against a captain's. Did a captain dock a sailor's pay because the sailor damaged freight, as he was entitled to under the law? Or was the captain simply self-dealing? Had a captain exceeded the powers of corporal punishment afforded him under the law? Or was his discipline justified? In many cases it was difficult to say. Further, the law itself regarding these matters could be unclear. Some sailors successfully sued their captains for merely pinching provisions. In other cases the law supported far more abusive captain conduct. In one case a captain beat his sailor with a one-and-half inch rope for cursing. The court found he "had Lawful provocation to Correct the Complainant and had not Exceeded the bounds of Humanity" and dismissed the sailor's claim.

Reputation also constrained some captain predation. Although the sailor population in the mid-eighteenth century approached eighty thousand, there were far fewer captains. The relatively small population of captains facilitated information sharing about captain behavior. Since merchant ships had to voluntarily attract sailors, this dampened some captains' predatory inclinations. Nevertheless, some captain-sailor relations were anonymous and nonrepeated. For instance, when in 1722 merchant ship captains Isham Randolph, Constantine Cane, and William Halladay petitioned the colonial governor of Virginia for greater authority to discipline their sailors (who they complained were insolent for want of "fear of correction"), they wrote: "It is frequently the misfortune of Masters of Ships at their fitting out in England, to be obliged to ship men for forreign Voyages of whose disposition and character they have no knowledge." Their letter suggests that in some cases the market for merchant sailors was anonymous. Captains sometimes didn't know the sailors they employed, which implies sailors sometimes didn't know the captains who employed them. A number of sailors were the "fair weather" sort, drifting between employment at land and at sea, as job and pay prospects permitted. Others went to sea between regular work and only had sporadic interaction with a few members of the maritime community. These features of the merchant sailor labor market made information sharing more difficult and rendered reputation a less-effective constraint on captain abuse.

In light of cases of captain predation like those discussed above, it's not surprising that "the too great severity their Commanders have used both as to their back and bellies" was near the top of pirates' list of reasons for entering their illicit trade. Pirate captain John Phillips, for example, called one merchant ship officer he captured "a Supercargo Son of a B—h, that he starved the Men, and that it was such Dogs as he that put Men a Pyrating." Pirate John Archer's last words before being put to death echo Phillips's remarks. As he lamented, "I could wish that Masters of Vessels would not use their Men with so much Severity, as many of them do, which exposes us to great Temptations." In 1726 the pirate William Fly pleaded similarly while awaiting his execution. *Our Captain and his Mate used us Barbarously. We poor Men can't have Justice done us. There is nothing said to our Commanders, let them never so much abuse us, and use us like Dogs.* The noose around his neck, Fly offered a final warning to the mob gathered to see him hanged: *He would advise the Masters of*

Vessels to carry it well to their Men, lest they should be put upon doing as he had done."

The potential for captain abuse on pirate ships is the subject of the next two chapters, so I won't spoil that discussion here. Suffice it to say, pirates organized their ships so they largely overcame this threat. In doing so, pirates created an improved work atmosphere on their vessels. Combined with the potential for substantially higher monetary rewards, for many sailors this created a more attractive total "compensation package" compared to what they could expect on merchant ships. Of course, unlike in merchant shipping, in piracy you could have a leg blown off by a canon ball or meet an untimely state-sanctioned death. But the lure of more money and better treatment was hard to resist. Indeed, it attracted some four thousand sailors to piracy between 1716 and 1726. These seamen entered their trade out of material concerns and, as I describe in later chapters, adopted their trademark practices to maximize the material rewards of life under the black flag.

A Compass for Navigating This Book

This book has six main chapters and a conclusion. Chapter 2 explores pirate democracy. In contrast to the organization of seventeenth- and eighteenth-century merchant ships and governments, pirates democratically elected their "leaders" and voted on all other important matters that affected their society's members. Pirates didn't adopt this democratic form of political organization by accident. It grew directly out of sailors' experiences on merchant ships where captains had autocratic authority that some abused with impunity. Merchant vessels' ownership structure drove this autocratic organization. However, pirates, who were criminals, and thus stole their ships, had a very different ownership structure for their vessels. This important difference—driven by pirates' criminality—allowed pirates to create a system of democratic checks and balances that held captains accountable and reduced captains' control over important aspects of life on pirate ships. By constraining captains' ability to benefit themselves at crew members' expense, democratic checks and balances facilitated piratical cooperation, and with it, pirates' criminal enterprise.

Chapter 3 delves deeper into the order and organization aboard pirate ships by examining the constitutions pirates used to govern their floating societies. For the better and more peaceful preservation of their criminal organization, pirates created "articles of agreement," or "pirate codes," which acted as constitutions aboard their ships. The rules and regulations these constitutions embodied prevented "negative externalities" that could abound on pirate vessels from undermining crew members' ability to cooperate for coordinated plunder. Pirate constitutions also created a "rule of law" that placed pirate officers on equal "legal" footing with other crew members. Pirates' system of constitutional democracy predated constitutional democracy in France, Spain, the United States, and arguably even England.

Chapter 4 applies the economic way of thinking to the pirates' infamous flag, the "Jolly Roger." It introduces an idea economists call "signaling" and illustrates how pirates capitalized on this mechanism to improve their bottom line. The skull-and-crossbones motif was more than a symbol of pirates' way of life. It was a rationally devised mechanism for encouraging targets to surrender without a fight. The Jolly Roger's success not only enhanced pirates' profit; it also "benefited" their victims by preventing unnecessary bloodshed and the loss of innocent life.

Chapter 5 applies the economics of reputation building to pirates' famous fondness for torture. Pirate victims were understandably reluctant to reveal booty to their attackers. Some victims even hid or destroyed their valuables. Such behavior threatened to reduce pirates' revenue. To prevent this, pirates invested in reputations of barbarity and insanity, creating a fearsome "brand name." Brutally torturing resistors was one important way they did this. But pirates used torture for other reasons too. One was to deter authorities from harassing them. The other was to bring justice to predatory merchant ship captains when government couldn't or wouldn't do so. In this last capacity, pirate torture may have contributed to the provision of an important public benefit for merchant sailors—the punishment of dishonest merchant captains, which stood to reduce merchant captain abuse.

Chapter 6 considers the economics of pirate conscription. According to popular depiction, pirates swelled their ranks by drafting innocent and unwilling sailors from the vessels they overtook. This chapter shows that in many cases the supposed "pirate press" was nothing more than a clever pirate ruse. In response to eighteenth-century legal changes that made pirating riskier, pirates pretended to conscript sailors to exploit a loophole in antipiracy law. Like all good businessmen, pirates developed solutions, such as this one, to advance their interests when rising costs threatened to cut against them.

Chapter 7 explores the economics of pirate tolerance. At a time when British merchant ships treated black slaves as, well, slaves, some pirate ships integrated black bondsmen into their crews as full-fledged, free members. Pirates' treatment of black sailors was far from consistent. Some pirates participated in the slave trade. Others granted equal rights to blacks and whites aboard their ships. Still others did both at the same time. Even so, pirates more consistently applied the ideas embodied in the preamble of the Declaration of Independence before this document was so much as written than Americans did nearly a century after their country was founded. Enlightened notions about equality or the universal rights of man didn't produce pirate tolerance, however. Instead, simple cost-benefit considerations driven by the compensation structure of pirates' criminal employment were responsible for this tolerance.

Chapter 8 concludes by discussing the secrets of pirate management and in particular the contemporary managerial lessons the economics of seventeenth- and eighteenth-century pirates provides.

Enough details; it's time to go a-pirating.

2 VOTE FOR BLACKBEARD
THE ECONOMICS OF PIRATE DEMOCRACY

The field of office-seekers has been whittled down to four. An ardent supporter of one candidate stands up to deliver an important speech. He addresses the electorate, imploring his fellow voters to elect a leader *"who by his Counsel and Bravery seems best able to defend this Commonwealth, and ward us from the Dangers and Tempests of an instable Element, and the fatal Consequences of Anarchy."* He finishes with a rousing endorsement of his man, *"and such a one I take Roberts to be. A Fellow! I think, in all Respects, worthy of your Esteem and Favour."*

If you had to place this scene, where would you put it? You might guess it was part of a presidential candidate's campaign tour. Perhaps it was taken from a national party convention. Maybe it describes a scene from a congressional rally in the months leading up to an election.

If you guessed anything along these lines, you'd be wrong. This scene has no connection to a legitimate political office. This veritable portrait of democracy took place aboard an eighteenth-century pirate ship, the *Royal Rover*. Crew member "Lord" Dennis delivered the speech, campaigning to his fellow outlaws for the election of the notorious pirate Bartholomew Roberts to be their captain. Dennis proved an effective campaigner. "This speech was loudly applauded by all but Lord *Sympson*," one of the competing candidates for office, "who had secret Expectations [of being elected captain] himself" and the pirate crew elected Roberts its new leader. If it was anything like other pirate elections, Roberts's postelection ceremony was attended by liberal quantities of "punch," a great deal of profanity, and a toast declaring "War against the whole World." "The Guns are then fired round, Shot and all" and the new captain "is saluted with three Chears."

It's truly remarkable to think that this model of democracy was staged not only on a pirate ship, of all places, but took place more than half a century before the Continental Congress approved the Declaration of Independence and only a little more than a decade after the British monarchy withheld Royal Assent for the last time. Pirate democracy extended the unrestricted right to pirates to have a say in the selection of their society's leaders nearly 150 years before the Second Reform Act of 1868 accomplished anything close to the same in Britain. What's more, as I discuss below, pirate democracy wasn't merely the crude "showing of hands" we're all familiar with. Pirates created and operated their democracy within a sophisticated and more elaborate system of institutionally separated power.

Pirates' institutional separation of power also predated seventeenth- and eighteenth-century governments' adoption of such institutions. France, for example, didn't experience such a separation until 1789. The first specter of separated power in Spain didn't appear until 1812. In contrast, pirates had divided, democratic "government" aboard their ships at least a century before this. Arguably, piratical checks and balances predated even England's adoption of similar institutions. England didn't experience a separation of power until the Glorious Revolution of 1688. However, the buccaneers, who used a similar, if not as thoroughgoing, system of democratically divided power as their pure pirate successors had partial democratic checks and balances in place almost ten years before the English Bill of Rights.

This isn't to say pirate society was the very first to organize democratically or divide authority, of course. The first democracy was in ancient Athens. Further, about when the buccaneers began converging on Tortuga, New England's colonies began experimenting with their own democratic government. In the 1630s Massachusetts Bay Colony—initially an English trading company—evolved into a representative democracy where popularly elected delegates from the colony's towns crafted legislation and elected their governor, and town residents voted on local legislation in now-famous "town-hall meetings." New England's early seventeenth-century democracy came from an even earlier democratic tradition rooted in its Puritan settlers' church organization.

Some systems of divided power also preceded that of pirates. Even under the reign of monarchial government in medieval Europe, for instance, the competing interests of church and crown, and feudal lords and king, served as partial checks on authorities' power. In the thirteenth century the Venetian Republic developed an explicit division of power in its government. And in the Roman Republic, where the Senate and Consuls exercised separated authority, there was some division of power too.

But these predecessor democracies and divisions of authority weren't as thoroughgoing as those of pirates. Unlike pirate democracy, under ancient Athenian and colonial New England democracy only a minority could actually vote. Athens restricted suffrage to free male citizens—those born to an Athenian mother and father. Massachusetts Bay Colony limited voting to male company shareholders, later to male members of a Puritan church, and when this restriction was lifted in some towns, to male property owners. Further, as I discuss below, pirates' division of authority located "supream Power . . . with the Community," not with a handful of aristocrats or politically privileged elites, as predecessor separations of power tended to do. Pirate democracy was radical, a "democracy that," according to historian Hugh Rankin, "bordered on anarchy." Anarchic, yes. But as I discuss here and in the next chapter, chaotic it was anything but.

Pirate democracy implies a pirate society that required collective decision making. Normally, we define and distinguish societies by individuals' citizenship of, residence in, and allegiance to particular nations and governments. None of these traditional demarcators of society make sense in the context of pirates, however. Although born as citizens of recognized countries, most pirates had abandoned associations with their governments before the age of thirty. Except for perhaps the buccaneers, who at times serviced various European governments as privateers, pirates heeded no flag but the black one they sailed under. They boasted that "they acknowledged no countrymen" but rather "had sold their country" and would "do all the mischief they could."

It's just as well pirates spurned government. Government viewed pirates with equal contempt. British law denied pirates the benefits of legitimate life. As an advocate general of Rhode Island put it, pirates *"have no Country, but by the nature of their Guilt, separate themselves, renouncing the benefit of all lawful Society."* A pirate, another state official declared, is "denied common humanity, and the very rights of Nature"; he is "as a wild & savage Beast, which every Man may lawfully destroy." Yet pirates' rejection of the legitimate world, and the legitimate world's rejection of them, doesn't mean pirates didn't have a world of their own. Captain Johnson may have been right when he referred to the community of pirates as "that abominable Society," but it was a society nonetheless.

One Pirate, One Vote: Pirate Democracy and the Paradox of Power

To lead this coarse crowd of criminals, each pirate ship required a leader. Many important piratical decisions, such as how to engage a potential target, the method to pursue when chasing a target or being chased by authorities, and how to react if attacked, required snap decision making. There was no time for disagreement or debate in these cases and conflicting voices would have made it impossible to undertake the most essential tasks. Furthermore, pirate ships, like all ships, needed some method of maintaining order, distributing victuals, payments, and administering discipline to unruly crew members. By addressing these issues the proper pirate leader could facilitate crew cooperation, enhancing pirates' ability to profit through plunder. Pirates fully appreciated this and "how shatter'd and weak a Condition their Government must be without a Head." To prevent such a "condition" and provide leadership to their floating societies, pirates had the office of captain. However, the need for captains posed a dilemma for pirates. A captain who wielded unquestioned authority in certain decisions was critical for success. But what was to prevent him from turning his power against his crew for personal benefit in the same manner predatory merchant captains did?

The combination of the need for an authority and the fact that the very introduction of such an authority generates strong incentives for him to abuse his power creates what political economists call the "paradox of power." In 1788 James Madison, American Founding Father and architect of the U.S. Constitution, famously described this paradox in the *Federalist Papers*. In Federalist No. 51 Madison wrote, "But what is government itself but the greatest of all reflections on human nature? If men were angels, no government would be necessary. If angels were to govern men, neither external nor internal controls on government would be necessary. In framing a government which is to be administered by men over men, the great difficulty lies in this: you must first enable the government to control the governed; and in the next place oblige it to control itself." In other words, because individuals are self-interested they require an authority to ensure they don't run amuck, to govern them, and to see to it that they serve their self-interests by cooperating with, rather than damaging, others. But by the same token, since the authority himself is only human and thus driven by his own self-interest, the governed need some way to ensure he doesn't use his power to serve himself at their expense. The trouble with "obliging" authority "to control itself," as Madison put it, is that, by definition, an authority strong enough to constrain itself is also strong enough to break those constraints when it's convenient.

If society can't overcome Madison's paradox of power, it has a serious problem. While those who have authority may benefit, everyone else will suffer. The highly dysfunctional countries of sub-Saharan Africa illustrate this failure. Unconstrained governments in many of these countries prey on their citizens, making them among the poorest in the world. This deterioration takes place for two reasons. First, since they're unconstrained, rulers in these nations transfer wealth from citizens to themselves, making the rulers richer and the citizens poorer. Second, citizens don't sit by passively faced with such predation. Rulers' predatory behavior shapes citizens' incentive to cooperate for mutual gain. If leaders are going to take nearly all the proceeds of production and exchange, why bother producing and exchanging? The resulting decline in cooperation impoverishes society. Thus, solving the paradox of power is crucial to a successful and flourishing society.

This was as true for pirate society as it is for any other. A failure to solve this paradox can bring a country to its knees; so, too, would such a failure have brought pirate society down before too long. If pirates couldn't constrain their captains, they would face the same treatment aboard pirate ships that they fled from aboard legitimate vessels. No pirate in his right mind would trade one poor and miserable life for another that carried the added possibility of a death sentence. And no pirates would sail together for long if a predatory captain scooped up all their booty. Without a solution to the paradox of power, pirates couldn't cooperate, which means they couldn't profit through criminal organization.

Remarkably, pirates avoided this fate by invoking Madison's solution to the paradox of power—nearly one hundred years before he suggested it. This solution was democracy. As Madison put it, *"A dependence on the people is, no doubt, the primary control on the government."* If citizens can popularly depose their leaders and replace them with new ones, leaders who want to retain their positions of authority must refrain from preying on their citizens. In this way, democracy is a fundamental "check and balance" on how leaders wield their power over society. And so it was with pirates.

Pirate democracy operated on the basis of one pirate, one vote, "the Rank of Captain being obtained by the Suffrage of the Majority." As Captain Johnson noted, "It was not of any great Signification who was dignify'd with [this] Title; for really and in Truth, all good Governments had (like theirs) the supream Power lodged with the Community, who might doubtless depute and revoke as suited Interest or Humour." Nevertheless, to affirm captains' commitment to use their power in crews' interests, some crews' postelection ceremonies reminded their captains of this necessity. This ceremony was similar to the one the American president participates in at his inaugural address after taking office, pledging to faithfully serve the public's interest, and so forth. The postelection ceremony following Nathaniel North's election, for example, pronounced the newly elected pirate captain's commitment to "doing every Thing which may conduce to the publick Good." In return, "the Company, promised to obey all his lawful Commands."

To constrain their captains democratically, pirates required the unrestricted right to depose any captain for any reason. Without this, the threat of popular removal wouldn't be credible, eliminating captains' incentive to abstain from preying on crew members. Thus, pirates indulged their democratic impulse with more enthusiasm than senior citizens in an election year. One crew went through thirteen captains in the space of a single voyage. Captain Benjamin Hornigold's crew, for example, deposed him from command because he "refused to take and plunder English Vessels." Pirates wanted to ensure captainship "falls on one superior for Knowledge and Boldness, Pistol Proof, (as they call it)," so they also removed captains who showed cowardice. For instance, Captain Charles Vane's "behaviour was obliged to stand the Test of a Vote, and a Resolution passed against his Honour and Dignity ... deposing him from the Command." Some pirates deposed their captains from command for violating pirate policy, such as the rule requiring them to mercilessly slaughter resistors, discussed in chapter 4. Captain Edward England, for example, "was turned out of Command" by his crew for this. Finally, pirates might depose their captains because they demonstrated poor judgment. Captain Christopher Moody's pirate crew, for instance, grew dissatisfied with his behavior and "at last forced him, with twelve others" who supported him, "into an open Boat ... and ... they were never heard of afterwards." Similarly, "a great difference falling out between [Captain] Low and his Men, they" also "discarded" their captain "and sent him away with two other Pirates." By liberally exercising

FIGURE 2.1. Democracy at work: Captain Edward England, popularly deposed by his crew. From Captain Charles Johnson, *A General and True History of the Lives and Actions of the most Famous Highwaymen, Murderers, Street-Robbers, &c.*, 1742.

their democratic right to elect and depose captains, pirates ensured "they only permit[ed] him to be Captain, on Condition, that they may be Captain over him."

Democracy was the primary, but not the only, mechanism pirates used to control their captains. In a few cases pirate crews physically punished their captains for behavior they deemed inconsistent with their interests. Oliver La Bouche's crew, for example, deprived him of his captainship and flogged him for attempting to desert them. Occasionally, crews also deserted predatory or incompetent captains. As one sailor reported of Captain William Kidd, for instance, "severall of his men have deserted him soe that he has not above five and twenty or thirty hands on board."

Pirates took the limitations they imposed on captains' authority through their system of checks and balances seriously. A speech one of the pirates aboard Captain Roberts's ship made testifies to this. As he told his crew, "*Should a Captain be so sawcy as to exceed Prescription at any time, why down with him! it will be a Caution after he is dead to his Successors, of what fatal Consequence any sort of assuming may be.*" This pirate was exaggerating—but only slightly. Crews quickly and readily deposed old captains and elected new ones when the former overstepped the limited power crews gave them.

The specter of pirate popular opinion looming over them like the Sword of Damocles, pirate captains faithfully executed their crews' wills. You can get an idea of this by considering one pirate contemporary's remarks, which point to the rarity of pirate captain predation. Perplexed by an anomalous pirate captain who abused his crew, he puzzled, "The captain is very severe to his people, by reason of his commission, and caries a very different form from what other Pirates use to do ... often calling for his pistols and threatening any that durst speak to the contrary of what he desireth, to knock out their brains." We can find further evidence of pirates' democratic control over their captains in the unsanctified status of pirate captains among their fellow rogues. As the Dutch governor of Mauritius marveled, "Every man had as much say as the captain."

Pirates' equal footing with their captains in everyday affairs extended to all aspects of life aboard the ship. Unlike merchant captains, pirate captains couldn't secure special privileges for themselves at their crews' expense. Their lodging, provisions, and even pay were similar to that of ordinary crew members. As Johnson described it, aboard pirate ships "every Man, as the Humour takes him . . . [may] intrude [into the captain's] Apartment, swear at him, seize a part of his Victuals and Drink, if they like it, without his offering to find Fault or contest it." And unlike on merchant or Royal Navy vessels, "any body might come and eat and drink" with the captain as they please. In other cases "the Captain himself not being allowed a Bed" had to sleep with rest of the crew in less comfortable conditions. Or, as one pirate observer exclaimed, "Even their Captain, or any other Officer, is allowed no more than another Man; nay, the Captain cannot [even] keep his own Cabbin to himself." According to Exquemelin, things were no different for buccaneer commanders. "The captain is allowed no better fare than the meanest on board. If they notice he has better food, the men bring the dish from their own mess and exchange it for the captain's." Among eighteenth-century pirates this was ensured by the division of power through the quartermaster, who I discuss later. As merchant captain Richard Hawkins described it, "At Meals the Quarter-Master overlooks the Cook, to see the Provisions equally distributed to each Mess." The success of pirate democracy in constraining captain predation helps explain why, counterintuitively, "the People [pirates overtook] were generally glad of an opportunity of entring with them," a phenomenon I'll examine in chapter 6.

The Separation of Piratical Powers

Pirate democracy prevented much captain predation. But by itself, democracy could go only so far. In the United States, for example, citizens not only democratically elect their rulers; they also divide authority, or separate powers, between various branches of government. The idea is that giving any person too much clout will make it easier for him to abuse it. Spreading authority around, in contrast, makes it more difficult for leaders to abuse their power since they don't have as much of it. James Madison's Federalist No. 51 is again useful to explain this. As we already discussed, according to Madison, "the primary control on the government" is "a dependence on the people"—democratic elections. However, Madison's next words are equally important. As he put it, "but experience has taught mankind the necessity of auxiliary precautions" for checking leaders' ability to prey on those beneath them. What are these "auxiliary precautions"? Madison continued, "The constant aim is to divide and arrange several offices in such a manner as that each may be a check on the other—that the private interest of every individual may be a sentinel over the public rights." In other words, to bolster democratic controls on authority, society requires separated powers.

To look at it, one could easily believe America's Founding Fathers used the pirates' system of democratic checks and balances in framing the United States government. To further constrain the possibility of captain predation, pirates instituted a separation of powers aboard their ships that looked and operated just like the "division" and "arrangement" of "several offices," "each" acting as "a check on the other," that Madison described—but more than half a century before he described it. As the pirate Walter Kennedy testified at his trial: "Most of them having suffered formerly from the ill-treatment of Officers, provided thus carefully against any such Evil now they had the choice in themselves ... for the due Execution thereof they constituted other Officers besides the Captain; so very industrious were they to avoid putting too much Power into the hands of one Man."

The primary "other officer" pirates constituted for this purpose was the quartermaster. The way this office worked is straightforward. Captains retained absolute authority in times of battle, enabling pirates to realize the benefits of autocratic control required for success in conflict. However, pirate crews transferred power to allocate provisions, select and distribute loot (there was rarely room aboard pirate ships to take all they seized from a prize), adjudicate crew member conflicts, and administer discipline to the quartermaster, whom they democratically elected:

> For the Punishment of small Offences ... there is a principal Officer among the Pyrates, called the Quarter-Master, of the Men's own choosing, who claims all Authority this Way, (excepting in Time of Battle:) If they disobey his Command, are quarrelsome and mutinous with one another, misuse Prisoners, plunder beyond his Order, and in particular, if they be negligent of their Arms, which he musters at Discretion, he punishes at his own dare without incurring the Lash from all the Ship's Company: In short, this Officer is Trustee for the whole, is the first on board any Prize, separating for the Company's Use, what he pleases, and returning what he thinks fit to the Owners, excepting Gold and Silver, which they have voted not returnable.

Others observed the same relationship between captain and quartermaster. At the trial of pirate captain Stede Bonnet, for instance, Ignatius Pell, Bonnet's boatswain, testified that the captain "went by that Name; but the Quarter-Master had more Power than he."

This separation of power removed captains' control over activities they traditionally used to prey on crew members, while empowering them sufficiently to direct plundering expeditions. According to Johnson, due to the institution of the quartermaster, aboard pirate ships "the Captain can undertake nothing which the Quarter-Master does not approve. We may say, the Quarter-Master is an humble Imitation of the Roman Tribune of the People; he speaks for, and looks after the Interest of the Crew." As noted above, the only exception to this was "in Chase, or in Battle" when crews desired autocratic authority and thus, "by their own Laws," "the Captain's Power is uncontroulable."

Under pirates' system of divided power, crew members democratically elected both captains *and* quartermasters. Indeed, pirates often elected quartermasters to replace deposed captains. After Charles Vane's crew removed him from command, for instance, it elected its quartermaster to captain in his place. This practice facilitated competition among pirate officers, which further constrained abuse and encouraged officers to serve their crews' interests. Once again, it appears pirates took a page right out of the Founding Fathers' book—or rather the other way around. As Madison wrote, for democratic checks and balances to work properly, "Ambition must be made to counteract ambition." Pirate captain-quartermaster competition achieved precisely this.

As with the right to elect and depose their captains, pirates took the separation of power aboard their ships very seriously. One pirate captive records an event in which the captains of a pirate fleet borrowed fancy clothes that were part of the loot their crews acquired in taking a recent prize. These captains hoped their stolen finery would attract local women on the nearby shore. Although the captains intended only to borrow the clothes, the crews became outraged at their captains who they saw as transgressing the limits of their narrowly circumscribed power. As the observer described it, "The Pirate Captains having taken these Cloaths without leave from the Quarter-master, it gave great Offence to all the Crew; who alledg'd, 'If they suffered such things, the Captains would for the future assume a Power, to take whatever they liked for themselves.'" This episode would be enough to make Madison's heart sing; if only all citizens guarded their polity's division of power as jealously as pirates.

Three Cheers for Criminals?

If pirates' system of democratic checks and balances isn't strange enough, the source of pirates' ability to use this system is: their criminality. Understanding the reason for this isn't difficult. But it requires us to leave the world of pirates for a moment so we can explore the world of merchant shipping instead. Merchant ships were owned by groups of typically a dozen or more landed merchants who purchased shares in various trading vessels and financed their voyages. In addition to supplying the capital required for ships' construction and continued maintenance, owners outfitted their vessels, supplied them with provisions, advanced sailor wages, and most important, solicited customers and negotiated terms of delivery and freight. Merchant shipowners were absentee owners of their vessels; they rarely sailed on their ships. They were landlubbers. Most merchant shipowners had no desire to take their chances with brutal life at sea, and in any event could earn more by specializing in their area of expertise—investment and commercial organization—hiring seamen to sail their ships instead. Because they were absentee owners, merchant shipowners confronted what economists call a "principal-agent problem" with respect to the crews they hired.

You're undoubtedly familiar with this problem, though you may call it something different. When you're at work and instead of working on the report you've been assigned you spend an hour browsing the Internet for a gift for your mother, you're a principal-agent problem. The idea is that there are principals, people with something at stake, who hire agents to help them in their duties when it's not possible or profitable for them to do so themselves. Your employer, for example, is a principal. You're her agent. The difficulty lies in the fact that your interests and her interests aren't always perfectly aligned. She wants you to finish the report because this is what she needs for her business to make money. You would rather troll around on the Internet because working on the report isn't as fun and your income doesn't depend significantly on how much money her business makes. Since she can't monitor you all the time, you spend some of your time surfing the Web instead of working on the report.

Merchant shipowners confronted a similar problem, albeit in a different context. Once a ship left port it could be gone for months. At sea, the owners' ship was beyond their watchful eyes or reach. Thus, shipowners couldn't directly monitor their sailors. This situation invited various kinds of sailor opportunism. Opportunism included negligence in caring for the ship, carelessness that damaged cargo, liberality with provisions, embezzlement of freight or advances required to finance the vessel's voyage, and outright theft of the vessel itself. To prevent this, shipowners appointed captains to their vessels to monitor crews in their stead. Centralizing power in a captain's hands to direct sailors' tasks, control the distribution of victuals and payment, and discipline and punish crew members allowed merchant shipowners to minimize sailor opportunism. As noted earlier, merchant ships tended to be quite small. Consequently, captains could cheaply monitor sailors' behavior to prevent activities (or inactivities) that were costly to shipowners and secure sailors' full effort. As we've already seen, Admiralty law facilitated captains' ability to do this by granting them authority to control their crews' behavior through corporal punishment. The law empowered captains to beat crew members with the infamous and ominous cat-o'-nine tails, imprison them, and administer other forms of physical "correction" to sailors who disobeyed orders, shirked in their duties, and so on. It also permitted captains to dock sailors' wages for damaging or stealing cargo and insubordination.

To align their interests with their captain's interests, owners used two devices. First, they hired captains who held small shares in the vessels they were commanding, or barring this, gave small shares to their captains who didn't. Merchant ship captains continued to draw regular fixed wages like the other sailors on their vessels. But unlike regular sailors, captains became partial stakeholders of the ships they controlled, aligning their interests with those of the absentee owners. Second, whenever possible, absentee owners appointed captains with familial connections to one of the members of their group. This ensured captains didn't behave opportunistically at the absentee owners' expense since, if they did, they were more likely to face punishment.

The reason merchant shipowners required *autocratic* captains to effectively serve their interests is straightforward. A captain who didn't have total authority over his crew couldn't successfully monitor and control sailors' behavior. Reducing the captain's power over victuals, payments, labor assignment, or discipline, and vesting it in some other sailor's hands instead, would reduce the captain's power to make sailors behave in the absentee owners' interest. Similarly, if merchant shipowners didn't appoint their captains as the permanent commanders of their voyages, but instead permitted a ship's sailors to popularly depose the captain and elect another crew member to this office at their will, the captain's capacity as acting manager of the ship's absentee owners would cease to exist. To see this, simply imagine what kind of captain merchant sailors would elect if given the power to democratically select him. Sailors' interests were best served by a lax, liberal captain who let them do as they pleased—exactly the opposite sort of captain that best served the owners' interests. Merchant ship autocracy was therefore essential to overcoming the owner-crew principal-agent problem, and thus to merchant ship profitability.

Merchant ship autocracy worked well in this respect. Although some sailors still managed to steal from the ships they sailed on, disobey command, and in several cases mutiny and abscond with the owners' ship, these were relatively unimportant exceptions to the general rule whereby merchant sailors, under the authority of autocratic captains, served their absentee owners' interests. However, while merchant ship autocracy overcame the principal-agent problem absentee owners confronted with respect to their crews, in doing so it created potential for a different kind of problem we've already examined: captain predation. The trouble was that a captain endowed with the authority required to manage his crew on the shipowners' behalf could also easily turn this authority against his seamen for personal benefit. Predatory captains who abused their authority created the miserable situations for sailors discussed in chapter 1. Some of these captains, such as the sadistic Captain Norman, were bad people. But many others were not; they were simply responding to the incentives merchant ship organization created for them. Since merchant captains had essentially unchecked authority over their sailors, the cost of serving themselves at sailors' expense was often low. So, a number of merchant captains predictably took advantage of their authority. In short, merchant ships failed to overcome Madison's paradox of power. This wasn't because merchant shippers were stupid. It was because merchant vessels' ownership structure dictated an unconstrained, or autocratic, leader.

With that under our belts, let's return to pirates. Similar to merchant ships, the particular, but very different, economic situation pirate ships confronted crucially shaped their organization. Most notably, pirates didn't confront the owner-crew, principal-agent problem merchant ships did. The reason for this is simple enough: pirates didn't acquire their ships legitimately. They stole them. Pirate ships therefore had no absentee owners. Instead, pirates jointly owned and operated their ship themselves. As historian Patrick Pringle described it, in this sense a pirate ship was like a "sea-going stock company." On a pirate ship, then, the principals were the agents. As we discussed previously, pirates still required captains. But they didn't require *autocratic* captains because there were no absentee owners to align the crew's interests with.

Since the pirates sailing a particular ship were both the principals and the agents, democracy didn't threaten to lead to captains who served the agents at the principals' expense. Given the opportunity to elect their captains, pirates had no incentive to "vote themselves a vacation" or, more accurately, to vote themselves a captain who would give them a vacation, as merchant sailors would've if given the same opportunity. On the contrary, pirate democracy ensured pirates got precisely the kind of captain they desired. Because they could popularly depose any captain who didn't suit them and elect another in his place, pirate captains' ability to prey on crew members was greatly constrained compared to merchant captains. Similarly, because pirates were both principals and agents of their ships, they could divide authority on their vessels to further check captains' ability to abuse crew members without loss. Unlike merchant ships, which couldn't afford a separation of power since this would have diminished the ability of the absentee owners' acting agent (the captain) to make the crew act in the owners' interests, pirate ships could and did adopt a system of democratically divided power.

In short, because pirates stole their ships they could organize their polity democratically. If, like legitimate sailors, pirates had merely been the agents of absentee shipowner principals, they would have had to organize their ships autocratically like merchant ships. And, given the predation problem this organization created, pirates would have faced the same problems merchant sailors did. If these problems had been severe enough, pirates wouldn't have found piracy sufficiently preferable to bother pirating at all. In fact, it's almost certain that if pirates had failed to solve the paradox of power, the problem of captain predation they faced would have been even worse than it was on merchant ships. Merchant sailors, recall from chapter 1, could at least appeal to government to prevent captain predation. As we already saw, in some cases such appeal was useless. But many other times it was effective. Pirates, in contrast, couldn't appeal to government to protect them from tyrannical captains any more than crack dealers can appeal to police to protect them from their distributors. In turning to sea banditry, pirates, we discussed above, "renounced the benefit of all lawful society." So, it was doubly important and difficult for pirates to overcome the threat of captain predation, which makes the fact they did so doubly impressive.

Pirate democracy highlights several important features of pirates. First, although they were motley and crude outlaws, pirates were members of societies. Pirate societies were floating ones, pirate ships. But like all others, these societies required leaders. Second, like all societies, pirate society—though criminally composed and directed—confronted the paradox of power, which requires a solution for society to function. Thus the fundamental problem pirates faced in this regard was the same one legitimate societies face. Third, pirate solutions to this problem were essentially the same ones the modern world uses to try and overcome Madison's dilemma. Pirates, however, "discovered" these solutions before their legitimate contemporaries.

Finally, pirate democracy didn't emerge out of pirates' adherence to romantic democratic ideals about man's right to have a say in who governs him. It emerged out of pirate profit seeking à la the "invisible hook." Pirates were interested in preventing captain predation, which threatened to undermine their ability to cooperate for coordinated plunder. In response, they developed democratic checks and balances. No outside authority centrally designed, directed, or imposed democracy on pirate society. Pirates' criminal self-interest led them to adopt this system without external prodding.

Similarly, pirate captains didn't display goodwill and faithful devotion to their crews' interests because they were nicer than merchant captains or cared more about fairness. Their better behavior resulted from a different institutional organization—democratically divided power—aboard pirate ships. The democratic institutions pirate captains operated under created incentives for them to behave differently than merchant ship captains who operated under an autocratic institutional regime. Pirate organization rewarded captains for being good stewards of the power they possessed and punished them for preying on their crews. Merchant ship organization often did very much the opposite.

Merchant and pirate ships' different institutional organizations resulted from the different economic situations each confronted. On merchant ships a principal-agent problem between shipowners and crew members necessitated an irrevocable autocratic captain to generate profits for their owners. Democracy would have destroyed this. On pirate ships the illicit nature of the enterprise prevented this principal-agent problem from coming into existence, making an autocratic captain unnecessary. Pirate ships were stolen and so had no remotely located owners. Consequently, pirates could elect their captains and divide power within their crews, which constrained pirate captains' ability to take advantage of their men. Strangely, then, pirates' self-interested *criminality* facilitated democratic checks and balances on their ships. The very outlawry pirates' contemporaries despised them for is responsible for pirates' reliance on the democratic mode of governance the modern world embraces as one its highest and most-cherished values.

3 AN-*ARRGH*-CHY
THE ECONOMICS OF
THE PIRATE CODE

The average person has a clear idea of what life was like as a pirate. The very occupational choice of these rogues is enough to paint a vivid picture. It was raucous, reckless, and brutally rapacious. Pirates were liars, cheaters, and traitors. They were thieves, murderers, and sailors to boot. Pirate society must have been as orderly and honest as an asylum for the criminally insane.

What's more, pirates had no government. In fact, according to a petition from "the General Officers of the Army" to King George I, pirates were "profess'd Enemys to all Order and Government." They consequently forswore the civilities afforded the members of legitimate societies who could rely on the state's apparatus of peace-keeping and order to lubricate the machinery of social cooperation. Pirates had no prisons, no police, and no parliament. They had no barristers, no bailiffs, and no royal bench. If these mechanisms of law and order are required to prevent barbarism and chaos in a society of mostly law-abiding citizens, one can only imagine what their absence must have meant in a society of violent criminals. Pirate society wasn't only an asylum for the criminally insane—it was one without a warden.

Although this intuition is very reasonable, it's also dead wrong. Contrary to conventional wisdom, pirate life was orderly and honest. This isn't counterintuitive on recollection of pirates' purpose, which was profit. To cooperate for mutual gain—indeed, to advance their criminal organization at all—pirates needed to prevent their outlaw society from degenerating into bedlam. Adam Smith expressed this necessity best. "Society," he noted, "cannot subsist among those who are at all times ready to hurt and injure one another. . . . If there is any society among robbers and murderers, they must at least . . . abstain from robbing and murdering one another." Pirates therefore had a strong incentive to secure social harmony without government. How did they do this? What did pirate order look like? And did it work? As in the previous chapters, pirates pose the questions; economics provides the answers.

The argument that society needs government is as old as government itself. In his book, appropriately entitled *Leviathan*, Thomas Hobbes supplied one of the most famous descriptions of what life would be like without government: "Solitary, poor, nasty, brutish, and short." Hobbes wrote his book in 1651, but his words have shaped almost everyone's thinking about anarchy to this day. Hobbes distinguished between the world without government—an anarchic world he called "the state of nature"—and the world with government, which he argued allowed for civilization. In the former there's perpetual conflict and fighting, a "war of all against all." In the latter there's widespread cooperation and peace.

Why would Hobbes characterize life under anarchy so differently from life under government? The reason, he argued, is man's self-interested nature. In chapter 2 we considered Madison's point in Federalist No. 51, which was that the need for "devices" such as democracy and separated powers "to control the abuses of government" is "a reflection on human nature."

Rulers' natural self-interest, left unconstrained, leads to abuse. Because "angels" don't "govern men," society needs "external" and "internal controls on government." We can think of Hobbes as providing an analogous argument but with regard to the governed. As Madison put it, "If men were angels, no government would be necessary." Because they're not, Hobbes contends, government is.

Our imaginations lend ready support to Hobbes's claim. Without government, who would supply rules and regulations to provide order to society? What would prevent strong people from stealing from weak ones? How would individuals resolve their disputes? What would prevent them from engaging in activities that harm others? For that matter, who would provide for the sick and injured, who can't provide for themselves? If people are self-interested, as Hobbes and Madison suggest, and this book has argued pirates were too, and there's no government to control them, what's to prevent cheating, lying, and stealing from running rampant? Without government, how can society avoid chaos?

To answer these questions, it's important to make an oft-ignored distinction between govern*ment* and govern*ance*. Government is an authority with a monopoly on coercion in the territory it presides over; it's based on force. That very monopoly on the right to force people to behave in ways they wouldn't voluntary choose to is supposed to give government the ability to prevent cheating and theft, and more generally create order. This same monopoly on the legitimized use of force is what gives government the power to provide for the sick and injured. Self-interested people won't provide for these individuals of their own accord, the argument goes, so we give government the right to forcibly take from people and redistribute to those in need.

Lest you doubt government is based on force, consider what would happen to you if you decided not follow one of government's rules or decided not to give government the money it demanded of you. The former is called breaking the law, which government punishes by imprisonment or fine. The latter is called tax evasion, which government punishes similarly. Everything a government does is therefore backed by the threat of coercion. Some governments' monopolies on force derive mostly from their rulers' superior strength, which they use to centralize and monopolize power over their citizens. In Stalin's Russia, for example, a relatively small proportion of citizens approved of how its government used force. Other governments' monopolies on force derive mostly from the approval of the populations they rule. In modern America, for instance, most citizens approve of how their government uses force. If you're one of these citizens, you may not mind many of the rules government requires you to obey or many of the fees it requires you to pay. But this is a happy coincidence for you. It doesn't change the fact that *if* you wanted to do otherwise, you couldn't without government punishing you. In fact, the very presence of a substantial number of people who desire to behave differently from the way government wants is one of the major reasons government is required in the first place—to compel these individuals to act differently than they desire. So, some people's willingness to go along with what government requires of them in many instances doesn't make government "voluntary." The coercive monopoly behind everything government does is the opposite of voluntary choice. There's nothing voluntary about it.

If this is government, what's governance? Governance is a broader concept than government. It refers only to the existence of some mechanisms or institutions that provide and enforce social rules and therefore create social order. Government is one kind of institution that provides governance, the kind based on a monopoly coercive power. But it's not the only kind.

Consider, for instance, a condominium association. A condominium association creates rules for its residents and stipulates punishments for breaking those rules. For example, if your condo association bylaws require you to pay $380 a month for the maintenance of common areas—to provide for landscaping, repainting the condo's exterior, and so on—and you don't pay your dues, the association reserves the right to kick you out. Condo associations also create rules that regulate resident behaviors that threaten to negatively affect other residents. For instance, the association's bylaws may prohibit residents from keeping barbeque grills on their balconies. Many condo associations also provide property protection for their residents. For example, out of the dues you pay the association, the association hires a private security guard or concierge who monitors and polices the building. Condo associations, then, provide governance to the members of their communities in many of the same ways governments provide governance to their citizens.

But condo associations aren't governments. To see why, think for a moment about how your government is fundamentally different from a condo association. While the former is based on force, the latter is purely voluntary. You don't have to submit to the rules of the condo association if you don't want to. You may dislike a particular element of the association's rules and choose not to purchase a condo in that association. You're free to go and purchase a different condo if you prefer, or no condo at all. If you do this, you don't owe the condo you turned down anything. You don't, for example, have to pay its association fees because you don't want to pay for its services. The condo association is a private organization and therefore can't use force to make you do anything you don't voluntarily agree to. Once you've agreed to follow the association's rules, you're bound to obey them. But no one forces you to agree to follow these rules in the first place.

Things are totally different with government. Government can and does use the threat of force to get you to obey its rules and pay its "association fees." If you don't like the rules government sets up, it's too bad. You don't have the choice of saying, as you do with a condo association, "no thank you, I don't much care for your rules, so I'm going to take my money and live according to my own rules." Whether you like its rules or not, government compels you to follow its rules and pay it your money. You might object: "But government provides me with services that are worth my money!" This might be true for you. But it's likely false for some others. Just because you think the local park is worth what you pay for it in taxes each year doesn't mean your neighbor does. And the fact that he receives the park's services even if he objects to paying for them doesn't change this. Imagine I came up to you and forced you at gunpoint to "buy" a candy bar from me. At the point of a gun I tell you, "Give me $5 for this candy bar." Even if you like candy bars, and even though I'm giving you something when I take your $5, wouldn't we still say I'm using force to steal from you?

You might also object, "If you don't like the government's rules, no one's stopping you from leaving the country. So, really it *is* a voluntary choice to live according to the government's rules." But this objection doesn't work either. Imagine I came into your house and threatened to break your legs if you didn't give me your wife's jewelry. Would you say I'm not forcing you to give me your wife's jewelry because you have the choice of not surrendering it, which involves me breaking your legs? Of course not. We always have options in a technical sense. But this isn't the same thing as voluntary choice. Voluntary choice requires that our options aren't framed under the threat of force. When I give you the option of surrendering your wife's jewelry or keeping it but having your legs broken, I'm using force to frame your options. Presumably, you should be allowed to keep your wife's jewelry and your legs because both are rightfully yours, not mine.

And so it is with government. While it's true I can stay in my home and follow the government's rules, or leave my home (and the nation it's located in) and avoid the government's rules by doing so, I can't stay in my home *and* avoid the government's rules. Government uses force to frame my options and removes the choice I would select if it weren't in the picture, which is to stay in my home and follow some other rules. If my house is mine, why should I have to leave it if I want to avoid the government's rules? Telling me I have the choice to leave, so there's nothing coercive about government, is like me telling you in the example above that you have the choice of having your legs broken, so there's nothing coercive about me stealing your wife's jewelry.

The fundamental distinction between government and governance, then, is that the former is always based on force, but the latter needn't be. When your government provides governance it's based on force. But when a private organization, such as a condo association, provides governance, it's based on voluntary agreement. The distinction between government and governance suggests an answer to the question this chapter began with: How can society achieve order and harmony without government? Quite easily, actually. Society can achieve this with private forms of governance instead. Hobbes's "state of nature," what we commonly call anarchy, doesn't mean the absence of rules, order, and cooperation. It merely means the absence of governance based on monopoly coercive power—the absence of government. Where government doesn't provide the rules and mechanisms for enforcing those rules that individuals require to cooperate for mutual gain, individuals don't simply throw up their hands and abandon their projects. The very prospect of mutual benefits—of profit—encourages them to privately provide these things instead. But could private governance fulfill these functions on pirate ships—veritable societies of violent criminals? Yes, and in fact it did.

The Three Keys of Successful Pirate Governance

Although pirates were lawless, they weren't without laws. Like all societies, pirates required some kind of governance—some system of rules, regulations, and punishments for those who broke the rules—to produce order and facilitate cooperation. It just so happens in pirates' case that this cooperation was aimed at plundering. We've already considered why, as outlaws, pirates couldn't rely on government for this purpose. The alternative to government, discussed above, is private governance. To be successful, private pirate governance needed to accomplish three primary goals.

First, pirate governance needed to provide rules to prevent conflict between pirates and a way of enforcing these rules. The reason for this is simple enough. If, for example, there were no rules defining private property rights on pirate ships, theft, cheating, and fighting would run rampant. This isn't because pirates were pirates. It's because pirates were people, guided by self-interest like the rest of us. And, in the absence of some kind of control on their behavior, their self-interest could lead them to transgress the property claims of one another, which in turn would create crew member conflict. A pirate ship divided against itself could not stand (or float). If crew members were constantly stealing from and fighting one another, they obviously couldn't cooperate for the purposes of their criminal enterprise. Sufficient conflict would cause the pirate ship—the pirate firm, if you will—to collapse. This is true in both a figurative and literal sense. Tension and mistrust among crew members would undermine pirates' ability to live and work together, to engage in their joint profit-seeking ventures. Furthermore, violence on pirate ships could destroy the ship. Like all early eighteenth-century marine vessels, pirate ships were constructed primarily of wood (the body) and cloth (the sails) and were therefore susceptible to damage by puncture or fire, among other things. If the members of a pirate crew in conflict with itself began shooting at one another, fire and other kinds of damage could tear the ship apart. Thus it was critical to prevent interpirate conflict if pirates were to cooperate for profit.

Second, successful pirate governance needed to regulate pirate behaviors that generated significant "negative externalities." Economists use the term *negative externalities* to describe the harmful side effects that result from an individual's behavior. Many of our actions not only directly affect ourselves, they also indirectly affect those around us. Pollution is one example of this. When a factory produces its products, it also produces pollution—toxins created during manufacture that the factory usually emits into the air. This imposes a cost on the people who live near the factory. Economists call this cost an "externality" since it falls on people who didn't fully produce it. Negative externalities emerge because individuals don't completely "internalize" the costs of their behavior. The factory, for example, doesn't incur a cost for emitting its pollution. If it did, it wouldn't pollute as much. Because polluting is free to the factory, however, it pollutes more than it otherwise would.

The key to preventing negative externalities is to make the individual who's generating them internalize the full costs of their behavior. Typically, introducing private property rights is the easiest and most effective way to do this. Using the pollution example again, if the factory owned the air, it would be damaging itself (in addition to its neighbors) when it polluted, as the value of the air it owns is presumably less when it's dirty.

To maximize the air's value, then, the factory needs to pollute less. Since the air's value ultimately affects the factory's bottom line, it has an incentive to take the air's quality into consideration; this will tend to lead the factory to pollute less. If no one owns the air, that incentive doesn't exist. This same principle can be applied to polluting rivers, and so on. By privatizing the good in question, the owner internalizes the costs of his behavior, which in turn encourages him to behave in a way that recognizes all the costs associated with his behavior.

Establishing private property rights isn't the only way to prevent negative externalities. Another option is to use regulation. Instead of creating property rights to the air, for instance, we could introduce a regulation that prohibits, or restricts, the emission of pollution. In most cases regulation is an inferior method of preventing negative externalities. But in some cases regulation makes sense because it's more cost effective than creating private property rights.

To see how this might be so, take the case of college dormitories. As any recent resident will tell you, college dormitory living presents serious negative externality threats. For instance, one person may want to blast his music at all hours of the night while others are trying to sleep. One way to solve this problem would be to create a private property right to "peace and quiet," which would require the person playing his music to pay the property right holders—the other people in the dorm—for the right to create noise, on the logic that the increased cost of playing music would lead the person to play his music less loudly or often. However, creating enforceable property rights to things like peace and quiet can be expensive in terms of what economists call "transaction costs." Transaction costs are the costs of making exchanges—the time, effort, grief, and sometimes financial costs—associated with coming to an agreement with someone else. In our example, each dorm resident would have to bargain separately with the person playing loud music over the price he'll have to pay to play his music as loud as he likes. Even if the bargaining process goes smoothly, with so many people individually "contracting" with the person playing music, the transaction costs of using property rights to handle this negative externality become large very quickly. So, rather than doing this, dormitories typically use regulation to prevent the negative externality of loud music by establishing "quiet hours" that restrict when loud music may be played.

Negative externalities don't only exist in legitimate society. They also existed in pirate society. Life on pirate ships was tight and cramped. This fact of life at sea made several behaviors that wouldn't generate negative externalities under "normal" circumstances prone to producing negative spillovers for others on pirate ships. For example, I don't care whether my neighbor drinks himself silly every night or not. He's in his house, I'm in mine, and any cost of his drunken stupor is contained within the walls of his home and stays out of mine. But on a pirate ship things could be different. All members of a pirate crew lived in the same house, so to speak. If one pirate decided to indulge in booze late in the evening, it could prevent other pirates from getting their sleep. Because of their close quarters, one pirate's excessive drinking generated a negative externality for other pirates.

Preventing negative externalities on pirate ships was important for two reasons. First, as in the drinking example above, some negative externalities threatened to create conflict between pirates, which as already discussed could undermine pirates' criminal enterprise. Second, other kinds of negative externalities on pirate ships could destroy the vessel. For example, if a pirate smoker dumped his pipe carelessly on the ship, it could ignite the large quantity of gunpowder the vessel was carrying, blowing the crew to smithereens. This would also undermine pirates' ability to cooperate for profit. To prevent negative externalities from threatening their operation's success, pirates therefore needed to prevent such externalities from running rampant on their ships—either by creating additional private property rights or by regulating activities.

Third, to be successful, private pirate governance had to provide important "public goods" for crew members. Economists define public goods as goods that are "nonexcludable" and "nonrivalrous." For our purposes the nonexcludable component is all that matters. If a good is nonexcludable, individuals who didn't contribute to its provision can't be excluded from enjoying the good after it's produced. A fireworks show is a good example of this. Once a fireworks show is underway, whether you've paid for it or not, you get to consume the display. It's not difficult to see the problem this creates. If everyone who wants to watch the fireworks show knows they can get away with watching it without paying, no one will be willing to pay for the show even though everyone wants to see it. The fireworks display's nonexcludability leads to "free riding." If everybody is free riding, though, the fireworks display never happens, even if everyone would have been willing to pay for it in the first place.

Pirates also confronted a free-riding problem on their ships, which left unsolved would prevent them from taking prizes. For a pirate ship to maximize its chances to take a prize, each crew member needed to exert his full effort. This meant remaining diligent in his daily duties, but especially giving his all in battle with a target, in extracting loot from victims, and so on. A dutiful pirates' job, then, could be very dangerous. In addition to the dangers of simply living and working aboard a ship, there was also the prospect of battle with quarries. Pirates faced a risk of being injured, which, in addition to imposing an immediate cost on them, might also make it more difficult for them to find future (pirate or nonpirate) employment. If any individual pirate slacked on the job, maybe not doing the most onerous part of his daily duties, or staying back a bit in the midst of battle so as not to get hurt, unless he played a critical role, the crew's probability of success would only be minimally diminished. In other words, with the exception of a few key pirates, the crew's success didn't depend on any individual pirate. Because of this, shirking wasn't costly to the individual pirate but exerting full effort was. This created an incentive for pirates to free ride on others' efforts.

The public good in this example is full pirate ship effort and the nonexcludable benefits are those of the ship's successful plunder. Of course, if a pirate weren't discreet about shirking, he could be identified as a slacker and excluded from any booty the crew subsequently captured. But if he did a good job of pretending to exert full effort, excluding him wasn't possible. From each individual pirate's perspective, then, the best thing to do was to pretend to exert full effort but in actuality slack off. But if all or even a significant number of pirates did this, the crew would be unsuccessful. To prevent this situation from undermining their criminal enterprise, private pirate governance therefore needed to provide for this public good and prevent pirate free riding.

To review, then, private pirate governance needed to provide rules to prevent interpirate conflict, and to enforce these rules; it needed to regulate pirate behavior that produced serious "negative externalities"; and it needed to provide important public goods and guard against the free-riding possibility these goods created. Although their particulars are different in important respects, these three features required for effective governance on pirate ships are fundamentally the same ones legitimate societies require for their success. In this way the problem of achieving successful pirate governance was no easier than the problem of achieving successful governance in the "civilized world." In fact, because pirates couldn't rely on a monopoly coercive power to overcome these obstacles as the legitimate world could through government, pirates' governance problem was that much more difficult to solve than "normal" society's governance problem. Despite this, private pirate governance successfully satisfied each of these features.

The Laws of Lawlessness: Pirate Constitutions

To create private governance pirate crews forged written constitutions, or "pirate codes," that specified their laws, punishments for breaking these laws, regulated negative externalities, and created a mechanism for overcoming the pirate free-rider problem discussed above. Additionally, pirate constitutions performed an important supplementary function in constraining officer behavior, discussed in chapter 2. Pirate constitutions originated with "articles of agreement" followed on buccaneer ships in the seventeenth century. The buccaneers called their articles a *chasse-partie*. These articles specified the division of booty among the officers and crew along with other terms of the buccaneers' organization. All sea bandits followed the basic rule of "no prey, no pay." Unless a pirating expedition was successful, no man received any payment. Alexander Exquemelin describes the chasse-partie that governed his crew's expedition in detail:

> The buccaneers resolve by common vote where they shall cruise. They also draw up an agreement or chasse partie, in which is specified what the captain shall have for himself and for the use of his vessel. Usually they agree on the following terms. Providing they capture a prize, first of all these amounts would be deducted from the whole

capital. The hunter's pay would generally be 200 pieces of eight. The carpenter, for his work in repairing and fitting out the ship, would be paid 100 or 150 pieces of eight. The surgeon would receive 200 or 250 for his medical supplies, according to the size of the ship.

Then came the agreed awards for the wounded, who might have lost a limb or suffered injuries. They would be compensated as follows: for the loss of a right arm, 600 pieces of eight or six slaves; for a left arm 500 pieces of eight or five slaves. The loss of a right leg also brought 500 pieces of eight or five slaves in compensation; a left leg 400 or four slaves; an eye, 100 or one slave, and the same award was made for the loss of a finger. If a man lost the use of an arm, he would get as much as if it had been cut off, and a severe internal injury which meant the victim had to have a pipe inserted in his body would receive 500 pieces of eight or five slaves in recompense.

These amounts having first been withdrawn from the capital, the rest of the prize would be divided into as many portions as men on the ship. The captain draws four or five men's portions for the use of the ship, perhaps even more, and two portions for himself. The rest of the men share uniformly, and the boys get half a man's share.

. . . When a ship is robbed, nobody must plunder and keep his loot to himself. Everything taken—money, jewels, precious stones and goods—must be shared among them all, without any man enjoying a penny more than his fair share. To prevent deceit, before the booty is distributed everyone has to swear an oath on the Bible that he has not kept for himself so much as the value of a sixpence, whether in silk, linen, wool, gold, silver, jewels, clothes or shot, from all the capture. And should any man be found to have made a false oath, he would be banished from the rovers, never more be allowed in their company.

Over time the buccaneers institutionalized their articles of agreement and social organization. The result was a system of customary law and meta-rules called the "Custom of the Coast," or the "Jamaica Discipline."

Eighteenth-century pirates built on this institutional framework in developing their own constitutions. Pirates created them "for the better Conservation of their Society, and doing Justice to one another." Each crew devised its own constitution, but pirate articles displayed strong similarities across crews. In describing the articles on Captain Roberts's ship, for instance, Johnson refers to "the Laws of this Company . . . principle Customs, and Government, of this roguish Commonwealth; which are pretty near the same with all Pyrates." Frequent intercrew interactions led to information sharing that facilitated constitutional commonality. More than 70 percent of Anglo-American pirates active between 1716 and 1726, for example, can be connected back to one of three pirate captains, Benjamin Hornigold, George Lowther, or Edward Low. Thus, the "pirate code," to the extent that it existed as a professionwide body of rules, emerged from piratical interactions and information sharing, not from a pirate king who centrally designed and imposed a common code on all current and future sea bandits.

Pirate articles of agreement required unanimous consent. Consequently, pirates democratically formed them in advance of launching pirating expeditions. "All [pirates] swore to 'em," sometimes on a Bible or, for one pirate crew, "upon a Hatchet for want of a Bible." The same was true for newcomers who joined pirate companies already under way. "When ever any enter on board of these Ships voluntarily, they are obliged to sign all their Articles of Agreement." Crews forged their articles alongside the election of a captain, quartermaster, and occasionally other smaller officers. Pirates sought agreement on their articles ex ante "to prevent Disputes and Ranglings afterwards." If a pirate disagreed with their conditions, he was free to search elsewhere for more satisfactory terms.

When multiple pirate ships joined together for an expedition they created similar articles establishing the terms of their partnership. On encountering one another at Grand Cayman, for example, Captain George Lowther and Edward Low's pirate crews forged such an agreement. Lowther "offering himself as an Ally; Low accepted of the Terms, and so the Treaty was presently sign'd without Plenipo's or any other Formalities." Likewise, crews that objected to the proposed articles or some other element of an intended multiship expedition were free to depart peaceably. In one such case, for example, "a Spirit of Discord" emerged between three pirate crews sailing in consort "upon which . . . [they] immediately parted, each steering a different Course."

The voluntary nature of consenting to a particular pirate ship's constitution facilitated what economists call "Tiebout competition" between pirate crews. Tiebout competition is the process whereby governments compete for citizens, so-named for the economist who first articulated this process, Charles Tiebout. The idea is a simple one. If citizens can "vote with their feet," governments must be more responsive to what citizens want. They must offer lower tax rates, better public services, and refrain from preying on citizens, or citizens will move to another jurisdiction that does. Governments care about this because their ability to raise tax revenues requires a tax base. And if citizens move out of one jurisdiction to another, in the jurisdiction citizens are fleeing from the tax base shrivels up. Pirates' voluntary governance structure means they didn't have governments. But the principle of Tiebout competition applies as

much to their floating societies as it does to competition between governments. To attract the men they needed pirate
crews had to offer favorable terms of employment. Since the
rules governing an expedition strongly affected the quality of a
pirate's life while he served as part of the crew, a significant element of the terms of employment was the desirability of a prospective crew's rules. Favorable employment terms also involved
nonpredatory officers, such as the captain and quartermaster.
Since pirates were free to enter or not enter into combination
with a particular crew's criminal enterprise, there was a strong
incentive to create favorable and effective rules.

Charles Johnson provides several examples of pirate constitutions, through which, as one court remarked, these rogues
were "wickedly united, and articled together." Consider, for instance, the articles aboard Captain Roberts's ship:

I. *Every Man has a Vote in the Affairs of Moment; has
equal Title to the fresh Provisions, or strong Liquors, at any
Time seized, and may use them at Pleasure, unless a Scarcity
make it necessary, for the Good of all, to vote a Retrenchment.*

II. *Every Man to be called fairly in Turn, by List, on board
of Prizes, because, (over and above their proper Share) they
were on these Occasions allowed a Shift of Cloaths: But if they
defrauded the Company to the Value of a Dollar, in Plate,
Jewels, or Money, Marooning was their Punishment. If the
Robbery was only betwixt one another, they contented themselves with slitting the Ears and Nose of him that was Guilty,
and set him on Shore, not in an uninhabited Place, but somewhere, where he was sure to encounter Hardships.*

III. *No person to Game at Cards or Dice for Money.*

IV. *The Lights and Candles to be put out at eight a-Clock
at Night: If any of the Crew, after that Hour, still remained
enclined for Drinking, they were to do it on the open Deck.*

V. *To keep their Piece, Pistols, and Cutlash clean, and fit for Service.*

VI. *No Boy or Woman to be allowed amongst them. If any Man were found seducing any of the latter Sex, and carry'd her to Sea, disguised, he was to suffer Death.*

VII. To *Desert the Ship, or their Quarters in Battle, was punished with Death or Marooning.*

VIII. *No striking one another on board, but every Man's Quarrels to be ended on Shore, at Sword and Pistol.*

IX. *No Man to talk of breaking up their Way of Living, till each shared a 1000 l. If in order to this, any Man should lose a Limb, or become a Cripple in their Service, he was to have 800 Dollars, out of the publick Stock, and for lesser Hurts, proportionately.*

X. *The Captain and Quarter-Master to receive two Shares of a Prize; the Master, Boatswain, and Gunner, one Share and a half, and other Officers one and a Quarter* [everyone else to receive one share].

XI. *The Musicians to have Rest on the Sabbath Day, but the other six Days and Nights, none without special Favour.*

Through such articles the pirates' private system of governance satisfied each of the three features required for successful governance discussed above. Let's look closer at how pirate articles satisfied these goals.

The Law and the Lash: Preventing Pirate Conflict

The first feature pirate governance required to be successful, remember, was laws to prevent conflict and provide for a peaceful and orderly pirate ship. Pirate articles achieved this by prohibiting the two big potential sources of social disorder, theft and violence. Sections II and VIII of Roberts's crew's articles, for example, regulated theft and violence respectively. Sections II and V of Edward Low's company's articles did the same, barring men to "to Strike or Abuse one another in any regard" or from "defrauding one another to the Value of a Ryal of Plate" and required that "if any Gold, Jewels, Silver, &c. be found on Board any Prize or Prizes to the value of a Piece of Eight . . . the finder" had to "deliver it to the Quarter Master in the space of 24 hours" lest he be considered guilty of stealing from the crew. Sections III and V on John Phillips's *Revenge* also declared it unlawful for "*any Man . . .* [to] *steal any Thing in the Company . . . to the Value of a Piece of Eight*" or to "*strike another whilst these Articles are in force.*" Pirate ships, then, weren't rock 'em–sock 'em, anything goes–type atmospheres. Although they did so privately, pirates created laws to facilitate social harmony and prevent social discord, just like legitimate societies do, and they did so for the same reason—because their ability to cooperate for mutual benefit required it. As Captain Johnson put it, "Nature, we see, teaches the most Illiterate the necessary Prudence for their Preservation, and Fear works Changes which Religion has lost the Power of doing."

Pirates' private system of governance also created punishments for law breakers and provided means for enforcing these penalties. Punishments for violating the laws on a pirate ship varied from physical tortures, such as "keel-hauling," which involved dragging the insolent pirate across the sharp and barnacled hull of the ship, to marooning—a practice pirate Joseph More described as "punishment among them for something notoriously villainous" whereby the offender is "put on shore on some uninhabited Cape or Island, with a Gun, some Shot, a Bottle of Powder, and a Bottle of Water, to subsist or starve." Pirates sometimes coupled marooning with ostracism if the transgressor managed to survive. Alternatively, they might downgrade the punishment of marooning instead of intensifying it if they considered the crime less severe. In Roberts's crew, for example, "*If the Robbery was only betwixt one another,*" as opposed to from the community plunder each crew member drew his pay from, "*they contented themselves with slitting the Ears and Nose of him that was Guilty, and set him on Shore, not in an uninhabited Place, but somewhere, where he was sure to encounter Hardships.*" To facilitate the enforcement of their laws against theft, pirates took additional simple but effective measures, such as employing random searches to hunt for anyone holding back loot. To ensure the quartermaster, who you'll recall from chapter 2 was in charge of watching over and distributing pirate booty, didn't hide plunder from the crew, some pirates prohibited their loot from being kept under lock-and-key. As pirate Peter Hooff described the situation on the *Whydah*, for instance, "Their Money was kept in Chests between Decks without any guard, but none was to take any without the Quarter Masters leave."

The articles on Captain John Phillips's ship provide a good idea of the range of punishments pirates applied for infractions of their other rules. Phillips's crew punished deserting with marooning, physical violence with "*Moses's Law (that is, 40 Stripes lacking one) on the bare back,*" and even capitally punished pirates who forced themselves on an unwilling woman. "*If at any Time we meet with a prudent Woman, that Man that offers to meddle with her, without her Consent, shall suffer present Death.*" Not too shabby for a group of godless "Hell-hounds."

Pirate articles didn't fully specify punishments for rule violations. In these cases violators didn't go unpunished, however. Instead, pirate articles stipulated that the wrongdoer "shall suffer what Punishment the Captain and Majority of the Company shall think fit." Similarly, for more severe infractions, crew members voted on punishments, "all the Pyrates Affairs being carried by that." As Richard Hawkins observed among his pirate captors, for instance, "If any one commits an Offence, he is try'd by the whole Company."

To settle inter–crew member disputes, such as allegations of theft, and to enforce the proscribed punishments if necessary, pirates relied on their democratically elected quartermasters. For minor accusations, crews left this duty exclusively to the quartermaster who "acts as a Sort of civil Magistrate on board a Pyrate Ship." If his mediation failed, the quartermaster refereed a duel between the parties on land to avoid damage to the ship. "The Quarter-Master of the Ship, when the Parties will not come to any Reconciliation, accompanies them on Shore with what Assistance he thinks proper, and turns the Disputants Back to Back, at so many paces Distance: At the Word of Command, they turn and fire immediately. . . . If both miss, they come to their Cutlashes, and then he is declared Victor who draws the first blood." Barbaric? Sure. But effective—both in terms of resolving crew conflicts and preventing conflicts between two pirates from damaging the vessel and thus spoiling things for the remaining crew. Far from lax or nonexistent, the piratical justice system was extensive and unforgiving. Pirate governance wasn't strict because pirates were sticklers. Pirate governance was strict because pirates couldn't rely on government to provide it for them. As historian Patrick Pringle put it, "They had no discipline, and therefore much self-discipline."

Though far from perfect, pirate articles worked well in preventing internal conflict and creating order aboard pirate ships. Although Blackbeard famously wrecked *Queen Anne's Revenge* and deserted part of its crew to increase the share out for him and his favorite crew members, and Walter Kennedy ripped off Bart Roberts's crew, sailing away with several accomplices and his fellow pirates' plunder, these were exceptions to the pirates' tendency to obey their rules and remain honest to their fellow rogues. According to one eighteenth-century commentator, the pirates' system of self-governance, "which kept Peace amongst one another, and under the Title of Articles, has produced a System of Government, which I think, (considering what the Persons were who fram'd it) as excellent for Policy as any Thing in *Plato*'s Commonwealth." That's pretty high praise for a "Pack of Sea Banditti."

Before discussing how pirates satisfied the other two features required for successful governance, we should highlight a few additional features of how pirate constitutions provided law and order. First, as discussed in chapter 2, pirate articles explicitly provided for a democratic form of governance: "*Every Man has a Vote in the Affairs of Moment.*" In this sense they were truly *constitutions*. Pirate articles not only established the rules governing pirate ships. They also established "rules about the rules"—that is, the decision-making criteria for the selection of laws and leadership. Pirate articles were therefore more than a simple list of social regulations. They governed how these regulations and the officers of their administration could be selected.

Second, pirate articles identified the terms of pirate compensation. In this way they were also like contracts between crew members. Putting these terms in writing helped prevent officers aboard pirate ships, such as the captain or quartermaster, from preying on crew members as some officers aboard navy and merchant vessels did. In particular, by making the terms of compensation explicit, pirate constitutions circumscribed the quartermaster's authority in dividing booty. When booty was indivisible, or there was a question as to its value and thus how many shares it counted for in payment, pirates sold the troublesome items or auctioned them at the mast and distributed the divisible proceeds accordingly. This practice prevented conflict between crew members and ensured a distribution of plunder consistent with the terms of the compensation agreement pirates signed on to. More important, it constrained the discretion of the quartermaster who might otherwise be in a position to circumvent the terms of compensation when loot was indivisible or of ambiguous value.

Notably, the pirate pay scale was very flat. On Roberts's ship, "*The Captain and Quarter-Master* [were] *to receive two Shares of a Prize; the Master, Boatswain, and Gunner, one Share and a half, and other Officers one and a Quarter*," with everyone else receiving one share. The difference between the highest and lowest paid person in this pirate crew was thus only a single share. The same scarcely progressive pay scale prevailed on pirate captain Edward Low's ship, whose articles stipulated: "The Captain is to have two full shares; the Master is to have one Share and one half; The Doctor, Mate, Gunner and Boatswain, one Share and one Quarter;" and everyone else one share. This was also true on Captain John Phillips's pirate ship whose articles read: "*The Captain shall have one full share and a half in all Prizes; the Master, Carpenter, Boatswain and Gunner shall have one Share and [a] quarter*," and everyone else a single share. This contrasts sharply with merchant vessels' pay scale where captains earned four or five times as much as regular sailors during peacetime.

One interpretation of the significantly smaller "wage gap" between pirates is that they were more interested in equality, "social justice," and egalitarian outcomes than merchant shipowners. But this is a downright peculiar interpretation given what we know about pirates, which is that they were as self-interested as anyone else and, given the opportunity, would happily take ten times as many shares as their fellow pirates if they could get away with it. The less romantic, but likely more accurate, explanation for the relative flatness of pirate pay scales is an economic one that goes back to pirates' lack of coercive government.

To ease the burden borne by their private system of governance, pirates needed to avoid as many opportunities for violent conflict that could erupt into fighting and tear their criminal organization apart as possible. Unsurprisingly, probably the greatest divisive force that threatened this possibility was money. Suspicions of unfairness, favoritism, and simple envy created unhappy specters for pirate ships. To minimize the chance of these natural human emotions disrupting or even totally undermining their profit-making purpose, pirates eliminated the greatest potential source of these emotions—large material inequalities. A relatively flat pay schedule that preserved some progressive elements but split booty roughly evenly accomplished this nicely and prevented undo stress on the pirates' private system of governance.

By more-or-less equally splitting their ill-gotten proceeds, pirates facilitated cooperation in another important way as well: through agreement about whether to continue plundering or to hang up the cutlass temporarily and dissolve the company instead. If nearly all pirates in a particular crew received the same payout from plunder, they were more likely to agree about whether to continue "on the account" or retire their expedition. This was important because it ensured that most pirates engaged in an ongoing plundering expedition had their hearts in it and would therefore exert full effort, improving the crew's chance of success. Contrast this with the situation that could prevail if different factions of a pirate crew had wildly different payouts from taking a prize. The faction that received a very large payout may be interested in ending the expedition right there. These pirates might have enough to live on for a while and not wish to go any further. The faction that received a very low payout, on the other hand, may be interested in keeping the whole crew together until its members have also earned enough to temporarily retire. The result would be intracrew conflict.

Thus, eminently reasonable economic considerations are likely responsible for pirate "egalitarianism," if one wants to call it that, not a quasi-socialist pirate ideology.

No Smoking, Please: Preventing Negative Externalities

The second feature pirate governance required to be successful was an ability to prevent negative externalities. Pirates' articles achieved this by establishing rules that carefully regulated activities likely to generate harmful spillovers that would inhibit the greater crew's ability to cooperate. The articles on Captain Roberts's ship, for example, required crew members to keep their weapons in good working order, or, as the article regulating this aspect of negative externalities on Phillips's ship read: "*That Man that shall not keep his Arms clean, fit for an Engagement, or neglect his Business, shall be cut off from his Share.*" Roberts's articles limited drunken raucousness to allow nonparticipant pirates to get sufficient sleep and to "give a Check to their Debauches"; prohibited onboard fighting that jeopardized the entire crew's ability to function; and prohibited activities, such as gambling, likely to lead to onboard fights. On similar grounds, some crews' articles prohibited women (and young boys), who might invite fighting or tension among crew members, aboard their ships. "This being a good political Rule to prevent disturbances amongst them," one pirate captive remarked, "it is strictly observed." In the same way, some pirate ships forbade activities such as firing one's guns or smoking in areas of the ship that carried combustible goods, such as gunpowder. According to the articles aboard John Phillips's ship, for example, "*That Man that shall snap his Arms, or smoak Tobacco in the Hold without a Cap to his Pipe, or carry a Candle lighted without a Lanthorn, shall suffer the same Punishment as in the former Article."*

Pirates relied on regulation instead of creating private property rights to address negative externalities for the same reasons college dormitories do. In pirates' particular situation, regulation was simply cheaper. Although in principle pirates could create property rights to overcome these externalities, the transaction costs of each individual pirate negotiating with all other members of his crew over how much he was to compensate them for the right to smoke in the hold, for instance, were prohibitively high. In contrast, it was comparatively inexpensive to create a rule restricting smoking in the hold.

The Sea Bandit Safety Net: Piratical Public Good Provision

Pirate articles satisfied the final feature required for successful governance—the provision of public goods, which in pirates' case referred to the need to solicit crew members' full effort—by creating an early form of social insurance, or workers' compensation. Pirate articles specified that before the proceeds of successful plunder were divided according to the pay scale established in the piratical contract, a certain sum would come out of the common purse to provide for those injured in the line of duty. As article IX of Captain Roberts's crew's constitution read, for instance: "*If . . . any Man should lose a Limb, or become a Cripple in their Service, he was to have 800 Dollars, out of the publick Stock, and for lesser Hurts, proportionately.*" Some pirate workers' compensation schemes were highly detailed. Different limbs were worth different amounts, reflecting the different values pirates attributed to these appendages, most likely in work-related purposes. Furthermore, in at least one crew, disability insurance payments continued indefinitely. As this ship's articles read, "*He that shall have the Misfortune to lose a Limb, in Time of Engagement, shall have the Sum of one hundred and fifty Pounds Sterling, and remain with the Company as long as he shall think fit,*" presumably drawing continual disability support from the crew's "publick Stock." The effect of pirate social insurance was to encourage full effort from each individual pirate, or at least to reduce the private disincentive to shirk, which improved pirates' ability to profit through plunder.

To further encourage full effort, pirate articles contained incentive provisions that paid bonuses to crew members who displayed exceptional courage in battle, were the first to spot potential targets, and so forth, out of the common purse. According to the buccaneers' rules, for instance, "Those who behaved courageously and performed any deed of extraordinary valour, or captured a ship, should be rewarded out of the common plunder." Similarly, according to section VIII of Ned Low's crew's articles, "He that sees a sail first, shall have the best Pistol or Small Arm aboard of her." These incentive provisions must have worked well since, as Johnson noted, "It must be observed, they [pirates] keep a good Look-out; for, according to their Articles, he who first espies a Sail, if she proves a Prize, is entitled the best Pair of Pistols on board, over and above his Dividend."

Pirate articles, then, satisfied each of the three features required for successful governance. What's even more incredible, they did so privately, without the aid of government. Since pirate constitutions were short and simple, they couldn't cover every contingency that might affect a crew. In this sense they were always incomplete. To deal with this, when a significant issue emerged, the crew gathered to act as a "judiciary" to interpret or apply the ship's articles to situations not clearly stipulated in the articles themselves: "In Case any Doubt should arise concerning the Construction of these Laws, and it should

FIGURE 3.1. Inside a pirate "courtroom": Captain Thomas Anstis's crew holds a mock trial. From Captain Charles Johnson, *A General History of the Robberies and Murders of the Most Notorious Pyrates*, 1724.

remain a Dispute whether the Party had infringed them or no, a Jury was appointed to explain them, and bring in a Verdict upon the Case in Doubt." The resulting "pirate council," as it's sometimes been called, created a quasi-judicial review process for pirate constitutions.

Alt for One and One for All: The Calculus of Piratical Consent

One important feature of pirate constitutions noted above that we haven't examined is how they required unanimous consent to enter into force. Why did pirates do this? The short answer is to facilitate their profit-making ability. The longer answer explains how constitutional unanimity facilitated pirates' profit-making ability in three ways.

The first of these ways is best understood in the context of a distinction between two kinds of costs of creating governance made by Nobel Prize–winning economist James Buchanan and Nobel Prize–deserving economist Gordon Tullock. One kind of cost is called "decision-making costs." Decision-making costs are the costs of arriving at a set of rules that will govern society. Debating the pros and cons of alternative rules and then actually taking votes on the various proposals are two forms decision-making costs can take. These costs are small when the population of voters is small. But they become large when this population grows.

The other major factor influencing the size of decision-making costs is the kind of voting rule used to make decisions. At one extreme is dictatorship. Since under dictatorship only one person determines the rules, there's no need for debate, no need for voting, and no need to secure anyone else's approval. Under dictatorship, decision-making costs are therefore extremely low.

At the other end of the spectrum is unanimity. Here, since a rule requires every single member of society's approval to pass, debate is likely to be intense and dragged out. Everyone must vote on the issue. And most important, since every person's consent is needed, a great deal of time, energy, and potentially other resources must be expended to convince every person of the desirability of the proposal. Under unanimity, decision-making costs are therefore very high. In between these polar ends of the decision-making cost spectrum are middle grounds, such as simple majority, which is more costly in terms of deci-sion-making costs than dictatorship, but less costly than una-nimity. There's also supermajority, which is more costly than simple majority, but still less costly than unanimity, and so on.

The other kind of cost of creating governance is called "ex-ternal costs." External costs are the costs borne by the members of society who disagree with the rules ultimately decided on. For example, if there's a ballot initiative in your town to decide whether to increase or decrease the speed limit on Main Street, and you vote to increase the limit but a majority of your fellow voters vote to decrease it, the speed limit is decreased and you suffer as a result. The main factor that influences the size of ex-ternal costs is the kind of voting rule society uses to make deci-sions. For example, if a new law only requires 10 percent of the voting population's approval to pass, the external costs of gover-nance are high. In principle a law may pass that 90 percent of the population views unfavorably. Closer to the other end of the spectrum, if, for instance, a new law requires a supermajority to pass, the external costs are much lower. Only a relatively small minority is at risk of living under a law it disagrees with using this voting rule. At the extreme end of this spectrum is unanim-ity. Since unanimity means everyone must agree to a law for it to pass, under unanimity nobody lives under a law he disagrees with. External costs under unanimity are therefore zero.

Since decision-making costs are higher when a rule requires a larger portion of society's approval to pass and external costs are lower when this is true, we face a trade-off in terms of these two costs of creating governance. We want to minimize the overall cost of creating governance, but by trying to reduce decision-making costs we increase external costs and vice versa. What's the right thing to do?

The answer to this question depends on how severe the increase in one kind of cost will be if we reduce the other. For example, if the issue being decided on is tremendously important, a decision-making rule closer to unanimity may be efficient. For a very important decision the external costs for those who disagree with the decision are very large. In this case it's worth bearing higher decision-making costs to prevent even more significant external costs. For instance, if a society is deciding how much income individuals will be allowed to earn, unanimity may be efficient even though it means higher decision-making costs. Contrast this with a situation in which the decision is essentially unimportant, for example, what kind of paper the rules will be written on. Here, since the decision-making costs of unanimity are extremely high, and the external costs of a simple majority or even a dictatorial decision are very low, a decision-making rule that requires only minimal public support is efficient.

This reasoning explains why pirates required unanimity for their articles. Since these articles set up the entire system of rules a consenting pirate would be required to live by for the remainder of his duration with his crew—from laws against theft, to division of booty, to workers' compensation coverage—the cost a pirate incurred if he disagreed with these rules but had to suffer under them nevertheless, that is, the external cost of anything other than unanimity, was huge. Contrast this situation with the simple majority rule pirates used to elect their captains and quartermasters, discussed in chapter 2. Here a simple majority made more economic sense than unanimity because the choice of captain and quartermaster, while very important, wasn't as important as the general overarching system of rules a pirate and his ship's officers had to live by. Since external costs were relatively lower in the case of deciding who would be captain or quartermaster, it made sense to accept some additional external costs in order to reduce decision-making costs. Thus, unlike their constitutions, pirates selected their captains and quartermasters by simple majority.

The second reason pirates required unanimity in creating their constitutions returns again to the issue of officer predation discussed in chapter 2. Recall that pirates checked captain predation through democratic elections for this office and by separating power through democratically electing a second officer—the quartermaster—who assumed a number of important powers otherwise concentrated in the captain's hands. Thus the quartermaster was in charge of distributing loot and provisions, and applying punishments to crew members who violated the ship's rules. By transferring these authorities to the quartermaster, a pirate crew could check the power of its captain. But what was to prevent the quartermaster from abusing his authority over these tasks to prey on the crew himself?

Democratic election to this office was one check on his ability to do this. Pirate constitutions were another. Pirate constitutions achieved this by making regulations, compensation, and punishments explicit, which circumscribed the quartermaster's discretion in his duties. This narrowed his latitude in exercising the power his crew endowed him with to check the captain's authority. For example, as noted earlier, a pirate crew's constitution explicitly identified what share of any booty each pirate was to receive. This circumscribed the quartermaster's discretion in distributing plunder, and thus his ability to cheat crew members. Similarly, the constitution also explicitly laid out what level of compensation each type of injury was worth, limiting the quartermaster's ability to cheat pirates along this dimension. Pirate constitutions also specified punishments for important infractions of their rules and reserved for crew members the right to vote on punishments for major violations, which constrained the quartermaster's discretion in punishing crew members and, as a result, his ability to abuse crew members as well.

Pirate constitutions not only created rules for quartermasters to follow. They also created what economists call "common knowledge" among crew members about when a quartermaster was overstepping his bounds. Since the constitution clearly delineated guidelines for the quartermaster to follow in administering the ship's rules, and constitutions were unanimously consented to, everyone knew when the quartermaster was transgressing his power and could agree that a transgression was in fact a transgression. This enabled pirates to coordinate on a common response to quartermaster abuse, which was to depose him and elect a new one. Since quartermasters knew everyone consented and agreed to the rules governing the ship, and furthermore, because the constitution made the rules quartermasters were to administer explicit, quartermasters also knew they couldn't get away with abusing their authority. If a quartermaster tried to abuse his power, the entire crew might react against him.

The historical record supports the effectiveness of pirate constitutions in this capacity, evidenced by the rarity of accounts of quartermaster abuse. Equally important, when abuse did occur, the evidence indicates crews successfully removed abusive quartermasters from power. For example, in 1691 quartermaster Samuel Burgess cheated his crew in the division of food. In response his crew marooned him. Similarly, when pirate captain John Gow's second in command, James Williams, grew violent and unruly, his crew "loaded him with Irons" and "resolved to put him on Board" a captured vessel "with Directions to the Master to deliver him on Board the first English Man of War they should meet with, in order to his being hang'd."

The third and final reason pirates required constitutional unanimity was to ensure harmony and "prevent Disputes and Ranglings" among the would-be pirate crew. In the absence of government to create peace and order on pirate ships, to avoid taxing their substitute private system of governance too much, it was important to assemble a crew that found the same rules and pay scheme agreeable. Constitutional unanimity achieved this by allowing pirates to self-sort at the outset. This not only prevented pirates with different ideas about how things should be run from coming into inevitable conflict once it was too late, it also helped enforce the rules decided on since no pirate who subsequently violated one of his ship's laws could claim he didn't know about or disagreed with them in his defense. In other words, unanimous consent at the constitutional stage promoted common knowledge about when a rule had been broken. This facilitated rule enforcement since everyone agreed on when a rule was violated and would therefore support the quartermaster in carrying out the constitutionally specified punishment. The punishments for breaking rules pirate articles identified thus posed credible threats to potential rule breakers who had strong incentives to adhere to the laws they agreed to be bound by.

Pirates' system of private governance was highly successful, a fact reflected in the success of piracy itself. One perceptive eighteenth-century seaman summarized the reason for this. As he put it, "As great robbers as they are to all besides," pirates "are precisely just among themselves; without which they could no more Subsist than a Structure without a Foundation." For their criminal enterprise to remain intact and produce sufficient crew member cooperation to successfully prey on target ships, pirates required "a Foundation." Since pirates were outlaws, government couldn't provide this foundation for them. But govern*ment*'s absence among pirates didn't mean govern*ance* was absent too. Pirates created private institutions to provide governance for themselves instead. Through the necessity of self-interest, disorderly, disagreeable, and violent delinquents managed to maintain surprisingly orderly, cooperative, and peaceful societies aboard their ships.

Oddly enough, probably the closest thing to seventeenth- and eighteenth-century pirate constitutions were seventeenth- and eighteenth-century Puritan church "covenants" forged by New England settlers. Their substance was very different from that of "pirate codes," of course. Further, church covenants didn't elaborate as many social rules as pirate constitutions did. Puritans had a more detailed document for that—the Bible. But their covenants were similar to pirate constitutions in that they created private governance for their societies' members—church members—and provided a consensual basis for authority.

Pirates weren't Puritans, of course. Nor did they create their elaborate system of private governance because of a special reverence for constitutions or fondness for following rules. They established rules because they recognized, as Captain Roberts did, that "it was every one's Interest to observe them, if they were minded to keep up so abominable a Combination." Adam Smith put it this way: "As society cannot subsist unless the laws of justice are tolerably observed, as no social intercourse can take place among men who do not generally abstain from injuring one another; the consideration of this necessity . . . was the ground upon which we approved of the enforcement of the laws of justice by the punishment of those who violated them." Smith was talking about legitimate society. But he might as well have been talking about pirates.

To secure profits, pirates needed to cooperate. And pirates could only cooperate if they could prevent conflict and provide order and incentives to work hard aboard their ships. In short, pirates created constitutions and adhered to their rules to achieve their profit-motivated goals. Pirates' self-interest made them understand "their greatest Security lay in this." According to one historian, as a result of their governance system, pirate ships were more orderly, peaceful, and well organized than many merchant ships, vessels of the Royal Navy, or indeed, even the British colonies. As an eighteenth-century observer described it, "At sea, they perform their duties with a great deal of order, better even than on the Ships of the Dutch East India Company; the pirates take a great deal of pride in doing things right."

4 SKULL & BONES
THE ECONOMICS OF
THE JOLLY ROGER

A two-hundred-ton ship appears on the horizon. From a distance it looks harmless. It's likely a merchantman, common in these waters, carrying cargo to the colonies. Your intuition is confirmed by the British ensign it flies, a red flag with the Union Jack in its upper-left corner. As she draws closer she hails and you oblige. You anticipate the standard civilities, perhaps to lend a helping hand. When the ship approaches nearer, however, you become suspicious. She's indeed a merchantman, but a highly modified one. Ominously, instead of the usual six guns, she's been reoutfitted with more than twenty. The deck of this beast is flush, the forecastle and quarterdeck having been removed and lowered. All ornament and superfluity is stripped away. Only cannons remain. What appeared to be a harmless merchantman is a menacing makeshift man-o'-war.

When the ship comes closer its formidable crew comes into sight. One hundred fifty motley pairs of eyes bear down on you. You look up and stare, quite literally, at death's head. Where the British ensign showed shortly ago, a black and beaten flag, emblazoned with skull and bones, ferociously stares back. The makeshift man-o'-war is a pirate ship. She fires a warning shot across your ship's bow and you hear the pirate's captain, who's shouting through a speaking trumpet, demand your captain come aboard and surrender. You panic, and rightfully so. What do you do?

You might try and run. But your ship is slow and lumbering, while theirs has been refitted for speed and agility. Your chances of escaping are slim. You could try and defeat the sleek and low-slung pirate. But she has 150 men and you have 15. What's more, for every gun on your ship, she has four. Most important, if you're feeling suicidal and decide to take your chances resisting this predator, when you lose you know you can expect no mercy. Your attacker's flag isn't for show. It communicates your fate should you be so saucy as to defy those who sail under it. The only option left is to submit to your well-armed predators, precisely what they're hoping for.

Perhaps the most recognizable of all pirate symbols is the skull and crossbones. It's nearly impossible to imagine a pirate ship without a black and skull-stippled flag flying ominously atop its mast. This image, so perfectly suited to common conceptions of pirates, is almost too good to be true. A flag of skull and bones seems more like an imaginative Hollywood producer's creation than something actual pirates invented. The skull-and-bones flag, however, is a genuine and important part of pirate history. The pirates called this flag the "Jolly Roger" and it played a central role in facilitating their profit-maximizing purpose.

Successful piracy was no easy task. Though drawn from the ranks of ordinary seamen, pirates weren't talentless hacks who camped out in one spot hijacking passersby. Nor did pirates wander aimlessly in the vast expanse of the sea. Although Captain Johnson described the process of pirating as "*going about like roaring Lions, seeking whom they might devour,*" it wasn't as easy as that. The average reader of this book, for example, couldn't simply decide to "go *on the Account,*" as pirates called it, which was their "term for Pyrating."

To do this, let alone do it effectively, you'd need an idea about how to sail a hundred-plus-ton vessel. If your oceangoing navigational skills are rusty, you're out of luck. In the time seventeenth- and most eighteenth-century pirates were operating, not even the marine chronometer, which might allow you to precisely determine longitude, had been invented yet. Instead, pirates relied on a navigational method called "dead reckoning." This method was about as sophisticated as it sounds. To "dead reckon" you needed to first determine your latitude. Lest your hopes be totally dashed, you had an instrument to aid you in this process. This instrument was the "backstaff," or "Davis quadrant," so-named for its inventor Captain John Davis. The backstaff amounted to a few wooden sticks, which when held to the navigator's face allowed him to simultaneously observe the position of the sun at noon determined by the location of its shadow cast along one of the sticks and the horizon. This permitted the viewer to measure the sun's altitude over the horizon, which could then be looked up in a series of printed tables that charted the sun's declination at the equator for each day of the year, describing the ship's latitude. After you measured your latitude at one spot, you could guess your longitude by measuring your speed and direction since your last latitude measurement. This was accomplished by throwing a wooden board, called a "chip log," over the side of the ship attached to rope, and with a "pegboard" upon which you charted any changes in speed or direction. The crudeness of this process shouldn't be mistaken for simplicity, however. Navigating a pirate ship also required intimate knowledge of the currents in different parts of the sea, the direction of winds, and a proper understanding of leeway. Piracy, like all early eighteenth-century maritime activity, was more art than science.

But to successfully pirate you'd need more than navigational expertise. You'd need to combine your navigational skills and oceanic agility with keen judgment and an ability to chase, run, and of course, wage battle with your vessel. Imagine approaching your target strategically to take advantage of current and wind conditions, and changes in these conditions on a moment's notice, as well as predicting your target's movements and responses to these conditions and your movements, all the while boxing it in and preparing for a fight. If this sounds tough, well, it was it was even tougher than it sounds. A pirate ship couldn't come barreling down some waterway like a squirrel sent down a waterslide, canons a-blazing and men scrambling every which way. Overwhelming a target was more like hunting a fox than lunging at a piñata.

Other things equal, the windward vessel had an advantage of speed and agility over the leeward vessel. With the wind at your back you were faster and better able to adapt to changes in wind direction than a ship sailing into the wind. For these reasons pirate ships made an effort to get themselves on the windward side of their targets. This wasn't a simple matter of getting upwind of their prey, however. Pirates had to do so without appearing threatening—if possible, without appearing even interested in the ship they hoped to attack. Furthermore, what the wind and tide conditions allowed the ship to do constrained the vessel's movement. Any number of wrong moves could raise the target's suspicion. Moving too quickly or nimbly is one example of this. As noted above, pirates modified their ships for speed and were noticeably faster than most merchant ships. If a ship was seen moving with too great speed or agility, it would send off red, or rather black, flags in the target's mind, alerting it to the possibility of an approaching pirate. Ideally, a pirate wanted to close in slowly on its target rather than launch headlong at the target full speed, which might scare it away. Once again, being windward of the prey facilitated this. A less obvious approach and all-out speed, which was needed after the ship's intent was discovered when the pirate ship was close, were easier to achieve of a leeward target. A windward target was possible as well, but more difficult to take.

To get close enough to their prey to take them, pirates used several ruses. The first was the flags of legitimate vessels. Pirates obtained these the same way they obtained their ships—by stealing them from the merchant crews they plundered. A pirate ship would carry a variety of stolen flags from different nations and fly the appropriate "colors" depending on where they were sailing or their prospective prize's nationality. Flags were critically important in the seventeenth and eighteenth centuries. Ships had little way of identifying one another without them. Pirates capitalized on this by tricking their targets with friendly colors, which allowed them to stealthily approach their unsuspecting prey until they could no longer hide their true identity.

Another tactic pirates used to hide their identity from targets was constructing canvas covers, colored to blend in with the ship's hull, which hid the pirate's gun ports. This made the pirate ship appear less well armed than it actually was, weaker and more merchantmanlike, so as not to prematurely scare its prey. On the other side of this, merchant ships played their own games, painting gun ports on their hulls or putting wooden "dummy" guns on their ships to appear better armed than they actually were in hopes of convincing potential attackers of their superior strength. In describing the 280-ton merchant ship he sailed on, for example, Edward Barlow, a late-seventeenth-century merchant sailor, noted its "twenty-four guns, with two wooden ones to make a show, as though we had more."

Another ploy pirates used to avoid detection was to put chicken coops and cargo on deck to look more like the merchant ships they pretended to be. To disguise their ship's speed, pirates sometimes tied barrels together, which they fixed to and threw over the ship's stern. The vessel would then drag the barrels behind it, which significantly reduced its pace. This enabled pirate ships to slowly approach targets without suspicion. Once within reach pirates would cut the barrels, producing a turbo boost that shot the ship forward, surprising the target, which by this time was unable to escape. Because of these ploys and because pirates modified their ships to be faster and more agile than most merchantmen they preyed on, if a target wanted to escape its attacker by fleeing, it had to decide this early when the approaching ship was still far away. This was certainly possible; but as historian Angus Konstam points out, "this wasn't always practical or expedient. Owners would have little time for merchant captains who greatly prolonged their voyages by running from every strange sail." Further, it wasn't uncommon for friendly ships to hail one another, requesting the other to heave to so assistance or information might be exchanged.

If a pirate tricked a merchantman into heaving to, the merchantman was as good as a sitting duck. The pirate ship could pull alongside the merchantman and at this distance, if need be, throw makeshift grenades, called "grenadoes," consisting of gunpowder, bits of metal, and fuse stuffed into a glass bottle, or "stinkpots," an early form of teargas similar to grenades but packed with rancid meat, fish, and other putrid items found on a ship. A seventeenth-century publication entitled, *Captain Sturmey's Magazine, or the Whole Art of Gunnery for Seamen 1669,* instructed sailors how to fashion an effective stinkpot. The list of recommended ingredients reads like a witch's brew: "Take of Powder 102, of Ship Pitch 60, of Tar 201, Saltpeter 81, Sulpher 81. Melt all together by a gentle Heat and being well melted, put in 21 of Cole dust, of the Filings of a Horse's Hoofs 61, of Assafoetida 31, of Sagapanam 11, and of Spatula Fetid half a pound." The only thing missing is "eye of newt." Needless to say, an appropriately concocted stinkpot worked wonders in disorienting the target crew. Pirates could then board the merchantman, which they achieved with grappling hooks.

But grappling distance wasn't necessary for pirates to "reach out and touch" their targets. The cannons a pirate ship carried could be as varied as its crew. Typical cannons, officially "guns" once aboard ship, were four- or six-pounders, called "minions" and "sakers" respectively. But larger guns were also used, including eight- and even twelve-pounders. A saker could reach a target nearly a mile away. The larger cannons could fire further accordingly. At the very least, then, a warning shot sufficient to give a good scare could be launched from a considerable distance. To break a target's hull closer proximity was needed. But at around 500 yards, a saker's effective range was nothing to sneeze at. Pirates had their choice of ammunition, which they selected depending on availability and their distance from a target. There were traditional canon balls, of course, or "roundshot," as they were called, but also "grapeshot," a mixture of musket balls and other metallic odds and ends shot out of cannon creating a shotgun-blast type effect, and "chainshot," in which two canon balls were shot simultaneously out of a ship's gun connected by rod or chain. The broader area chainshot covered allowed it to do a different kind of damage, taking out masts and rigging as it slung through the air.

Pirates' superior strength, in conjunction with our image of them as blood-lusting, battle-loving, and downright fiendish curs, would seem to suggest they were happy to engage in, and indeed devilishly hoping for, a good brawl, complete with booming canons and clashing cutlasses. But just the opposite was true. Pirates were loath to engage in a fight, even with a target they easily dominated. This is another case where pirate myth conflicts sharply with pirate reality. And, like other pirate myths, the key to piercing this one lies in understanding pirates' profit-seeking purpose.

Peace-Loving Pirates?

Among the chief obstacles pirates confronted in attempting to maximize profit from plundering expeditions was keeping their costs down. Piratical costs of production included, among other things, the costs associated with battling potential prizes. Since armed robbery was the primary means of piratical plunder, pirates faced the sorts of problems any organized band of armed thieves would face. Foremost among these was minimizing violent conflict. If pirates failed to do this, they incurred several profit-eating costs. First, conflict with a target meant the possibility of crew casualties. In addition to deaths, pirates found incapacitating injuries or other kinds of maiming costly to their crews. For instance, to keep pirate insurance claims, discussed in chapter 3, from becoming overbearing, pirates needed to minimize battle-related injuries.

The second profit-eating cost of violent battle was the potential for damage to the pirate ship. This was problematic on two fronts. First, it reduced pirates' effectiveness in chasing and defeating later prey. A pirate ship with a hole in it, for example, would be slower and less agile than an undamaged vessel. Further, since pirate ships were stolen, a damaged ship reduced pirates' ability to take undamaged ships as replacements. Because of this, a damaged ship needed to be repaired. Many repairs, however, had to be undertaken by pirate carpenters on or near land. Pirates identified a number of small hidden landings from which they could undertake such repairs. But additional time spent in repair reduced the time spent plundering merchant ships and increased the probability of capture by authorities. When on or near the shore undertaking repairs or otherwise tending to the maintenance of their ships, pirate crews were vulnerable to attack. To "careen" their ships, for instance—the process of removing sea debris that accumulated on a ship's hull—pirates had to remove the ship's guns, cargo, and topmast, and heel her over with blocks and tackle fastened to the mast and trees ashore, allowing the ship to tilt sufficiently to expose one side of her bottom for cleaning and repair. Then the ship would need to be heeled over on her other side to expose the other half of the vessel's bottom for cleaning and repair. Exposed in this state, pirates were easy targets for navy ships or other pirate hunters. Walter Moore, for instance, captain of the *Eagle*, captured George Lowther's pirate crew while it careened on an island off Venezuela. To avoid these costs of a damaged ship, pirates needed to minimize the frequency and duration of repairs, which in turn required minimizing violent engagement with targets that damaged their ships.

Finally, battle between a pirate and its prey could damage the prize. Stolen ships had value to pirates since they sometimes "traded up" when they took a superior vessel. Of course, a damaged ship was less valuable to them than an undamaged one. In the extreme, if pirates inadvertently sunk their target, the entire prize would be lost. In this way, violent conflict not only contributed to the cost side of pirating expeditions but could diminish the revenue side as well.

To reduce these cost of taking prey pirates sought to overwhelm victims without violence. "Their whole policy was directed towards taking prizes without having to fight for them." Actually achieving this was harder than it sounds, however. Although pirate ships frequently outmanned and outgunned their quarries by a factor of three or more, merchant ships weren't defenseless. Most carried several guns and some succeeded in damaging and escaping their pirate attackers. To minimize merchant ship resistance and thus the costs discussed above, pirates developed their infamous flag, the "Jolly Roger." The origin of the Jolly Roger's name is debated, but probably came from an antiquated and impolite nickname for the devil, "Old Roger." Another possibility is that the name derives from the original French buccaneers' red flag, the *jolie rouge*, or "pretty red." Ironically, rather than an emblem of blood-thirsty pirates, the Jolly Roger reflects pirates' strong desire to avoid violent conflict with their prey.

Pirate flags originated with the buccaneers in the seventeenth century. The buccaneers flew red flags, which communicated to targets they would take "no quarter" if they were resisted. If the red flag was displayed and the target resisted, the assaulting pirates mercilessly slaughtered the target's crew. Eighteenth-century pirates substituted black flags, often adorned with skulls and bones, for the buccaneers' red ones. The first recorded account of the Jolly Roger is on the French pirate Emanuel Wynne's ship in 1700. A witness described it as "A Sable Flag with a White Death's Head and Crossed Bones in the Fly." By 1717 references to the Jolly Roger begin to appear regularly. The skull-and-crossbones motif has received the most attention. Captain Samuel Bellamy's crew, for instance, flew the classic pirate ensign, a "large black Flag, with a Death's Head and Bones a-cross." An eyewitness described the flags in Blackbeard's fleet similarly, these being "Black Flags and Deaths Heads in them." Some pirates never retired the red flag. Several ships in Blackbeard's consort, for instance, flew "Bloody Flags." Other pirates used the black and red flag together. As Richard Hawkins, who was taken prisoner by pirates in 1724, explained it: "When they fight under *Jolly Roger*, they give Quarter, which they do not when they fight under the Red or Bloody Flag."

However, pirate flags were considerably more varied than either the classic skull-and-bones on black or plain red varieties suggest. They also depicted hourglasses, full skeletons, flexing arms, swords, bleeding hearts, and related symbols of strength, death, and destruction. One pirate ship Captain Johnson discussed, for example, "let fly her Jack, Ensign and Pendant, in which was the Figure of a Man, with a Sword in his Hand, and an Hour-Glass before him, with a Death's Head and Bones." Another "had the Figure of a Skeleton in it, and a Man pourtray'd with a flaming Sword in his Hand, intimating a Defiance of Death itself." Pirate captain Francis Spriggs's crew favored a "*Jolly Roger*, (for so they call their black Ensign, in the middle of which is a large white Skeleton, with a dart in one hand, striking a bleeding Heart, and in the other an Hour Glass)." An unusual Jolly Roger one witness reported was a photonegative of the traditional pirate flag, "a white Ensign with the figure of a dead man spread in it."

Several pirates coupled the Jolly Roger with the official flag of England or other countries. One witness, for instance, described Bartholomew Roberts's ship, "English Colours flying, their Pirate Flagg at the Topmast-Head, with Deaths Head and Cutlash." According to another eyewitness, Captain Roberts's pirate fleet sailed under a veritable rainbow of national and pirate emblems. "The Colours they fought under (beside the Black Flag) were a red English Ensign, a King's Jack, and a Dutch Pendant."

Roberts customized his ship's flag to send a pointed message to the governors of Barbados and Martinique who dared to send warships after the notorious pirate captain to bring him to justice. According to Johnson, "*Roberts* was so enraged at the Attempts that had been made for taking him, by the Governors of *Barbadoes* and *Martinico*, that he ordered a new Jack to be made, which they ever after hoisted." Thereafter, this crew had "a black Silk Flag flying at their Mizen-Peek, and a Jack and Pendant of the same: The Flag had a Death's Head on it, with an Hour-Glass in one Hand, and cross Bones in the other, a Dart by it, and underneath a Heart dropping three Drops of Blood— The Jack had a Man pourtray'd in it, with a flaming Sword in his Hand, and standing on two Skulls, subscribed *A.B.H.* and *A.M.H. i.e.* a *Barbadian*'s and a *Martincan*'s Head."

FIGURE 4.1. Jolly Roger: Captain Bartholomew Roberts's pirate flags wave in the background. From Captain Charles Johnson, *A General History of the Robberies and Murders of the Most Notorious Pyrates*, 1724.

Although the specific images on pirate flags varied, the purpose was the same in each case. As Snelgrave described it, this was "to terrify Merchant-Men." The hourglass communicated time was running out, the swords, fierce battle, and the skulls and skeletons, death for resistors. Countless historians of piracy have echoed Snelgrave's rationale for the Jolly Roger. But on closer inspection the traditional explanation for pirate flags— to frighten targets—by itself, anyway, leaves something to be desired. Being threatened by an attacker several times stronger than you would certainly strike fear into your heart. And, as noted above, the gap between pirate and prey strength could easily be this size or larger. But it's difficult to see how flying a skull-emblazoned flag would add substantially to this fear. Pirates' superior strength alone would seem to be enough to lead targets to surrender. After all, what's the point of waging a battle you know you'll lose? It's puzzling, then, why pirates bothered with the trouble of constructing the Jolly Roger and hoisting it when they were in striking distance of their prey.

The Pirate and the Peacock

A bit of economic theory may resolve this puzzle, if only speculatively and incompletely. In hoisting the Jolly Roger pirates may have been engaged in what economists call "signaling." Signaling works a lot like it sounds. Individuals engage in certain behaviors, such as wearing a tie, or getting an education, that send signals about the kind of person they want others to think they "really are." All of us signal everyday. We dress in uncomfortable clothes to fit in at the office; we send flowers to our loved ones and take important people out to expensive dinners. Although we enjoy doing these things to some extent, we also do them to communicate something it's in our interest for others to believe about our intelligence, wealth, and overall quality— whether that something's true or not.

The key to a successful signal is that it must be more costly for some types of individuals to send than for others. If not, the people for whom it's false will have an incentive to send it too. Wearing sweatpants to the office, for example, wouldn't convey that you're "a professional" to those around you. In fact, it would almost certainly signal exactly the opposite. Likewise, taking your date to McDonald's wouldn't signal high income. The reason "cheap talk" doesn't work as an effective signal is because the signal is equally inexpensive for both the kind of person you're trying to suggest you are and the kind of person you're trying to suggest you're not. Because of this, the signal contains no useful information. The signal receiver can't tell if you took her to McDonald's because you're poor, or you're rich but have poor taste. Cheap talk signals result in what economists call a "pooling equilibrium." In a pooling equilibrium both the "high-quality" and "low-quality" types of individuals send the same signal, preventing receivers from distinguishing which people are high quality and which are low quality. Costly signals, in contrast, can prevent this situation. It's more difficult for a low-intelligence person to make it through MIT than it is for a high-intelligence person. So, by getting a degree from MIT, an individual is able to successfully signal her intelligence to potential employers who know that because she made it through MIT she must be a high-quality potential employee. The reason this works is because of the signal's costliness, and in particular, because the signal is more costly for one type of person to send than for another.

If you go to a zoo, you can observe successful signaling in the animal kingdom. Ever wonder why peacocks have such large plumes? It seems like this would be an evolutionary disadvantage because their big, brilliant feathers make them easier prey for predators. Biologist Amotz Zahavi suggested a solution to this puzzle in the 1970s, which is rooted in the idea of signaling. Imagine a world of peacocks, some of which have large plumage and others of which don't. Precisely because those with plumage are more susceptible to predators, Zahavi reasoned, they signal they've passed the test of nature, avoiding or fending off predators. Peacocks with plumage are therefore more attractive mates, leading them to reproduce, while those without lavish tails die out.

The peacock's feathers in this example are the costly signal— a behavior that's more "expensive" for weak, inept peacock's than for strong, successful ones. Because of this, potential mates can identify and procreate with the "good" peacocks—those

with plumage—leading the "bad" peacocks—those without—
to be weeded out through sexual selection. This signal results in
what economists call a "separating equilibrium," where signal
receivers can distinguish between the different types of signal
senders. In terms of using costly signals to distinguish themselves from others, pirates may have been a lot like peacocks.

During most of the great decade of piracy from 1716 to 1726,
when the Jolly Roger made its most frequent appearance, the
maritime powers of Europe were officially at peace with one another. Despite this, throughout the period French and Spanish
ships continued to attack British and other merchant vessels.
Both France and Spain had "coast guards," government-com-
missioned warships charged with protecting their respective
coasts from illicit foreign traders called "interlopers." The Spanish Guarda Costa was the most enthusiastic enforcer of its
country's trade monopoly. Officially, the Spanish coast guard
was restricted to taking interlopers near the coasts it protected.
But in practice these ships often cruised the waters far from
shore in search of merchant vessels carrying any goods they
could use to justify seizing in alleged violation of the law that restricted trade with Spain's possessions in and around the Caribbean. From the end of the War of the Spanish Succession in
1713 through the end of the Golden Age of Piracy in the late
1720s, British colonial officials in the West Indies and North
America complained of the overzealous Spanish coast guard,
which was capturing and condemning British trading vessels
against the peace created by the Treaty of Utrecht. Virginia governor Alexander Spotswood, for instance, wrote to the members of the Council of Trade and Plantations in 1717 to inform
them "that the Spaniards" had recently taken a "man and his
vessell on the high seas without being near any of their Dominions, and without any hostility offered on his part." Spotswood
added that "every vessell belonging to H.M. subjects may expect

the like treatment" if the Guarda Costa were allowed to continue. This wasn't an isolated incident. Over the next ten years, colonial officials repeatedly complained of unscrupulous coast guards plundering innocent merchant ships.

The Spanish coast guard didn't take merchant vessels on anything like the scale that privateers did in official times of war. Further, these ships confined their activity to the waters of the Caribbean and never went as far as the Indian Ocean, where pirates sometimes traveled. Nevertheless, beginning in the years following the end of the War of the Spanish Succession and continuing beyond the rapid decline of piracy in the 1720s, there were other potential attackers in many of the areas pirates frequented. In addition to French and Spanish coast guard vessels, between 1718 and 1720 British and Spanish privateers also inhabited the waters surrounding the West Indies. A few traversed the water lanes encompassing portions of the greater Pirate Round, sailing as far as the South Sea to the west and Africa's Atlantic coast to the east. The short and consequently oft-forgotten War of the Quadruple Alliance thus gave rise to another class of potential attackers, albeit in small numbers, that sought to seize merchant ships at the same time and in some of the same parts of the ocean as pirates.

The presence of these other belligerent marine vessels provides a clue why pirates went through the trouble of using the Jolly Roger when they attacked their prey: Pirates wanted to distinguish themselves from the other assaulting vessels merchant ships might encounter. Britain criticized the Spanish Guarda Costa for inhumanely treating some British prisoners it captured. Nevertheless, at least in principle, the viciousness coast guard vessels could show toward merchant crews they assaulted was limited because they were government-sanctioned cruisers. They weren't permitted to wantonly slaughter merchant crews that resisted them after these crews cried out for quarter, for instance. In contrast, pirates weren't even theoretically constrained in how they treated those they overcame. Pirates were outlaws and would be hanged if authorities captured them whether they massacred merchant crews they attacked or not. In this sense, for pirates, massacring resistors was essentially costless. A piratical threat to kill all those who didn't immediately surrender to them peacefully was consequently a very credible one. This threat's credibility facilitated a simple pirate policy one pirate described as "No Quarter should be given to any Captain that offered to defend his Ship."

An angry pirate therefore posed a greater danger to merchant ships than an angry Spanish coast guard or privateer vessel. Because of this, merchant ships may have been more willing to attempt resisting these "legitimate" attackers than their piratical counterparts. This would explain the answer captain William Wyer's crew members gave him when Wyer asked if they would defend their vessel against an approaching, unknown belligerent: "Asking them if they would stand by him and defend the ship, they answered, if they were Spaniards they would stand by him as they had Life, but if they were Pirates they would not Fight." When Wyer's men determined it was Captain Blackbeard's crew bearing down on them, they "all declared they would not Fight and quitted the Ship believing they would be Murthered by the Sloops Company."

To achieve their goal of taking prizes without a costly fight, it was therefore important for pirates to distinguish themselves from other ships also taking prizes on the seas. The Jolly Roger offered pirates a way to do this by signaling to targets that the sailors assaulting them were the totally unconstrained variety—those who could murder the entire crew if it resisted. As one witness described it, the "black Flag with a Death's Head in it . . . is their Signal to intimate, that they will neither give nor take Quarter." The Jolly Roger, then, signaled "pirate," which meant two things. If you resist us, we'll slaughter you. If you submit to us peacefully, we'll let you live. As Snelgrave summarized it, the Jolly Roger's message to merchantmen was "to surrender on penalty of being murdered if they do not." The skulls, swords, and bleeding hearts that graced many black flags left little room for interpretation. "Everybody knew what these images were meant to convey."

And woe to the few who resisted nonetheless. Pirate captain Edward Low, for example, "had [a victim's] Ears cut off close to his Head, for only proposing to resist ... [his] black Flag." In another case Low's crew came upon a ship, "and because at first they shewed Inclinations to defend themselves and what they had, the Pyrates cut and mangled them in a barbarous Manner." Bartholomew Roberts's crew assaulted a Dutch interloper, which, after "mentaining an obstinate defence for four hours ... killed a great many of the pirates." Ultimately, however, the interloper "being overpower'd was forced to submit and what men the pirates found alive on board they put to death after several cruel methods."

Edward England's pirate crew, which sought to capture Captain James Macrae's East Indiaman, also illustrates the credibility of pirates' commitment to following through on the Jolly Roger's deadly promise. England's crew ultimately overcame the East Indiaman, but only "after a desperate resistance." Captain England, it seems, grew soft on Macrae and didn't want to murder him as pirate policy—per the Jolly Roger—dictated. However, his crew's response to this ill-founded mercy that violated piratical protocol points to the seriousness with which pirates took their policy. "*England* was inclined to favour Captain *Mackra*; but he was so free to let him know, that his Interest was declining amongst them; and that the Pyrates were so provok'd at the Resistance he made against them, that he was afraid he should hardly be able to protect him." In the end, England succeeded in protecting the resistant merchant ship captain. But true to the effectiveness of pirates' democratic system of checks and balances discussed in chapter 2, "Captain *England* having sided so much with Captain *Mackra's* Interest, was a Means of making him many Enemies among the Crew; they thinking such good Usage inconsistent with their Polity, because it looked like procuring Favour at the Aggravation of their Crimes; therefore . . . he was soon *abdicated* or pulled out of his Government, and marooned."

For the most part, pirates also stuck to the sunny side of the Jolly Roger's promise: mercy for those who peacefully surrendered. According to William Snelgrave, for example, one of his pirate captors informed him they "observe strictly that Maxim established amongst them not to permit any ill usage to their Prisoners after Quarter given." Captain Low's company enshrined this policy in its articles, which stipulated "Good Quarters to be given when Craved."

The Jolly Roger worked marvelously in limiting violent conflict. As the *Boston News-Letter* reported, those merchant crews "that have made Resistance have been most barbarously butchered, without any Quarter given them, which so intimidates our Sailors that they refuse to fight when the Pirates attack them." Pirates "deliberately publicized [the] policy" behind their flags, "which was so effective that they hardly ever needed to kill." Captain Johnson, for example, describes one case in which two French cruisers chased Bartholomew Roberts's crew, mistakenly believing Roberts's vessel to be a foreign merchant ship prohibited by French monopoly from trading in such waters. "Supposing him to be one of these prohibited Traders, [the cruisers] chased with all the Sail they could make, to come up with him; but their Hopes, which had brought them very nigh, too late deceived them, for on hoisting of *Jolly Roger*, (the Name they give their black Flag) their *French*

Hearts failed, and they both surrendered without out any, or at least very little Resistance." Surely part of the fear motivating this surrender was the knowledge that, as pirates, Roberts's men could and would slaughter the French crews for resisting them.

Thus most merchant crews responded to pirate attack in the way Benjamin Edwards's crew members did when George Lowther's pirates assaulted them. "Fearing the Consequence of too obstinate a Resistance against those lawless Fellows," they peacefully submitted to their pirate attackers. Indeed, pirate captain Ned Low simultaneously attacked several vessels and managed to take them all without spending so much as a bullet. "He threaten'd all with present Death who resisted, which stuck such a Terror to them, that they yielded themselves up a Prey to the Villains, without firing a Gun." The Jolly Roger's success explains the surprising confidence one tiny pirate crew exhibited. Though they had only five crew members among them, they "sail'd away down the Coast, making them a black Flag, which they merrily said, would be as good as fifty Men more, *i.e.* would carry as much Terror."

Though plastered with images of death and destruction, the pirate flag wasn't all gloom and doom. Pirate targets were, of course, worse off as a result of pirate attack. They had to surrender their goods to thieves. However, given that merchant ships couldn't avoid this fate in most cases, the Jolly Roger operated to *save* merchant sailor lives, not take them. Pirates used the Jolly Roger to enhance their profit through plunder. But it was the profit motive that led them to overtake victims in the least violent manner possible. By signaling pirates' identity to potential targets, the Jolly Roger prevented bloody battle that would needlessly injure or kill not only pirates, but also innocent merchant seamen. Ironically, then, the effect of the death head's symbolism was closer to a dove carrying an olive branch.

Pirates, Pretenders, and Pooling Equilibrium

We've passed over an important part of the story here, however. Recall that for a signal to successfully distinguish various types of potential senders, it must be more costly for one type to send than for the other. For the Jolly Roger to successfully signal to potential prizes that its attackers were pirates rather than privateers or coast guard attackers, then, it needed to be more expensive for legitimate attackers to use than it was for pirates. If it weren't, legitimate attackers would also want to fly the Jolly Roger, rendering it useless for pirates. So, how was the Jolly Roger cheap for pirates but expensive for legitimate ships?

The Jolly Roger was a well-known symbol of piracy. As the court declared at the trial of Bartholomew Roberts's crew, for instance, the accused had acted "under a Black Flag, flagrantly by that, denoting your selves common Robbers, Opposers and Violators of all Laws, Human and Divine." Ships attacking under the death head's toothy grin were therefore considered criminal and could be captured and prosecuted as pirates. Since pirates were criminals anyway, for them, flying the Jolly Roger was costless. If they were captured, the penalty was the same whether they used the Jolly Roger or not—the hangman's noose. For legitimate ships, however, things were different. To retain at least a veneer of legitimacy, privateers and Spanish coast guard ships couldn't sail under pirate colors. If they did, they could be hunted and hanged as pirates. For example, Governor Hart of St. Christophers sent a man-of-war "who is now cruizing among the French and Spanish Islands of these practices, of the Spanish guarda de la costa's; who is resolv'd to bring in all such pirates, where he shall find a black flag." Because of this, while the Jolly Roger signal was "free" for pirates to send, it was expensive for legitimate ships to send. As a result, pirates were more likely to use it than "legitimate" sea raiders. On seeing the Jolly Roger hoisted, merchant ships could therefore reasonably conclude they were under pirate, as opposed to coast guard or privateer, attack. Knowing this, they knew it was better to surrender without resisting.

Despite this, in some cases legitimate belligerent ships couldn't resist the benefits of hoisting the Jolly Roger to take targets. One colonial official who complained about the Spanish coast guard problem, for instance, suggested that one of these supposedly legitimate vessels—captained by a former pirate—was out cruising, taking British ships under pirate colors. "When he finds any vessel he can overpower, [he] hoists a black flag, and acts like a pirate. But if he meets any ship of war, or others that are too strong for him, he then produces a Commission from the Governor of Porto Rico, as a Guarda de la Costa." This coast guard captain evidently remembered the benefits of marauding under pirate colors. He wasn't alone. "To intimidate" merchant ships into surrenduring, several coast guard vessels "frequently hoisted and fought under pirate's colours." These vessels were trying to exploit the easier surrender the Jolly Roger enabled by pretending they were pirates. So, although flying the black flag was costly for legitimate belligerent vessels, it wasn't costly enough to prevent them from doing so altogether, a fact that undoubtedly irked many pirates.

The Jolly Roger, then, wasn't able to establish a perfect separating equilibrium. But it must have avoided perfect pooling as well, or else pirates, and "legitimate" belligerents who sometimes pretended to be pirates, wouldn't have found any benefit in using it. Indeed, a comment from the anonymous author of a paper on the sugar trade who complained of coast guard vessels co-opting the Jolly Roger for their own purposes suggests that despite this contamination of the separating equilibrium pirates sought to establish with their flag, the Jolly Roger managed to preserve its purpose. Writing in 1724, this author remarked that navigation is made "as dangerous as it now is by pirates and the guard de coast vessels, the latter of which are undoubtedly supported underhand by the Spaniards in Europe." He added that "on the faith of treaties our merchants fit out large adventures and fall into the hands of an enemy one dreams nothing of [the Spanish coast guard], and for that reason no resistance is made, but if there is up goe the pirate colours, at sight whereof our men will defend their ship no longer." The implication of this fellow's comments is clear. When merchantmen believed their attackers were nonpirates they might resist. But when merchantmen saw the Jolly Roger they concluded they were under pirate attack and surrendered without further ado. Thus, although some Spanish coast guard ships illicitly appropriated the pirate flag, this confirms the Jolly Roger signal was effective. Of course, if all "legitimate" belligerent vessels had done the same all the time, the Jolly Roger would have been rendered ineffective. But because of the high cost of doing so pointed to above, they didn't, allowing the pirate flag to work its magic despite pirate pretenders who sometimes adopted it.

A different, but related, problem also threatened to undermine the Jolly Roger's effectiveness. This one, however, came from within the pirates' camp rather than outside it. Weaker pirate crews had an incentive to free ride on the skull-and-bones imagery. Not all pirate crews were large and powerful. If a weak crew hoisted the Jolly Roger to overtake its prey without a fight, but its prey took its chances in battling the crew nonetheless, the prey might defeat the pirate crew indicating to other merchant ships that the Jolly Roger wasn't so fearsome after all. If this happened, even strong pirate crews might find their prey resisting them, destroying the signaling power of the black flag and eroding pirates' precious profit.

One likely reason this problem didn't plague pirates is that, as discussed above, many pirate crews customized their flags.

Flags were similar enough to signal "pirate," but different enough to communicate a more specific identity—namely, which particular pirate crew was attacking. Bart Roberts's crew, recall, sailed under a flag that featured its captain standing atop "a *Barbadian's* and a *Martincan's* Head." Other pirate crews' Jolly Rogers depicted hourglasses, bleeding hearts, and full skeletons. If particular flags became associated with particular pirate crews, stronger sea scoundrels could internalize the benefit of their crew's Jolly Roger, overcoming the black flag free-rider problem.

The economics of the Jolly Roger sheds light on several important features of eighteenth-century pirates. First, piracy was no easy task. In addition to the sailing expertise required for successful piracy, there was the all-important art of plunder. To get within cornering distance, pirate ships had to fool merchant ships into thinking they were harmless or friendly. Pirates modified their vessels to enhance their speed and agility to feign innocuous approaches and to chase down and corner targets, flew false flags, and used other ploys to get within striking distance of potential prizes. On the other side of this dance were merchantmen, which took steps to ward off potential piratical predators, such as "arming" their ships with dummy guns and painting pretend canon ports on their vessels. In the end, however, pirates usually had the upper hand. Their ships were stronger, faster, and carried more men.

Despite this, pirates still faced a significant problem in taking prey. They didn't want to use their muscle to overpower potential prizes. In fact, contrary to popular perception, which portrays pirates as great lovers of violent conflict and bloody mayhem, pirates wanted to overcome potential prizes peacefully.

This wasn't because pirates were pacifists. Their desire to avoid violence stemmed from their desire to maximize profit. A violent clash was costly to pirates. It could cause pirate injuries or deaths, damage their primary tool of plunder—the pirate ship— or even worse, do irreparable damage to booty. Battle, therefore, not only raised pirates' operating costs, but also threatened to reduce piratical revenue.

To strengthen their targets' incentive to peacefully submit, pirates developed the Jolly Roger. Existing explanations for the Jolly Roger focus on its effect in terrifying merchantmen into surrender. However, they fall short in explaining why a pirate ship many times stronger than its victim would need to resort to a skull-emblazoned flag to achieve this. The economics of signaling suggests a possible answer to this puzzle. By distinguishing pirate attackers from "legitimate" potential attackers prowling the sea that weren't quite as fearsome to resist as pirates, the Jolly Roger allowed pirates to capitalize on their status as total outlaws who could credibly commit to murdering entire crews if they resisted. The Jolly Roger communicated pirates' policy toward targets very clearly. When merchantmen saw it they knew what choices they faced. Rather than risking resistance and subsequently slaughter, most prizes surrendered without a fight.

Finally, and perhaps most important, pirates' pursuit of profit, which led them to adopt the Jolly Roger, operated to enhance the welfare of pirates and their prey. Targets would have undoubtedly been better off if they weren't accosted by sea bandits. But conditional on pirates' presence, the Jolly Roger ensured a "peaceful theft" instead of a violent and bloody battle. Thus, although the Jolly Roger is one of history's most recognizable symbols of death and destruction, this symbolism is only half the story. The other half is the lives the pirates' ominous ensign preserved.

5 WALK THE PLANK
THE ECONOMICS OF PIRATE TORTURE

One of the most popular pirate images is the brute and bearded captain, perhaps with a hook for a hand and a parrot on one shoulder, barking at a prisoner with sadistic pleasure, "Walk the plank!" In the movies, the captain, standing at the edge of his ship, is surrounded by a mob of encouraging pirates, while the poor captive stands on a wooden beam jutting from the vessel's side. Below him swirl the ominous and devouring waves of the sea, or perhaps even the fins of circling sharks. Movies and books depict this torture as a pirate pastime, a source of amusement and play. However entertaining, the basic "facts" of this oft-depicted pirate picture are purely fictional. There are, in fact, no recorded cases of seventeenth- or eighteenth-century pirates, hook-handed or otherwise, forcing captives to jump off wooden planks. Further, pirates weren't sadists who tortured everyone they encountered for fun. A few actually showed downright charity to their targets.

Despite this, it's easy to think of pirates as bloodthirsty fiends—as men, one of their prisoners reported, "to whom it was a sport to do Mischief." Many pirate contemporaries described them as such. Charles Johnson, for example, described Bartholomew Roberts's crew's apparent violent madness as follows: "It is impossible to particularly recount the Destruction and Havock," which these pirates committed "without Remorse or Compunction; for nothing is so deplorable as Power in mean and ignorant Hands, it makes Men wanton and giddy.... *They are like mad Men, that cast Fire-Brands, Arrows, and Death, and say, are not we in Sport?*" "Like their Patron, the Devil," Johnson observed, pirates "must make Mischief their Sport, Cruelty their Delight, and damning of Souls their constant Employment."

Modern perceptions of pirates remain wedded to this depiction. Fictional pirates are sometimes portrayed as funny, charming, and even loveable fellows; but for every "Captain Jack Sparrow" there are a dozen depraved, feral, and sadistic sea bandits to do his dirty work. There were some psychopathic pirates, to be sure. But most pirates comported more with the attitude Captain Sam Bellamy expressed when he said, "*I scorn to do any one a Mischief, when it is not for my Advantage.*" Pirates did in many cases torture captives. But they did so rationally to increase their profit, "when it was for their advantage," to use Bellamy's wording. Pirates skillfully deployed their infamous instruments of terror, generating a reputation for cruelty and madness that spread throughout the maritime world. They did this so skillfully that they elevated their reputation to the status of a piratical "brand name." As a result of this brand name pirates improved their efficiency on the account, reaping greater rewards from their plunder. Unfortunately for the objects of pirate barbarity, the piratical brand name didn't permit any tortures as kind or quick as walking the plank.

Pirates tortured captives for three main reasons. First, they did so to elicit information, usually regarding the whereabouts of hidden valuables aboard captured ships. Second, pirates tortured captives to punish government officials for attempting to capture them or for capturing and hanging fellow pirates. Third, pirates used torture to punish unscrupulous or abusive merchant captains. The first two motives for torture directly contributed to pirates' welfare and were part of their profit-seeking purpose. The third didn't but instead satisfied a piratical "justice motive." Perhaps most important, however, this application of pirate torture may have improved merchant sailors' treatment on the seas.

It's Nothing Personal: Discovering Hidden Booty

Violent conflict wasn't the only hurdle pirates faced in maximizing profits from their expeditions. Equally damaging to this endeavor was lost loot. Unsurprisingly, crew members aboard captured vessels weren't always as forthcoming with the location of certain valuables aboard their ships as pirates would've liked. Even though pirate prey overwhelmingly surrendered to their attackers without a fight at the sight of the Jolly Roger, some victims tried to foil pirates' plunder in nonviolent, less detectable ways once they were boarded. For example, captured crew members sometimes hid valuables to keep them out of pirate hands. In other cases a captured vessel's passengers might destroy booty to prevent pirates from taking it. One merchant captain who Edward Low attacked, for example, "hung eleven thousand moydores of gold in a bag out of the cabbin window, and as soon as he was taken by the said Lowe, cutt the rope and lett them drop into the sea." Since retrieving goods from the murky depths of the ocean floor wasn't possible, destroying valuables was like cutting off one's nose to spite one's face. Still, desperation drove some pirate captives, like Low's victim above, to try and destroy booty.

Pirates weren't only keen to discover the location of money, however. In some cases they were equally interested in discovering papers that might provide them with valuable information, such as news of the course authorities had taken, or a suggestion of where the next rich prize might be sailing. After Blackbeard's crew seized one vessel, for example, "all their Papers were perused with the same Diligence as tho' it had been at the Secretary's Office here in England." If such papers were on board but pirates couldn't find them because their captives had hidden or destroyed them, pirates might miss an opportunity to increase their haul.

Captives' passive resistance therefore posed a threat to pirates' profit. If captured crew members hid or destroyed booty, revenue from even a successful plundering expedition would fall, resulting in a smaller share out to each pirate. Pirates developed their much-famed practice of torturing captives in response to this problem. By inflicting heinous tortures on those who hid or destroyed valuables, or who were suspected of hiding or destroying them, pirates could prevent behaviors that would otherwise erode their revenue. Even more important than its ability to reveal stashed valuables on the prize a pirate crew had just taken, however, heinous pirate torture prevented crew members on *future* prizes from attempting to withhold valuable booty. Torture accomplished this by creating a reputation for pirate barbarity that spread throughout the maritime world. Pirates actively cultivated, and then cashed in on, this reputation, which scared most victims into surrendering everything they had that their pirate attackers wanted. Who would dare hide loot from a blood-crazed mob of "Barbarous and Inhumane Wretches"? Virtually no one, which is precisely why pirates endeavored to appear in this way.

Any business that wants to remain in business must develop and maintain a reputation. Businesses go about this in various ways. One way is simply to produce high-quality products and then to rely on word of mouth to spread this information. This generates a positive reputation that allows firms to retain existing customers and attract new ones. On the other hand, if a producer offers a shoddy product, this information also spreads, destroying the seller's reputation and with it his customer base. To make money, then, businesses must consistently behave in ways that contribute to the kind of reputations they desire to foster.

Businesses can grow their reputations by investing in brand names. Brand names institutionalize reputations. When you think of Mercedes-Benz, for example, you think of high-quality automobiles. This car manufacturer's brand name is connected in our minds with a reputation for quality, luxury, and exclusivity. Honda also has a brand name, but it conjures up a different reputation in our minds. We associate Honda with durability, value, and accessibility. Thus different producers seek to develop different brand names that occupy different niches, depending on the customers they're catering to. There are many ways businesses can invest in brand names, but perhaps the most common way is through advertisement. By projecting particular images of themselves publicly, businesses build and institutionalize reputations for the attributes they wish to be known for.

In this respect the business of piracy was no different from the business of selling cars. Pirates weren't selling a product. But their enterprise's profitability relied on a reputation and "brand name," which pirates sought to cultivate. To prevent captives from withholding booty in the ways described above, for instance, pirates required a reputation for cruelty and barbarity. And, as I discuss below, adding madness to the piratical reputation didn't hurt either. Pirates institutionalized their reputation for ferocity and insanity into a piratical brand name through the same means Mercedes-Benz uses for this purpose: word of mouth and advertisement. Pirates didn't take out glossy ads in magazines. But they did make a point of publicizing their barbarity and madness so their reputation could strengthen and spread. What's more, pirates received advertisement for their reputation in popular eighteenth-century newspapers, which unwittingly contributed to pirates' ruthless brand name, indirectly facilitating pirates' profit.

To develop a reputation for viciousness, pirates sought to impose the highest cost possible on captives who resisted their demands by hiding or destroying valuables. This is why pirates spent so much time, as one court remarked, "*making their Hellish Inventions for unheard of Barbarities.*" Relatively painless tortures, like the apocryphal walking of the plank, couldn't create a reputation that would lead victims to surrender everything in their possession. But the prospect of being cooked alive or forced to eat the severed ears from their own heads could. When pirates boarded a prize they therefore enquired into the whereabouts of valuables. If captives weren't forthcoming with this information, pirates launched into a torturous frenzy that gave the Inquisition a run for its money. Thus, in response to the merchant captain discussed above who threw a bag of gold into the ocean to prevent Edward Low's pirate crew from taking it, "Lowe cutt off the said Masters lipps and broyl'd them before his face, and afterwards murder'd the whole crew being thirty two persons." In a newspaper article in the *American Weekly Mercury*, a witness described how Low's crew treated other resistant prisoners: "They cut and whiped some and others they burnt with Matches between their Fingers to the bone to make them confess where their Money was." Apparently it worked. Low's pirates "took to the value of a Thousand Pistoles from Passengers and others," the article noted.

This response to passive pirate prisoner resistance wasn't unique to Low. Pirate captain Charles Vane "bound [one captive's] hands and feet and ty'd (upon his back) down to the bowsprit with matches to his eyes burning and a pistol loaded with the muzzle into his mouth, thereby to oblige him to confess what money was on board." Captain Edward England "threatned to sink" a victim's "vessell and throw him overboard with a double headed shot about his neck, if he concealed where his money was." Pirate captain George Lowther also resorted to torture to reveal the location of hidden valuables, "placing lighted matches between the fingers of" his prisoners "to make them discover where the gold was." A less imaginative pirate captain "threatened to shoot" a captive "for not discovering forty Ounces of Gold" the captive had apparently hidden aboard the ship. Even the "gentleman pirate" Major Stede Bonnet wasn't above torturing captives who weren't forthcoming with their booty. According to an article in the *Boston News-Letter*, Bonnet's crew "barbarously used" merchant ship captain "Mac Clenan for hiding his money."

The buccaneers had a particular skill for inflicting pain on prisoners who refused to surrender booty. Their practice of "woolding" illustrates this well. Exquemelin describes this torture, which the buccaneers administered to one recalcitrant prisoner: "they strappado'd him until both his arms were entirely dislocated, then knotted the cord so tight round the forehead that his eyes bulged out, big as eggs. Since he still would not admit where the coffer was, they hung him up by his male parts, while one struck him, another sliced off his nose, yet another an ear, and another scorched him with fire." To another pitiful fellow who refused to divulge the whereabouts of booty, "they tied long cords to his thumbs and his big toes and spreadeagled him to four stakes. Then four of them came and beat on the cords with their sticks, making his body jerk and shudder and stretching his sinews. Still not satisfied, they put a stone weighing at least two hundred-weight on his loins and lit a fire of palm leaves under him, burning his face and setting his hair alight." The French buccaneer Francois L'Ollonais added a special flair to his torture of several stubborn Spanish prisoners who refused to lead him to their hiding compatriots and money. L'Ollonais "being possessed of a devil's fury, ripped open one of the prisoners with his cutlass, tore the living heart out of his body, gnawed at it, and then hurled it in the face of one of the others."

Taking a cue from their woolding forefathers, some eighteenth-century pirates literally squeezed valuable information from their prisoners. Pirate captive Richard Lazenby, for instance, described how Captain John Taylor's crew treated several such prisoners. According to Lazenby, Taylor's men "squeezed their [prisoners'] joints in a vice to extort confession." Not to be outdone by their buccaneering predecessors' inventiveness, eighteenth-century pirates developed their own special tortures. Consider, for instance, "the sweat." "The Manner of a Sweat," one pirate prisoner explained in the pages of the *British Journal*, "is thus: Between the Decks they stick Candles round the Mizen-Mast, and about twenty five Men surround it with Points of Swords, Penknives, Compasses, Forks, &c. in each of their Hands: *Culprit* enters the Circle; the Violin plays a merry Jig, and he must run for about ten Minutes, while each Man runs his Instrument into his Posteriors."

Pirates sometimes got carried away in their zeal to prevent prisoners from concealing or destroying valuables. In one case, for instance, an unfortunate woman who several buccaneers captured "was by some set bare upon a baking stone and roasted, because she did not confess of money which she had only in their conceit." But pirates couldn't afford to torture prisoners indiscriminately. Wrongly torturing on such suspicion too often would render torture ineffective for pirates' purpose. If pirates developed a reputation for assured torture, and thus captives expected to be brutalized whether they delivered up their valuables or not, captives wouldn't find it costly to

Figure 5.1. Building a reputation: Captain Spriggs's crew administers "the sweat." From Captain Charles Johnson, *A General History of the Robberies and Murders of the Most Notorious Pyrates*, unknown edition.

hide loot. For torture to constitute a penalty, when captives acquiesced to pirate demands, pirates needed to spare them such cruelty. Philip Ashton, for instance, "learned from some" of his pirate captors "that it was one of their Articles Not to Draw Blood, or take away the Life of any Man, after they had given him Quarter." This explains the seeming generosity of the quartermaster on Captain Roberts's ship who observed one of his men abusing a captive. When he saw this "the Quarter-master came forward, and took the Pyrate off from beating him, asking him how he wou'd like it were he a Prisoner." Thus, while pirates had an incentive to torture when they genuinely suspected captive resistance, it wasn't in their interest to do so wantonly.

Understanding pirate torture as a rationally chosen means to develop a reputation for terror provides a rather different interpretation to Captain Johnson's comment that "in the Commonwealth of Pyrates, he who goes the greatest Length of Wickedness, is looked upon with a certain kind of Envy amongst them." Because the reputation this "wickedness" created contributed to a threatening brand name, heinous pirate torture reduced pirates' costs of passive captive resistance, enhancing their revenue.

Critical to the word-of-mouth process pirate barbarity depended on, pirates required survivors who could relay the consequences of resisting their demands and spread tales of their wickedness to others. "Dead men tell no tales." But this is why pirates had a strong incentive to avoid slaughtering compliant captives. Although in some cases it was "good Policy" to sink a captured vessel after relieving her of plunder "to prevent her returning to tell Tales at Home," pirates often released some or all of the crew members who didn't join them to return home where they could communicate their experience to others. Pirate captain John Phillips established a reputation as a "bloody, merciless ruffian" with the "diabolical disposition of an infernal fiend" this way. Thus, when Phillips captured John Fillmore, for instance, Fillmore was "dread to fall into [Phillips's] hands," he later recorded, "having heard of the cruelties committed by that execrable pirate."

Just as the Jolly Roger confronted a potential free-riding problem within the pirate community, piratical torture did too. A wimpy pirate crew without the strength or stomach to inflict heinous tortures on captives who hid or destroyed booty might try and free ride on pirate crews that did. If a captive were brave enough to test such a crew, he would learn this, and by spreading the word, could undermine the threat of piratical torture for preventing costly captive behaviors. As with the Jolly Roger, however, pirates could overcome this free-rider problem if within the broader piratical brand name, particular pirate captains, for instance, enjoyed their own individual reputations. And it seems they did. As discussed above, Captain John Phillips, for example, enjoyed a fearsome reputation particular to him. And as I discuss below, so did Blackbeard and other pirates. Pirate-specific brand names prevented the torture free-riding problem by permitting specific pirates and pirate crews to internalize their reputation's benefit.

The most public form of communication about pirates in the seventeenth and eighteenth centuries was through newspapers published in London and New England. In addition to relating information about pirate movements, captures, and facts about crew composition, newspapers also related information from pirate victims and released pirate prisoners. As Joel Baer points out, in these published accounts "Something about [the pirates'] temper might be included to help persons that confront[ed] them in the future." Newspaper reporting on "piratical character" provided pirates further opportunity to build their reputations as insane, heartless heathens. One way they did this was by broadcasting their fiendish deeds to the legitimate persons they interacted with, who then might relate these deeds to a newspaper that would publish the account. For instance, according to one pirate captive's information published in the *American Weekly Mercury*, "The Pyrates gave us an account of" several of their violent depredations, including their slaughter of crews, burning of ships, and a particularly proud act in which they "cut off one of the Masters Ears and slit his Nose." The captive was astonished that "all this they confessed themselves." But this isn't astonishing at all given the helpful effects such boasting had on pirates' reputation.

Another way pirates capitalized on newspaper reporting about their character was by fostering a "devil-may-care" image among the legitimate persons they interacted with, who again might relate this attitude to newspapers that would publish their experiences. For instance, pirates loudly proclaimed to those they overwhelmed that they feared neither death nor the law. As the *British Journal* reported, for instance, the members of one pirate crew declared to their captives that "they have no Thoughts of ever being taken, but swear, with the most dire Imprecations, that if ever they should find themselves overpower'd, they would immediately blow their Ship up, rather than do *Jolly Roger* the Disgrace to be struck, or suffer themselves, to be hang'd like Dogs." Or, as the *Boston News-Letter* reported, according to another pirate prisoner, his captors went about "often saying they would not go to Hope Point in the River of Thames to be hung up in Gibbets a Sundrying . . . for if it should chance they should be Attacked by any Superiour Power or Force, which they could not master, they would immediately put fire with one of their Pistols to their Powder, and go all merrily to Hell together!"

Pirates projected this attitude often enough that it became something of a sea-dog slogan. As Bartholomew Roberts famously boasted, for example, "A merry Life and a short one, *shall be my Motto.*" The operative word here was *short.* In part, declarations like Roberts's were simple statements of fact. Few pirates managed to survive life on the account for more than a few years. But equally important, the pirate motto was also a useful way for pirates to signal that they had what economists call a "high discount rate": that is, that the future meant very little to them. This was a useful tactic since, if potential victims or authorities viewed pirates as reckless with their own lives, they would be less willing to risk engaging them or raising their ire for fear of an irrational and kamikazelike response. This explains pirate comments, such as the remark one of William Snelgrave's pirate captors made, that "as to his part, he hoped he should be sent to Hell one of these days by a Cannon Ball." Even the melo-dramatics of Blackbeard's last stand against Lieutenant Robert Maynard, reported in the *Boston News-Letter* for the public to consume, helped solidify pirates' reputation as short-sighted demons. As the newspaper described it, before engaging May-nard, "Teach called for a Glass of Wine, and swore Damnation to himself if he either took or gave Quarters."

Pirates' desire to build their brand name for cruelty and in-sanity may also explain the seemingly senseless destruction of cargo pirates engaged in after taking some prizes, such as throw-ing parcels of goods overboard and torching ships that weren't up to their piratical standards. Just as newspapers publicized pi-rates' declarations of their high discount rates, they also publi-cized these images of pirate madness. Consider, for example, how a victim of Bartholomew Roberts's crew described his predators' antics in the *Boston News-Letter*. According to the victim, Roberts's men proceeded "with madness and rage to tare up the Hatches" and then "enter[ed] the Hould like a Parcel of Furies, where with Axes, Cutlashes, &c they cut, tore, and broke open Trunks, Boxes, Cases, and Bales, and when any of the Goods came upon Deck which they did not like to carry with them aboard their Ship ... they threw them over board into the Sea ... There was nothing heard among the Pirates all the while but Cursing, Swearing, Damning, and Blaspheming to the greatest degree imaginable." Richard Hawkins, who pirate captain Francis Spriggs victimized, described a similar scene of madness about his encounter in the *British Journal*, noting "every Thing that please them not they threw over board ... every individual Thing they destroy'd; broke all my Windows, knock'd down the Cabbin ... and then deliver'd me my Ship in a despicable Condition." One pirate victim's account, published in the *Boston News-Letter*, spoke specifically to pirates' apparent godlessness and confirmed the popular perception that pirates were "in the Possession of the Devil" and "*laughing* at the very thunders of God." "In ravaging the Vessel," this victim reported, "they met with two or three Bibles, at the sight whereof some started and said, They had nothing to do with them; or with God, nor any thing Above."

The same brand-name considerations likely motivated pirates' pyromania. Captain Johnson provides a list of reasons why pirates frequently burned ships, which he notes was "sometimes to prevent giving Intelligence, sometimes because they did not leave men to navigate them, and at other Times out of Wantonness, or because they were displeased with the Master's Behaviour." A later section in this chapter discusses pirates' punishment of merchant captains. But the "Wanton" destruction Johnson describes was more likely a deliberate effort to foster an image of insanity and fearsomeness, as discussed above. For example, when a prisoner asked pirate John Phillips why his crew needlessly burned ships, Phillips "answer'd, it was for fun." Those who witnessed such destruction "for fun" or read about it in newspapers were shocked by this behavior, which corroborated the picture of pirates Boston's advocate general painted when he described pirates as having "declared themselves to live in opposition to the rules of Equity and Reason." In short, pirate "madness" had precisely the effect pirates desired.

A few pirates took name branding their fearsomeness a step further. Edward Teach, the "notorious pyrate better known by the name of Blackbeard," is the best example of this. By creating a horrible and intimidating physical appearance, Teach cut an image so terrifying that it created a bloodcurdling reputation, which over time evolved into a Blackbeard brand name. According to Captain Johnson, for example, "his Beard . . . did not a little contribute towards making his Name so terrible." Johnson describes the effect Blackbeard achieved with his appearance as follows:

> Captain *Teach*, assumed the Cognomen of *Black-beard*, from that large Quantity of Hair, which, like a frightful Meteor, covered his whole Face, and frightened *America* more than any Comet that has appeared there in a long Time.
>
> This Beard was black, which he suffered to grow of an extravagant Length; as to Breadth, it came up to his Eyes; he was accustomed to twist it with Ribbons, in small Tails ... and then turn them about his Ears: three Brace of Pistols, hanging in Holsters like Bandaliers; and stuck lighted Matches under his Hat, which appearing on each Side of his Face, his Eyes naturally looking fierce and wild, made him altogether such a Figure, that Imagination cannot form an Idea of a Fury, from Hell, to look more frightful.

Rather than resulting from flamboyance, madness, or eccentricity, pirates like Blackbeard deliberately constructed their bizarre and frightful physical appearances to facilitate piratical plunder. "There is no doubt that Blackbeard," for instance, "was conscious of the public image he had created" and worked diligently to maintain it. Of course, most pirates looked more like the one this witness described: "He is a middle-sized man, of a swarthy complexion, inclinable by his aspect to be of a churlish constitution; his own hair short and brown, and apt, when in drink, to utter some Portugese or Moorish words." Nevertheless, pirates could invest in appearances such as Blackbeard's to complement their reputations for cruelty and insanity, which reduced victim resistance, and in turn promoted profits. For Blackbeard, at least, this investment paid off. According to

FIGURE 5.2. Blackbeard's brand name: The terrible image of Captain Edward Teach. From Captain Charles Johnson, *A General and True History of the Lives and Actions of the most Famous Highwaymen, Murderers, Street-Robbers, &c.,* 1742.

Angus Konstam who has investigated Blackbeard's life and piratical career extensively, until Blackbeard's final battle with the lieutenant of HMS *Pearl*, Robert Maynard, who took the bearded icon's life, the world's most notorious and fearsome pirate hadn't so much as killed a single man. Apparently he didn't need to.

Mess with a Pirate, Get the Hook: Deterring Capture

In addition to preventing captives from withholding valuables, pirates inflicted barbarous tortures and more generally fostered a devilish brand name for another reason as well: to deter authorities from clamping down on them. The pirate M.O. proceeded along the lines described above, only here, instead of inflicting punishment on stubborn victims, pirates directed their barbarity at government officials who tried to capture sea bandits or, failing them, those officials' citizens. As noted in chapter 4, for instance, in response to the governors of Barbados and Martinique seeking to capture him, Captain Roberts constructed a special flag communicating his new policy: death for any Barbadians and Martinicans he might take on the account. Roberts squelched any doubts about his threat's credibility when he captured and "murther'd the French Governor of" Martinique, hanging the good governor from the yardarm of his own ship, "and hang'd the First Mate for some Minutes, because the said Governor executed one his best Men."

Other pirates adopted a similar policy, albeit with less panache than Roberts. Captain Low, for example, was said to have an "irreconcileable Aversion to New-England Men" and consequently "let none of that Country depart without some Marks of his Rage." Low's "aversion" stemmed from the audaciousness of the New York–based man-o'-war HMS *Greyhound*, which once attacked Low and succeeded in capturing his pirate consort, Charles Harris. Low announced he would have his revenge by brutalizing subsequent New England vessels he encountered. He was good to his word. The next two ships Low captured happened to be from Plymouth. As the *Boston-New Letter* reported the episode, Low slashed one of the captains open alive, "taking out his Heart," "roasting" it, "and then made" the captain's "Mate eat it." Low served the other merchant captain a tasty treat of his own, "slashing and mauling" the master, "and then cutting off his Ears," the pirate captain "made him eat them."

Several other pirates shared Low's animosity toward New England. For pirate captain Francis Spriggs, who sailed with Low and Harris, the reason for revenge was the same as Low's. But the New England–directed rage of several other sea bandits traced back to the Boston hanging of a handful of pirates who sailed with Sam Bellamy's *Whydah*, which wrecked during a violent storm. Several members of the pirate community swore revenge for these pirates' capture. Blackbeard, for example, informed Captain William Wyer, whose ship he'd recently taken, of the sad news that he'd have to "burn his Ship because she belonged to Boston, adding he would burn all Vessels belonging to New England for executing the six pirates at Boston." Similarly, merchant ship captain Thomas Fox testified that the pirates who captured his vessel swore that "if the Prisoners [in Boston] Suffered they would Kill every Body they took belonging to New England."

Pirates didn't limit their hostility to avenging Bellamy's men, however. They viciously avenged officials' mistreatment of any of their "brethren." Captain Low, for example, met with a ship "manned partly with English and partly Portuguese; the latter Low caused to be hang'd, by Way of Reprisal, for some of his own Men sent thither." The English got off easier since Low had no axe to grind with them. These "he thrust into their own Boat to shift for themselves." Bart Roberts used similar tactics to send a message to those acquainted with Captain Rogers, the man who led the two-ship expedition sent to attack him off the coast of Barbados. As one of Roberts's victims publicized in the *Boston News-Letter*, "The Pirates seem much enraged at Bristol Men, for Capt. *Rogers* sake." When Roberts's crew members took a ship from Bristol, "They us'd" its captain "barbarously, because his Countryman, Captain *Rogers* . . . was of the City of *Bristol*." Further, "when any Ship belonging to that Island [Barbados] fell in his Way, he was more particularly severe to them than others." Similarly, pirate captain Charles Vane instituted a policy of mistreating Bermudan vessels because Bermuda's governor arrested pirate Thomas Brown. As mariner Samuel Cooper deposed, "They beat the Bermudians and cut away their masts upon account of one Thomas Brown who was (some time) detain'd in these Islands upon suspicion of piracy etc."

Pirates' threats of revenge caused more than a little concern for a few of the more actively antipirate colonial officials. Virginia governor Alexander Spotswood, for example, couldn't have been pleased when he learned from one of Bartholomew Roberts's victims in 1721 that Roberts "expected to be joined by another ship and would then visit Virginia, and avenge the pirates who have been executed here." If this frightened Spotswood, he must have wet himself a year earlier when he wrote to the Council of Trade and Plantations that if those "barbarous wretches can be moved to cutt off the nose and ears of a master for but correcting his own sailors, what inhuman treatment must I expect, should I fall within their power, who have been markt as ye principal object of their vengeance, for cutting off their arch-pirate Thatch, with all his grand designs, and making so many of their fraternity to swing in the open air of Virginia." But Spotswood wasn't alone. Lieutenant Governor Hope of Bermuda, for instance, had his own pirate vendetta to fear, the rogues having "endeavour'd my destruction," as Hope put it, "because that I have put the laws and H.M. Instructions in execution upon them."

According to Marcus Rediker, in at least some cases these sorts of pirate threats—backed by implementation—actually worked. As one Bermudan colonial official complained, for example, the island's residents "fear'd that this very execution [of two pirates] wou'd make our vessels fare the worse for it, when they happen'd to fall into the pyrates' hands" and so were reluctant to provide the testimony needed to condemn them. The threat of pirate retribution, deemed credible because of pirates' reputation for barbarity, put pressure on government officials to think twice about zealously pursuing sea bandits. In turn, this eased the pressure on pirates coming from some authorities.

Mixing Business and Pleasure: Pirate Justice

Pirates used barbarous torture for one other purpose: to bring "justice" to predatory captains. As William Snelgrave put it, "They pretend one reason for these villainies is to do justice to sailors." Unlike torture for the purposes considered above, this motivation for cruelty had a more personal edge. As discussed in chapter 2, several pirates identified captain mistreatment of merchant sailors as their reason for turning to piracy. In their part as pirates, some of these sailors took it on themselves to return the favor. Like the other motivations for piratical barbarity, the justice motive also contributed to pirates' reputation as madmen who shouldn't be trifled with. Further, by punishing abusive merchant captains, pirates contributed to a positive reputation among merchant sailors. This could help with recruiting, make merchant crews more willing to surrender to pirate attack, and might even incline merchant sailors to help their captors in other ways, such as providing them with information about the whereabouts of prospective prizes.

Unlike the previous motivations, however, in the case of vigilante justice it doesn't seem pirates had profit seeking in mind. This doesn't mean justice-based torture resulted from pirate altruism—unless revenge for "ill usage" could be considered public spirited. Nonetheless, administering "justice" to unscrupulous merchant captains may have generated public benefits for other men employed on the seas.

Recall from chapter 1 that to prevent situations of captain predation, British law included several protections for merchant sailors. But official legal protections could and did fail, leaving sailors without effective, or at least immediate, shelter from captain abuse. Where the law failed to reign in predatory merchant captains, pirates, oddly enough, picked up the slack. In principle, the British government could have adopted policies to improve sailors' protection against merchant captain abuse. For instance, it could have placed government officials on every merchant ship leaving British ports. Similarly, it could have deployed its naval vessels to troll the waters, stopping merchant ships wherever the navy encountered them to inspect the status of the crew vis-à-vis the ship's officers. But clearly such policies would have been impractical. First, they would have been incredibly costly to government and a strain on naval resources. Second, if actually adhered to, they would have substantially slowed the flow of merchant vessels and burdened the very commercial activity Britain hoped to encourage.

In terms of the costs and benefits they faced of bringing justice to abusive merchant ship captains on the high seas, pirates were better suited for this task than government. Although even at its height the pirate population was only 15 percent of the Royal Navy, pirates were still numerous. Further, for pirates, the additional cost of administering justice to predatory merchant ship captains was very low. Pirates were searching for and stopping merchant vessels to plunder them anyway. Inquiring of an overtaken crew how its master treated sailors and then dispensing justice accordingly required little additional time or effort. Any benefit pirates derived from avenging their own formerly abusive captains was likely plenty to compensate for this small cost. And, for the reasons already mentioned, because pirates were criminals—and perceived as maniacal ones at that—the threat of pirate justice was highly credible.

After taking a ship, pirates would "examin[e] the Men concerning their Master's Usage of them, according to the Custom of other Pyrates." If the crew informed their captors that its captain had "misbehaved," the pirates punished him. Pirates did this with torture, including some of the methods described earlier. On taking a "whole Salt Fleet, consisting of about 20 Sail," pirate captain Christopher Condent, for example, "enquir[ed] into the Manner of the Commanders' Behaviour to their Men, and those, against whom Complaint was made, he whipp'd and pickled"—a torture that involved lashing the abusive officers and pouring brine on their open wounds.

Particularly unlucky captains might happen into the hands of pirates who used to sail under them as merchant sailors. Woe to such a captain if he'd wronged his sailors. One of Edward England's pirates, for instance, immediately recognized Captain Skinner, whom he'd previously sailed under as boatswain, when England's crew captured Skinner's ship. Apparently Skinner had misbehaved as his captain. The pirate addressed his former master as follows: "*Ah, Captain Skinner! It is you? The only Man I wished to see; I am much in your Debt, and now I shall pay you all in your own Coin.*" The pirates tied Skinner "to the Windless, and there pelted him with Glass Bottles, which cut him in a sad Manner; after which they whipp'd him about the Deck, till they were weary." England's men finished Captain Skinner with a "shot . . . thro' the Head." Captain Thomas Tarlton must have been equally distressed to encounter a prisoner aboard Bartholomew Roberts's ship whom he'd refused help to in the past. The prisoner "could not spare using some Reproaches of" Tarlton "for what he thought was Inhumanity." This "getting to the Ears of *Roberts*, he took upon him, as a Dispenser of Justice, the Correction of this *Tarlton*, beating and misusing him grievously."

Conversely, if a captured merchant crew spoke well of its captain, the pirates not only spared him punishment, but might even reward the captain for his humanity and good conduct. For instance, when Thomas Cocklyn's pirate crew took William Snelgrave's ship and "endeavoured to beat out my Brains," as Snelgrave put it, for ordering his sailors to defend their vessel, "some of my People that were on the Quarter-Deck observing, cried out aloud, 'For God's sake don't kill our Captain, for we never were with a better Man.'" Not only was Snelgrave's life "safe provided none of my people Complained against me," the pirate quartermaster informed him, but by the end of Snelgrave's captivity his captors were so impressed with him, they offered to gift him a ship loaded with valuable cargo. Captain Hawkins's honest conduct toward his sailors similarly spared him from pirate torture. When his pirate captors suggested "sweating" the merchant captain, several who knew Hawkins "did intreat earnestly for me, alledging, That I never did any Man any ill; that I had done them no Injustice," so the pirates excused him. Pirates who knew merchant captain Henry Fowle also reprieved him and informed their fellow rogues that "he was an honest Fellow that never abused any Sailors . . . which hinder'd" Fowle's ship "from being burnt."

Pirates might also make gifts to merchant ship captains if they believed they could forge friendships with these men that could serve them in the future. Pirate captain William Lewis, for example, took a ship "belonging to *Carolina*, commanded by [a] Captain *Smith.*" "*Lewis* used him very civilly, and gave him as much, or more in Value, than he took from him, and let him go, saying, he would come to *Carolina* when he had made Money on the Coast, and would rely on his Friendship." Similarly, Sam Bellamy's pirates showed surprising kindness to Captain Lawrence Prince who they'd recently plundered. "They gave the ship taken from Capt. *Richards* [another recent prize] to Capt. *Prince,* and loaded her with as much of the best and finest goods as She could carry, and gave Capt. *Prince* above Twenty Pounds in Silver and Gold to bear his charges." To strengthen merchantmen's incentive to yield to them, some pirates even "paid" freight to their victims, which harmed the cargo's owners, but left the captain and sailors no worse for wear. As Alexander Spotswood observed, "It is a common practice among the Pirats to make presents to Masters of Ships and Seamen of such Commoditys they have less use of, in lieu of what they take away." Merchant ship captain Knott, for example, couldn't have been too disappointed at his crew's capture in 1720. His pirate attackers "took what they wanted out of the merchantman and gave him money and goods of a very considerable value for the same." Captain John Gow's pirates felt particularly compelled to "ma[k]e a Reparation" to some of their victims, "giving" to one "what they had taken Violently from another" in "a strange Medley of Mock-Justice made up of Rapine and Generosity blended together."

It's impossible to say how effective the threat of private, pirate-applied justice was in reducing captain predation. But a letter from three merchant shipmasters to Virginia's governor in 1722 suggests it had some effect. "The far greater hazard, which we run in case of meeting with Pyrates," they wrote, is "we are sure to suffer all the tortures wch such an abandoned Crew can invent, upon the least intimation of our striking any of our men." Merchant captains who feared pirate justice may have lessened their severity toward sailors; and in this capacity, pirates may have contributed to merchant seamen's welfare.

Of course, pirate justice wasn't all upside. While it may have filled a void that the high costs of state-administered justice created, pirate justice suffered from the absence of any controls. For instance, instead of fitting the crime, pirate punishments were likely to vastly exceed this limit. While an official court would financially punish many captain abuses, pirates were partial to the death sentence and went out of their way to make executions cruel and unusual. Furthermore, the only participants in pirates' private justice system were disgruntled sailors and pirates. Captains received no hearing for their part. Thus there was no objectivity under pirate justice. Pirates were liable to kill or torture innocent merchant ship captains even if they sought impartiality (which they didn't) and relied only on sailors' "testimony." For instance, angry merchant sailors might indict captains who "corrected" them or put them on short rations even when such discipline was legitimate. In short, the pirate "justice system" for merchant captains was probably as reasonable as the justice prison inmates would administer to their wardens if given the chance. Surely some unscrupulous characters who would have escaped punishment if they had been left to the official legal system received their dues. But it's equally certain that others who didn't deserve punishment suffered at pirate hands.

Pirate torture, while often heinous, was rarely arbitrary. Instead, pirates primarily used grizzly tactics to serve their profit-seeking purpose. Through barbarous torture, pirates created and diligently tended to their reputation for insanity, cruelty, and murderous destruction. In doing so, these "Fury of unreasonable Hell," as one contemporary styled them, "gave you the Liveliest

Picture of Hell," fostering a brand name so frightening few dared to resist them. Captives relinquished valuables they might otherwise have hidden from their attackers and some authorities thought twice before capturing and condemning pirates for fear of retribution against them and their citizens. Although pirates certainly appeared to be, as one court put it, "Instigated by the Devil," in reality "the Folly and Madness among Pyrates" so many pirate contemporaries described was rational, reasonable, and even carefully calculated to achieve a brand name as barely better than, or perhaps worse than, wild animals.

Besides torturing their captives for profit, pirates also tortured for "justice." Allegedly wronged by their masters when they sailed as common tars on merchant ships, pirates were more than happy to punish merchant captains they came upon whom one of their members had formerly suffered under or whose crew claimed was predatory. On the one hand, pirate justice for merchant ship captains may have operated to tame these captains' abuses, contributing to merchant sailors' welfare in cases when government was unable to do so. On the other hand, absent any controls, pirate justice could be unfair, excessive, and in more than a few cases was probably totally unwarranted.

Finally, although pirates overwhelmingly tortured "with purpose," there are cases that were no more than sadism as well. I've focused on the former since the latter is well known and paints a distorted picture of pirate torture that wrongly portrays brutality for sport as the rule instead of the exception. Nevertheless, we shouldn't forget that, like a minority of merchant captains, navy captains, and landlubbers, a minority of pirates were also simply psychopaths. Francis Spriggs, for example, forced merchant captain Richard Hawkins to eat "a Dish of Candles" for his amusement. But Spriggs's wanton torture looks like fraternity hazing next to the tortures of truly sadistic pirates, such as Edward Low. Low, for example, burned one victim alive for no other reason than, "being a greazy Fellow," he thought he "would fry well in the Fire."

Even Low, however, didn't brutalize everyone he encountered. Rather, he often reserved his perverse passions for times when unleashing them could profit him. As noted in an earlier example in this chapter, for instance, Low released English prisoners he captured with whom he had no axe to grind. More generally, Low seems to have recognized the importance of not overindulging his sadistic desires. Doing so would undermine his crew's ultimate goal—to take prizes with as little resistance as possible. In one case, for example, Low captured an old man who he used as a hostage to extort water from the governor of Madeira. The pirates "threaten'd to hang [the old man] at the Yard-Arm" if the governor refused, "but the Thing being comply'd with, the old Man was honourably (as the Pyrates say) discharged" and returned home "much handsomer cloathed than when" the pirates took him. Reneging on this agreement would have ruined Low's word and made it more difficult to ransom prisoners in the future. Apparently the profit motive was sometimes strong enough to overcome even the most sadistic pirate's inclinations.

6 PRESSING PEGLEG
THE ECONOMICS OF PIRATE CONSCRIPTION

n most people's minds, conscription is as integral to pirate
lore as parrots and peglegs. Popular pirate fiction repeatedly
portrays the infamous "pirate press." The press was as simple as it was terrible. On taking their prey, pirates gave captives
two options: join the pirate crew or die. Confronted with this
"choice," many captives entered the pirate company. The frequency with which popular pirate culture has repeated this
theme has created the perception that pirates conscripted virtually *all* their members. It plays into the perception, discussed in
chapters 4 and 5, that pirates were blood-crazed killers who
would just as soon murder everyone in their path for fun. If pirates held their victims' lives in such low esteem, it's not a
stretch to assume most seamen who joined pirate crews did so
at the point of a cutlass.

Like many infamous pirate practices, there's a grain of truth
to the rumors about the popularity of the pirate press. Pirates
did compel some sailors to join them. But pirate conscription
was the exception instead of the rule. In reality, most sailors entered piracy voluntarily. Like other counterintuitive pirate behaviors, this one, too, was the result of pirates' self-interest rather
than benevolence. Pirates generally augmented their ranks with
volunteers out of simple cost-benefit considerations. Ironically,
similar cost-benefit considerations perpetuated the perception
that pirates overwhelmingly conscripted their members. The

key to resolving this apparent contradiction again lies in the hidden economics of pirates.

The Costs and Benefits of Conscription

Unlike the Royal Navy, which often had to impress men to get the sailors it needed, "pirates had no difficulty in recruiting ordinary seamen to their ranks" without force. As detailed in chapter 1, life on seventeenth- and eighteenth-century merchant ships was difficult, sometimes cruel, and offered minimal income-earning potential for most ordinary sailors. Life aboard pirate ships was no picnic either but was considerably easier, less abusive, and offered substantially greater income-earning possibilities. If a pirate captive could overcome his moral dilemma, in many cases the choice to join his captors was probably not difficult to make at all. As one of William Snelgrave's pirate captors informed him, for instance, "The People were generally glad of an opportunity of entring with them."

Although many sailors may have been ready to sign on with their pirate captors, the question remains, why would pirates have signed them on as free men instead of conscripts? Pirates' benefit of conscripting sailors was clear enough. Free men received a full share of booty; conscripts, on the other hand, often received no share. Pirates could therefore increase their own shares by forcing captured merchant sailors—even those who wanted to join them—instead of admitting them as volunteers. Since pirates were already outlaws, they incurred no additional "legal cost" of conscripting sailors. Pressing seamen should've been a no-brainer for sea robbers.

It only seems this way, however, if we ignore the extralegal costs pirates incurred by conscripting sailors. Recall that pirate self-governance was critical to their criminal enterprise's success.

Pirates couldn't rely on government to maintain cooperation between them, to squelch discontent, and so forth; they had to do this themselves. They achieved this through privately created constitutions. Pirate crews unanimously consented to the articles governing their ships. This prevented conflicts and disagreements that might otherwise jeopardize their ability to cooperate for plunder. While a pirate crew could compel coerced seamen to sign its articles, since these seamen didn't do so voluntarily, they didn't consent to the ship's laws in the same way as the rest of the crew. By undermining the unanimity pirates used to secure cooperation on their ships, conscription could undermine the very purpose the articles served. Pirate captain Bart Roberts seems to have understood this well. Conscripts, Roberts appreciated, "might hazard, and, in Time, destroy his Government."

In addition to posing a threat to piratical harmony, conscripted seamen could be the undoing of a pirate company if they revolted against their pirate pressers. Pirate captain John Phillips discovered this when seven forced men in his crew, led by pressed carpenter Edward Cheeseman, designed "to overthrow the pyratical Government" on Phillips's ship and succeeded owing to "how few voluntary Pyrates there were on board." Cheeseman and the other conscripts revolted, delivered their pirate captors to the authorities, and must have been pleased when officials convicted and executed the brutes. Forced men also overwhelmed pirate captain William Fly on *Fame's Revenge*, delivering Fly and his pirates to the authorities who ultimately condemned the pirates to death. Similarly, if authorities ever captured a pirate ship, prisoners, such as conscripted crew members, would be the first to turn on their captors and, as witnesses to the latter's piratical acts, could supply damning evidence against them. In Virginia, for example, "a Man and a Woman" "who had been Prisoners among the Pyrates ... became the principal Evidences to convict" their captors.

Conscripts were also prone to desert their pirate pressers at the first chance. If they constituted a substantial portion of the crew they were deserting, their departure could leave the pirates high and dry, with insufficient sailors to man the ship in overtaking prizes. For example, forty-eight conscripts on pirate captain John Finn's *Morning Star* deserted Finn "on the grand Comanos . . . which was a design'd thing, there being so many forced men on Board." An escaped conscript could also provide authorities with information they could use to capture or convict pirates. A forced man on pirate captain John Gow's *Revenge*, for instance, escaped, "surrender'd himself to the Government . . . and inform'd them who Gow was, and what the Ship's Crew were, and upon what Business they were Abroad; with what else he knew of their Designs." Even if conscripts never managed to escape, provided they comprised a significant proportion of the crew, they nevertheless significantly weakened the ship they sailed on. Forced men, of course, were less willing to "give it their all" in battle and might even deliberately "give little" so their crew would be captured. For instance, Captain Cornelius, who shortsightedly stocked his pirate crew with seventy conscripts, spotted several Men of War and "was for giving Chase, but finding his Men unwilling, there being, as they gave for Reason 70 forc'd Men on board," had no choice but to sail elsewhere. Similarly, Captain Gow's pirates had to flee from a prospective French quarry, Gow giving "as a Reason against engaging with the Martinico Ship, that he had a great many Prisoners on Board."

Because of these costs of pressing sailors, pirates were reluctant to force unwilling seamen to join them. Some pirates went to great lengths to avoid conscripting the sailors they needed. When Edward Low captured Philip Ashton, for instance, he began with the pirates' traditional inquiry of the captured crew about who would join them. As Ashton put it, "according to the

Pirates usual custom . . . [he] asked me, *If I would sign their Articles, and go along with them.*" A man of strong moral fiber, Ashton declined. When this failed Low returned to him later and "asked the Old Question, Whether we would Sign their Articles, and go along with them?" When Ashton refused again, Low waited and then reapproached Ashton, this time demanding "with Sterness and Threats, whether I would Joyn with them?" On his third refusal the pirates "assaulted" Ashton— but not with fists. Rather, they subjected the upright sailor to "temptations of another kind, in hopes to win me over . . . [they] treated me with an abundance of Respect and Kindness," offering Ashton a drink and doing all they could to "sooth my Sorrows." Only when Ashton rebuffed the fourth advance did a frustrated Low resort to violent intimidation, declaring, *"If you will not Sign our Articles, and go along with me, I'll shoot you thro' the Head.*" Much to Low's consternation, Ashton remained obstinate, and the pirate captain dragged Ashton with him anyway. But clearly Low appreciated the high cost of a conscript and the benefit of a volunteer. Why else would he try so hard to convince Ashton to sign his crew's articles?

Despite his captor's advances, Ashton stuck to his guns. He was an unusually righteous fellow in this respect. Many other captured sailors didn't share Ashton's rectitude. Rather, as Snelgrave observed, they "were generally glad of an opportunity" to join the pirates. Several pirate observers confirm this and attest to pirates' aversion to conscripting sailors. As Governor Bennett of Bermuda complained to the Council of Trade and Plantations, for example, "I fear they will soon multiply for to many are willing to joyn with them when taken." Alexander Spotswood similarly lamented to the commissioner of the Admiralty that the pirates' "strength increases daily by the addition of new men from those Ships that fall in their way, though they give out that they will force no man into their Service." A late-seventeenth-century pirate contemporary observed this feature of pirates as well. In describing one pirate crew that augmented its ranks after taking a prize, for instance, he noted, "This was dun . . . without any force or Compulshon, as the pyrats themselves did declare That thay did not nor would not force him nor sundry more which did intend To goo with them." Pirate captive John Brett testified at the trial of a member of Sam Bellamy's crew that "it was the Custome among the Pyrates to force no Prisoners, but those that remained with them were Voluntiers."

Some seamen didn't just enter willingly with the pirates who overtook them. They begged to join their aggressors. For instance, when Bartholomew Roberts's crew captured the *Onslow*, a frigate transporting soldiers, eager volunteers overwhelmed the pirates. As one witness reported, far from needing to force anyone, "more would have enter'd than they would accept of." According to another witness, "the Pyrates despised most of" the *Onslow*'s volunteers "that enter'd with them, and received them, on their Petitions, only out of Charity." Rather than conscripting sailors indiscriminately, some pirates were selective in who they allowed to join them. Ned Low, for instance, refused married men in his crew, "that he might have none with him under the Influence of such powerful attractives, as a Wife & Children, lest they should grow uneasy in his Service, and have an Inclination to Desert him, and return home for the sake of their Families." Bartholomew Roberts's pirates wouldn't allow landlubbers to join them, taking "none but Sailors into their Company." Neither would Roberts permit Irishmen to enter his crew, "which Country Folks was against the Pyrates Rules to accept of, because they had been formerly cheated by one *Kennedy* an *Irish* Man, who run away with their Money."

Although pirates' cost of forcing an ordinary merchant sailor to join them often exceeded the benefit, for some skilled varieties of sailors things were different. Like merchant ships, pirate ships also needed certain skilled sailors in their crews. However, unlike unskilled sailors, skilled varieties were harder to come by. Furthermore, in contrast to unskilled seamen who were more-or-less easily substitutable among one another in terms of the labor they performed on the ship, and none of whom individually was especially important to the crew's overall success, skilled seamen couldn't be easily substituted with other men and their presence was critical to the rest of the crew's ability to function. This doesn't mean pirates always conscripted skilled sailors. Sometimes skilled seamen volunteered to join their captors. But these factors significantly increased the benefit of pressing skilled sailors, which in turn increased the frequency with which pirates pressed them if volunteers weren't forthcoming.

Skilled sailors comprised a small part of the typical pirate crew. But they comprised an important part because of their expertise. Who were these skilled sailors? Pirate captain Thomas Howard's crew, which "forced on board all Carpenters, Cawlkers, Armorers, Surgeons, and Musicians," provides a good example of the kinds of highly skilled seamen pirates most frequently pressed. Surgeons were critical for obvious reasons. Wounded or sick pirates required medical attention just like seamen on legitimate sailing vessels. Carpenters were equally indispensable for success at sea. Ships, pirate and nonpirate, commonly confronted situations that could damage them. Rocks, storms, and of course, violent conflict, threatened the integrity of seventeenth- and eighteenth-century marine vessels. A deteriorating or damaged vessel was slower and could sink, preventing successful sail. The carpenter's job was to fix this.

Carpenters were also important for undertaking the important task of careening, "a Light Pair of Heels being of great Use either to take, or escape being taken." And they were responsible for caulking, which involved sealing gaps between the ship's planks with oakum and pitch, when a caulker wasn't readily available. The other seamen Howard's crew conscripted performed similar specialized roles, comparably important and difficult to fill. Coopers, for instance, were in charge of maintaining the ship's wooden barrels that stored provisions. A good cooper was crucial to keep victuals fresh as long as possible. Musicians, on the other hand, were important for supplying piratical entertainment and for providing the soundtrack for pirate tortures that involved dancing or jigs. Ned Low's crew, for example, pressed a boy out of the *Sycamore Galley* "because he could play upon a violin."

Although pirates primarily limited conscription to skilled sailors such as these, they didn't take a principled stance against forcing unskilled sailors if they needed them and couldn't find volunteers. Even in these cases, however, some initially forced men, after only a brief time pirating, grew to rather enjoy their new occupation and joined the crew as volunteers. As one eighteenth-century observer put it, "Doubtless 'tis possible for a man to prove a hearty Rogue after he is forced into the Service of the Pirates, however Honest he was before, and however Undesignedly or against his Consent he at first come among them." One captured merchant captain, for example, remarked that two of his men "were at first forc'd" by his pirate attackers, "but," he added, "I have Reason to believe they turn'd Pyrates afterwards." Similarly, pirate prisoner Harry Glasby commented at Robert Crow's trial that although he believed Crow might have been "forced at first" by his pirate captors, he "since had done as others (*i.e.*) robb'd and pillaged when he went on board Prizes in his turn." Some prisoners "converted" because pirate crews denied conscripts the rights afforded to volunteers, such as participation in the ship's democratic decision making, the right to their shares of plunder, and the right to settle disputes with other crew members by duel. Pirate conscript Joseph Williams, for example, was "drubb'd" by Robert Bland, a volunteer pirate in the crew he was forced into. "*Williams* that he might revenge himself, and have Liberty to fight *Bland*, went that Instant and entered himself as Voluntier in the Ship's Books, and ask'd Leave to fight *Bland*, which was allowed him."

Perhaps the most famous pirate conscript who ultimately embraced pirate life as a full-fledged volunteer, however, is piracy's most successful captain, Bartholomew Roberts, who captured an estimated four hundred ships in his short-lived career between 1719 and 1722. Originally a sailor aboard a slaving vessel, Roberts was pressed into piracy by Captain Howell Davis when Davis captured the slaver off Guinea. "In the Beginning" Roberts "was very averse to this Sort of Life, and would certainly have escaped from them, had a fair Opportunity presented it self; yet afterwards he changed his Principles" and upon Davis's death accepted the crew's election of him to the office of captain. Roberts tried to cheer up conscript Benjamin Parr with his own story of conversion. Parr "begg'd of *Roberts* with Tears . . . that he would let him go from them, to which *Roberts* reply'd, that he had shed as many Crocodile Tears as himself when he was first taken," but had gotten over it, implying Parr would as well.

Force Me, Please

Although pirates didn't see themselves as "pressers," a glance at pirate testimony suggests they almost universally conscripted their members. At their trials pirates time and again claimed "that they were forc'd men," compelled against their wills into piracy. Sailors commonly pleaded they joined the pirates only because their captors "would, have shot them on Refusal" to serve with them. How do we reconcile these remarks with observers' contradictory comments, discussed above, which suggest most pirates were volunteers?

To answer this question it's crucial to understand the changing circumstances pirates faced in pursuing profit over time. Of particular importance is government's changing attitude toward the growing piracy problem in the eighteenth century, which made it increasingly difficult for pirates to get away with maritime banditry. This shift in attitude manifested itself partly through the introduction of more stringent antipiracy laws. These legal changes increased the risk of being a pirate and thus the cost of going on the account. In the very early days of piracy, between 1340 and 1536, England tried pirates under the civil law in special courts with jurisdiction over crimes committed on the high seas called Admiralty courts. The pre-1536 law relating to piracy was deficient in many respects. Most significantly, to convict someone of piracy required either the accused to confess or two eyewitnesses, neither of whom could be accomplices, to testify to his alleged act of piracy. In 1536 England introduced the Offenses at Sea Act, which rectified this deficiency by mandating that acts of piracy be tried according to common law procedure—a procedure that permitted accomplice testimony. This mandate put pirates' fate in the hands of a jury of twelve "peers," which heard cases at special Admiralty sessions in England's criminal courts.

Like the law relating to piracy before 1536, piracy law under the Offenses at Sea Act was also flawed. Most significantly, it didn't provide a practical way for England's growing colonies to handle the pirates they captured. Although some colonies adopted their own legal procedures relating to piracy, colonial piracy trials were rare and the High Court of Admiralty could overturn their decisions. In 1684 most colonial trials halted when the English government decided the colonies didn't have jurisdiction to try any cases of piracy. The 1536 statute obligated colonial officials to ship accused pirates and witnesses to England to attend trial. Since a great deal of piracy took place in and around England's distant colonies, the Offenses at Sea Act left a serious impediment to effectively dealing with sea bandits. As a later law read:

It hath been found by experience, that Persons committing Piracies, Robberies, and Felonies on the Seas, in or near the East and West Indies, and in Places very remote, cannot be brought to condign Punishment without great Trouble and Charges in sending them into England to be tried within the Realm, as the said Statute directs, insomuch that many idle and profligate Persons have been thereby encouraged to turn Pirates, and betake themselves to that sort of wicked Life, trusting that they shall not, or at least cannot be easily questioned for such their Piracies and Robberies, by reason of the great trouble and expense that will necessarily fall upon such as shall attempt to apprehend and prosecute them for the same.

In response to this problem, in 1700 England introduced the Act for the More Effectual Suppression of Piracy. The new statute empowered colonies with commissions from the crown or Admiralty to preside over Vice Admiralty courts to try and punish pirates on location. According to the act:

That all Piracies, Felonies & Robberies committed in or upon the Sea, or in any Haven, River, Creek or Place, where the Admiral or Admirals have Power, Authority or Jurisdiction may be examined, inquired of, tried, heard and determined, and adjudged, according to the Directions of this Act, in any Place at Sea, or upon Land in any of His Majesty's Islands, Plantations, Colonies, Dominions, Forts or Factories, to be appointed for that purpose by the King's Commission or Commissions under the Great Seal of England, or the Seal of the Admiralty of England.

In Vice Admiralty courts seven or more commissioners sat in judgment of accused pirates. Trial by jury per common law procedure, which an accused pirate still enjoyed if he were tried in England, was not (with a single exception) afforded him if he were tried in one of the colonies, as was increasingly the case. The creation of regular colonial courts with the authority to try pirates proved a tremendous boon to government's assault on sea robbers. Parliament originally stipulated that the 1700 act would expire in only seven years. But owing to the great effect it had in permitting the more regular prosecution of pirates, parliament renewed it several times following the War of the Spanish Succession and made the law permanent in 1719.

The Act for the More Effectual Suppression of Piracy stuck two additional thorns in the side of pirates. First, it treated active pirate sympathizers as accessories to piracy and stipulated the same punishments for them—death and property forfeiture—as for actual pirates. According to the act:

> AND whereas several evil-disposed Persons in the Plantations and elsewhere, have contributed very much towards the Increase and Encouragement of Pirates. . . . Be it enacted by the Authority aforesaid, That all and every Person and Persons whatsoever, who . . . shall either on Land, or upon the Seas, wittingly or knowingly set forth any Pirate, or Aid and Assist, or Maintain, Procure, Command, Counsel or Advise any Person or Persons whatsoever, to do or commit any Piracies or Robberies upon the Seas . . . . [or shall] receive, entertain or conceal any such Pirate or Robber, or receive or take into his Custody any Ships, Vessels, Goods or Chattels, which have by any such Pirate or Robber piratically and feloniously taken . . . are hereby likewise declared . . . to be Accessary to such

Piracy and Robbery.... And ... shall and may be ... Adjudged ... as the Principals of such Piracies and Robberies.

Second, the law encouraged merchantmen to defend themselves against pirate attacks by providing them a reward "not exceeding Two Pounds per Cent. Of the Freight, and of the Ship and Goods so defended." By 1717 England not only rewarded individuals for defensively resisting pirate aggression; it also rewarded them for offensively initiating aggression against pirates. These rewards, published in the *Boston News-Letter*, awarded *"for every Commander of any Pirate-Ship as Vessel the Sum of One hundred Pounds; for every Lieutenant, Master, Boatswain, Carpenter, and Gunner the Sum of Forty Pounds; for every Inferior Officer the Sum of Thirty Pounds; And for every Private Man the Sum of Twenty Pounds."*

In September 1717 Britain offered pirates a pardon to try and curb their activities. The initial "Act of Grace" expired on September 5, 1718, but government subsequently extended the pardon deadline to July 1, 1719. A number of pirates accepted the government's pardon. But fewer did so with the intention government had in mind when offering clemency. Accepting His Majesty's gracious pardon was good business for pirates whether they intended to give up their trade or not. The terms of pardon wiped the slate clean for all piracies previously committed. So, even if a pirate had no intention of permanently renouncing his wicked way of life, it still behooved him to accept any pardon Britain offered.

Although many pirates accepted pardon, then, as the attorney general at one pirate trial remarked, "like Dogs to their Vomits," many "returned to their old detestable way of living." In 1718, for example, Woodes Rogers, the man who did the most to extinguish eighteenth-century sea bandits, "reduc'd above a thousand" pirates at New Providence "to accept his

Majesty's Pardon." But as several British military officers re-marked, although these rogues "submitted to his Majesty's Act of Grace, and sworn allegiance &c. taking Certificates of their Submission, yet most of them retained their piratical Principles." Rogers estimated that a hundred of the six hundred New Providence pirates who initially accepted the king's par-don returned to their old trade within three months of accept-ing it.

In 1721 parliament bolstered antipiracy law again, now to hold accountable anyone who traded with pirates. Under the new the law any person who "any wise trade with any pirate, by truck, barter, exchange, or any other manner" was "deemed, ad-judged and taken to be guilty of piracy" and punished as the same. Further, to the carrot of reward money, which the 1700 law promised merchantmen that successfully defended their ships and cargo against pirate attack, the 1721 law added the stick of wage forfeiture and six months imprisonment for armed merchantmen that didn't try to defend themselves against pi-rate aggression.

Another important addition in the 1721 law punished naval vessels charged with hunting sea rovers and protecting mer-chant ships from pirates for engaging in trade instead. It seems His Majesty's warships had taken to using the government's vessels as their personal trading convoys rather than to defend merchantmen and capture pirates. In 1718, for example, Jamai-ca's governor complained to the Council of Trade and Planta-tions of "the neglect of the Commanders of H.M. ships of warr, who are said to be appointed for the suppressing of pyrates and for a security to this Island, and protection of the trade thereof, but in reality by their conduct, have not the least regard to the service they are designed for" and are instead engaged in "trans-porting goods and merchandize which otherwise would be done by vessels belonging to the Island." By introducing stiff penalties for such behavior the 1721 law reduced this problem, putting stronger screws to the pirates.

In addition to punishing private individuals who aided and abetted pirates, these legal changes could be used to prosecute public officials, some of whom weren't exactly on adversarial terms with pirates. Besides corrupting some merchant sailors, piracy's potential riches corrupted some men in government too. As Alexander Spotswood put it, "People are easily led to favor these Pests of Mankind when they have hopes of Sharing in their ill-gotten Wealth." In the face of strong punishments for showing such favor, the law could indirectly squeeze pirates who relied on "legitimate" citizens to carry on their criminal trade.

Together, these legal changes made piracy in the second and third decades of the eighteenth century a considerably riskier employment than it had been before. Pirates rationally responded to this increased risk with their own tricks for circumventing punishment under the law. The primary trick they employed for this purpose was conscription. This conscription had one catch, however; in many cases it wasn't real. More than a few sailors who pirates forced to join them were, in the words of Captain Johnson, "willing to be forced."

Once authorities apprehended them, most pirates had little to offer in their defense at their trials. As a result, lame arguments abounded. A key piece of William Taylor's defense, for instance, was that he was "given to Reading, not swearing and bullying like others of them." This argument failed to persuade the court. The one defense that did occasionally prove effective, however, was that pirates had pressed a sailor into their service when they captured his ship. The law harshly punished individuals who willingly robbed on the sea. Most convicted pirates were hanged. However, courts were reluctant to condemn men who pirates compelled into service under the threat of death or bodily harm. If accused pirates could demonstrate to the court that they were in fact pressed men, they could escape their trials unscathed. As Captain Johnson observed, "The plea of Force was only the best Artifice they had to shelter themselves under, in Case they should be taken." Under the law "The court acquitted all those who could prove that they had been forced to join the pirates."

The court that tried several of Bartholomew Roberts's crew members in 1722, for instance, identified "the three Circumstances that compleat a Pyrate; first, being a Voluntier amongst them at the Beginning; secondly, being a Voluntier at the taking or robbing of any Ship; or lastly, voluntarily accepting a Share in the Booty of those that did." Or, as the court that tried William Kidd indicated, "There must go an Intention of Mind and Freedom of the Will to the committing an Act of Felony or Pyracy. A Pyrate is not to be understood to be under Constraint, but a free Agent; fir in this Case, the bare Act will not make a Man guilty, unless the Will make it so." Clearly, voluntarily complicity with a pirate crew was important to establishing guilt. Pirates exploited this loophole by pretending to conscript seamen who joined their ranks voluntarily. Since, as discussed above, pirates genuinely compelled some seamen to join their companies, court officials considered the impressment defense plausible.

For their ruse to work, pirates needed to concoct evidence that they were conscripts. Although many pirates attempted to escape punishment by simply claiming they were forced, absent corroborating evidence to this effect the impressment defense didn't usually persuade. Pirates generated convincing evidence of their impressment in two ways. First, conscripts, real and pretend, asked their captured fellow sailors who the pirates released to advertise their impressment in one of the popular London or New England newspapers. If authorities ever captured the pirates the "conscripts" sailed with, "conscripts" could use the newspaper ads verifying their forced status as evidence in their defense. After being "forced on Board" Captain Roberts's ship, for instance, Edward Thornden "desired one of his Ship-Mates . . . to take notice of it, and incert it in the *Gazette*." Out of guilt, pity, or perhaps even complicity, most released sailors were only too willing to place them for their unfortunate friends. If they weren't, a little palm grease could help things along. Sailors considered these ads such important evidence of their innocence that they had no compunction about paying fellow crew members to place them. Nicholas Brattle, for example, "gave all his Wages" to his captain "to put him in the *Gazette* as a forced Man."

"Ads of force" were a marvelous invention for conscripted sailors. But they were equally useful to volunteers who wanted to insure themselves against conviction in the event of their capture. Such sailors could join the pirates, ask their released colleagues to place an ad verifying their conscription in the paper, and proceed to go roving about with the comforting knowledge that if the law ever caught up with them, they had at least a reasonable shot of getting off as forced men. What's more, this invention was an excellent recruiting tool for pirates. By reducing the cost of piracy, "ads of force" made it easier for pirates to find volunteers in the face of a more dangerous legal environment. Thus, far from objecting to these ads, in some cases at least, pirates actively encouraged them. Aboard one ship, for instance, "*the Quarter-Master of the Pirate Publickly Declared, they would carry them* [captives], *and let them send to New England and Publish it if they pleased.*" Pirate captain John Phillips went a step further and demanded that his (alleged) conscripts' colleagues represent them as such in the news. When he forced John Burrell into his crew he "*ordered*" Jethro Furber, Burell's captain, "*to declare upon his return home, that the said* Burell *was a Forc'd Man: And that if the said* Furber *should neglect to do it, when he met with him again he would Cut off his Ears."*

The second ruse seamen who were eager to join the pirates used to insure themselves against conviction if captured worked to enhance the first. Such sailors staged "shows" of pirate impressment in coordination with their attackers, acted out in front of their more scrupulous sailing companions who had no intention of becoming "Brethren in Iniquity." When pirates attacked a merchant ship, for example, the ship's crew members who wanted to join the pirates might devise a plan whereby one of the aspiring sea bandits would pull aside the pirate captain or quartermaster and inform him of their desire to join the company. The eager sailors would then request their pirate captor to make a public spectacle of compelling their service to convince their fellow crew members who didn't desire to join that they were conscripted. "Their request was granted with much waving of cutlasses and brandishing of pistols and shouting in the hearing of the officers and men on the merchant ship who were not going to join the pirates." Captain Roberts, for instance, asked one prize's crew members "whether they were willing to go with him? for that he would force no body; but they making no Answer, he cry'd, these Fellows want a show of Force" and pretended to conscript the sailors, who in reality had "agree[d] one with another to enter." As Captain Johnson put it, "The pretended Constraint of *Roberts*, on them, was very often a Complotment between Parties equally willing."

Shows of force helped legitimize the advertisements pretend conscripts used to insure themselves against the risk of conviction if authorities captured them. Since honest captives believed they had witnessed their comrades' conscription, they had no scruples about placing ads publicizing the "victims'" names in the newspaper. Further, since witnesses to shows of force believed this force was genuine, they could supply compelling testimony of their former crewmen's compelled status at trial if authorities later captured the pirates.

According to historian Patrick Pringle, "this ruse often worked." It often worked because courts relied on observer testimony about accused pirates' free or coerced status in determining their guilt or innocence. For instance, pirate prisoners Stephen Thomas, Harry Glasby, and Henry Dawson testified on accused pirate Richard Scot's behalf at his trial. All three testified Scot "was a forced Man." What persuaded them of this was Scot's demeanor and behavior while among the pirate crew. Scot, they deposed, "lamented his Wife and Child . . . with Tears in his Eyes" and "received no Share" in the pirates' plunder. "The Court from these several Circumstances concluded he must be a forced Man" and acquitted him.

Similarly, eyewitness testimony that a sailor seemed to act freely or was pleased to be among the pirates could be crucial in establishing his guilt. According to the testimony of one pirate captive, for example, "I was a Prisoner, Sir, with the Pyrates when their Boat was ordered upon that Service, and found, upon a Resolution of going, Word was pass'd thro' the Company, Who would go? And I saw all that did, did it voluntarily; no Compulsion, but rather pressing who should be foremost." The court found the pirates he testified against guilty and sentenced them to hang. By the same token, a sailor stupid enough to publicly declare his piratical desires could expect eyewitness testimony to this effect at his trial if pirates later captured his crew and he went along with them. One such sailor, Samuel Fletcher, whose fellow seamen heard him say "several times [he] wish'd to God Almighty they might meet the Pyrates," and later in fact did, was confronted with his wish at his trial and found guilty of piracy.

The artificial pirate press wasn't an iron-clad way to escape punishment. Courts naturally viewed the common claim of conscription with considerable suspicion, the "*Plea of constraint or force, (in the mouth of every Pirate)*," as one prosecutor put it. If a prisoner's testimony contradicted an accused pirate's claim that others forced him, this was doubly so. For instance, Peter Hooff, a pirate in Sam Bellamy's crew, argued at his trial "that the said Bellamy's Company Swore they would kill him unless he would joyn with them in their Unlawful Designs." Unfortunately for Hooff, actual prisoners aboard the *Whydah*, such as Thomas Checkley, informed the court that "at that time [Bellamy's crew] forced no Body to go with them; and said they would take no Body against their Wills." Commissioners at piracy trials often needed to negotiate conflicting claims like these. This is where the harder evidence of a newspaper ad proved especially helpful to accused pirates claiming to be conscripts. Sadly, Hooff had no such ad. The court found him guilty and sentenced him, along with several others, to "be hanged up by the Neck until you & each of you are Dead; And the Lord have Mercy on your Souls."

Even with an ad of force as evidence, however, an accused pirate might not manage to weasel his way out of conviction. Court officials were weary of "*that Hackney Defense made by every Pirate upon Trial, namely, That he was a forced Man,*" as one advocate general put it, even if less so when such a defense relied on the newspaper ads discussed above. Joseph Libbey, for instance, who "said he was a forced Man, and was detained by *Low*, and produced an Advertisement of it" was nevertheless convicted of piracy and sentenced to hang. Still, the pirates' ploy was sometimes effective. The same court that condemned Libbey acquitted Joseph Swetser whose defense was an ad stating Captain Low forced him to serve with the pirates. Perhaps Swetser really was a conscript. Or, like many others, he may

Aovertifements.

JOhn Smith of Bofton in New-England late Mate of the Briganteen Rebecca of Charlftown, burthen about Ninety Tons,
whereof James Flucker was late Commander, and Charles
Meffon of Bofton aforefaid Mariner, late belonging to the faid
Briganteen, Severally Declare and fay, 'I hat the faid Briganteen
in her Voyage from St. Chriftophers of Bofton, on the Twenty-
eighth day of May laft paft, being in the Latitude of Thirty-
eight degrees and odd Minutes North, the faid Briganteen was
taken by a Pirate Sloop Commanded by one Lowder, having
near One Hundred Men and Eight Guns Mounted, and the day
after the faid Briganteen was taken, the faid Pirate parted
their Company, Forty of them went on board the faid Briganteen Commanded by Edward Loe of Bofton aforefaid, Mariner,
and the reft of the faid Pirates went on board the Sloop Commanded by the faid Lowder ; and the Declarents further fay,
That Jofeph Sweetfer of Charleftown aforefai,d and Richard
Rich, and Robert Willis of London, Mariners, all belonging to
the faid Briganteen, were forc'd and Compelled againft their
Wills to go with the faid Pirates, viz Jofeph Sweetfer and
Richard Rich on board the Briganteen, and Robert Willis on
board the Sloop ; The faid Willis having broke his Arm by a
fall from the Maft, Defired that confidering his Condition they
would let him go, but they utterly refufed and forced him
away with them.

Signum

John Smith,
Charles C l Meffon.

Suffolk ff.

Bofton June 15th. 1722.

The above named John Smith and Charles Meffon perfonally
appearing made Oath to the Truth of the above-written
Declaration.

Coram me J. Willard, *Secr. &* Juft. Peace.

FIGURE 6.1. Conscript or volunteer? Joseph Swetser's "ad of force." From *Boston News-Letter*, June 11–June 18, 1722.

have simply manipulated the court's judgment with his ad of force. We'll never know. And the point is, neither did the court.

Contrary to popular perception, most pirates were volunteers, not conscripts. Pirates sought willing companions instead of forced men because of simple cost-benefit considerations, not because of a principled objection to using force to get what they wanted. On the one hand, in many cases pirates simply didn't have to resort to coercion to increase their numbers. The better treatment and opportunity for vastly superior pay on pirate ships was plenty incentive for many sailors to sign on under the black flag when given the opportunity. The benefit of conscripting ordinary sailors was therefore quite low. On the other hand, the costs of pressing sailors could be very large. Forced men threatened to destroy the harmony pirates' system of private governance was based on. Conscripts were liabilities to pirates in other ways as well. They could escape, informing authorities, or leaving the remaining crew too small to take advantage of the ship. Even if conscripts didn't manage to escape, a crew with a sizeable portion of forced men was less likely to succeed since conscripts didn't have the same incentive to participate as volunteers. For some specially skilled sailors, such as surgeons, coopers, and navigators, the cost-benefit calculus pirates confronted was different. Since these seamen were necessary and difficult to come by, and furthermore, since they were relatively few and therefore taxed pirates' governance system little, pirates conscripted skilled sailors more often.

Although the historical record contains many claims of pirate conscription, these claims must be analyzed more closely. In response to legal changes in the early eighteenth century that raised the risk of pirating, pirates rationally reacted to protect themselves. They did this by feigning conscription through staged "shows" to fool their more scrupulous fellow sailors who didn't want to join the pirates, and through newspaper ads that publicized their "forced" status. These two ruses generated evidence of innocence pirates could use at their trials if they were captured. If these tricks had worked for pirates even half as well as they've worked to create the modern perception that most sea bandits were forced men, nary a pirate would've swung from the gallows.

7 EQUAL PAY FOR EQUAL PREY
THE ECONOMICS OF PIRATE TOLERANCE

Centuries before the civil rights movement, the ACLU, or the Equal Opportunity Act, some pirates had already adopted a policy of "hiring" black sailors in their crews. What's more, these pirates extended suffrage to their black members and subscribed to the practice of "equal pay for equal work," or rather, "equal pay for equal prey." This is startling considering the views and policies towards blacks in the rest of the seventeenth- and eighteenth-century world. In England government didn't abolish slavery until 1772; and slaves in the British colonies didn't enjoy freedom until 1833. In the United States slavery persisted until 1865. Blacks didn't enjoy equal rights as citizens, politically or in the workplace, until even later than that. In contrast, some pirate crews granted black sailors the same perquisites and privileges of "citizenship" in their floating societies as white sailors in the early 1700s.

Pirates weren't the only seventeenth- and eighteenth-century mariners to have black crew members. Merchant ships, Royal Navy vessels, and slavers also relied on black sailors for labor. Some blacks even nominally captained smaller ships engaged in coastal or interisland transport. A few of these black seamen were freemen. However, most were slaves, operating on behalf of, or hired out by, their owners, or runaways who found employment on vessels in need of men. Pirate ships had a larger proportion of black crew members than their legitimate counterparts, and as noted above, they sometimes enjoyed the same rights as their white colleagues. In contrast, on legitimate vessels, slave sailors were invariably treated as, well, slaves. Most significantly, this meant they sailed without pay or voice in their crews.

Were pirates early abolitionists, predecessors of the great Harriet Tubman and Booker T. Washington, and harbingers of enlightened color-blind thinking? Far from it. Economic concerns, not lofty ideals, drove pirates to enroll black sailors as paid, full-fledged crew members. Simple self-interest, in the unique context in which pirates operated, explains some pirates' progressive racial practices. The invisible hook, it turns out, may have fostered pirate tolerance.

Black Pirates

W. Jeffrey Bolster, whose book, *Black Jacks*, extensively explores black seamen in the age of sail, notes that although data are hard to come by, "the impression is that" black sailors in pirate crews "were more numerous than the proportion of black sailors in commercial or naval service at that time." In 1718, for instance, eighty members of Captain Edward England's pirate crew were black. Eighty-eight pirates who went on the account with Captain Roberts's crew in 1721 were as well. Sixty black pirates sailed on one of Blackbeard's ships in 1717. And at least one of these was close to Blackbeard personally. This pirate's name was Caesar, "a resolute Fellow, a Negroe, whom he had bred up."

Historian Kenneth Kinkor has performed an invaluable service in compiling the racial composition of several pirate crews. Table 7.1 presents his data, which identifies the racial makeup of twenty-three pirate companies active between 1682 and 1726. The data portray highly racially mixed pirate crews. The percentage of black crew members in Kinkor's sample ranges from 13

TABLE 7.1.
The racial composition of 23 pirate crews, 1682–1726

| Captain | Year | Crew | | | |
		Total	White	Black	% Black
Anstis	1723	60	40	20	33
Bellamy	1717	180	<153	>27	>15
Charpes	1713	68	48	20	29
Cooper	1726	19	15	4	20
Davis		250	<210	>39	>16
Edmonson	1726	10	6	4	40
England (est. one)	1718	180	130	<50	<28
England (est. two)	1719	380	300	80	21
Franco	1691	89	39	50	56
Hamann	1717	25	1	24	96
Hamlin	1682	36	16	22	61
Harris	1723	48	42	6	13
La Bouche	1719	64			50
Lewis		80	40	40	50
Lowther	1724	23	16	9	39
Philips	1724	20	17	3	15
Roberts (est. one)	1721	368	280	88	24
Roberts (est. two)	1722	267	197	70	26
Shipton	1725	13	9	4	31
Thatch (est. one)	1717	100	40	60	60
Thatch (est. two)	1718	14	9	5	36
Unnamed	1721	50	1	<49	<98
Williams	1717	40	<25	>15	>38

Source: Kinkor, "Black Men under the Black Flag," 201.

to 98 percent. None of these pirate companies were all white. In seven of the twenty-three crews, or nearly a third, half or more of the pirate crew was of African descent. If this sample is representative, an astonishing 25 to 30 percent of the average pirate crew operating in the height of piracy's golden age was black.

Historians disagree about the status of black crewmen on pirate ships. David Cordingly suggests they were mostly slaves. As he puts it, "The pirates shared the same prejudices as other white men in the Western world." There's good reason to believe this statement. As this book has emphasized throughout, pirates were profit seekers and therefore opportunists. They had no qualms about doing what was necessary to enhance their hauls. Sometimes this meant selling captured slaves. Other times it meant keeping the slaves they captured for the menial tasks aboard their ships. Further, there's nothing in the historical record to suggest pirates were racially enlightened compared to their legitimate contemporaries. But just because pirates probably shared the same racist *beliefs* as their legitimate contemporaries doesn't mean pirates must have always *behaved* as prejudicially as their legitimate contemporaries did. Contradictory as it may seem, pirates holding contempt for black sailors and simultaneously treating them as equals isn't contradictory at all.

The reason for this is that indulging one's beliefs or preferences can be very expensive. This costliness can lead people to behave in ways at odds with what they actually prefer. To see this more clearly, consider a bigoted employer who loves brunettes but loathes redheads. Our bigoted employer owns a shoe factory and needs employees. Redheads and brunettes are equally productive; a redhead with 60 hours of training and a brunette with 60 hours of training produce the same number of shoes per hour. But redheads are willing to work at the shoe factory for $10 per hour, whereas brunettes demand $20 per hour for the same labor.

CHAPTER 7

What will the bigoted employer do? He hates redheads. But for every redhead he hires instead of a brunette, he pockets an additional $10 per hour in profit. In other words, if he wants to indulge his prejudice, it's going to cost him $10 per hour for every brunette worker he employs. If the bigoted shoe factory owner is as greedy as he is bigoted, he'll hire redheads even though he despises them. The profit motive "forces" him to behave in his hiring decisions as though he weren't prejudiced at all. In fact, the profit motive leads the redhead-hating employer to behave as though he actually preferred redheaded workers. Provided redheaded workers charge less per hour than brunette workers, it pays the prejudiced employer to discriminate against brunettes, hiring only redheads instead.

The bigoted, but profit-motivated, employer's actions—hiring redheads and letting go of brunettes—also serves to bring the wages of redheads and brunettes into parity. As he purchases more redheaded labor, redheaded workers' wages rise. At the same time, as he purchases less brunette labor, brunette workers' wages fall. The former will rise and the latter will fall until there's no longer a gap the employer can exploit for his own profit, that is, until redhead and brunette worker wages are the same.

Of course, our bigoted employer *could* choose to indulge his antiredhead thinking in practice. In this example, there's no law preventing him from discriminating against redheaded workers. But if he's interested in making as much money as possible, this doesn't matter. The bigoted employer still *acts as if* he loves redheads rather than loathes them. His antiredhead preferences and proredhead behavior coexist without contradiction because there's a cost of catering to the former, which leads him to act in accordance with the latter. Incidentally, if the bigoted employer decided to indulge his antiredhead thinking even though he'd lose money by doing so, it's unlikely he'd remain in business for

160

long if he has competitors. A more profit-motivated competitor could hire all the less expensive redheaded workers, lower his prices accordingly, and drive the bigoted employer, who's paying more for brunette workers and thus can't lower his prices to compete, out of business.

The relevance of this example for pirates is what it tells us, or rather doesn't tell us, about how pirate racism influenced the status of black crew members on pirate ships. Like the bigoted shoe factory employer above, it's possible pirates "thought racist" without "acting racist" when it came to their enterprise. In short, it's wrong to conclude that because pirates held the same detestable views about blacks as their legitimate contemporaries that pirates necessarily treated blacks in the same detestable ways as their legitimate contemporaries. Pirates, after all, were profit seekers, which means they cared more about gold and silver than they cared about black and white.

It's impossible to say what percentage of black pirates identified in table 7.1 was free and what percentage of them was slaves. But several facts suggest a significant number of black sailors on pirate ships—and certainly more than on legitimate vessels—were "regular" pirate crew members in good standing. For example, some black sailors in pirate companies carried arms and actively participated in battle. Several black pirates fought alongside Blackbeard, for instance. Similarly, a black pirate in Bartholomew Sharp's crew fought as hard as any of his white colleagues. This "Negro, who had his Leg shot off, being offered quarter, refused it, and killed four or five of their Men, before he was shot dead on the spot." Unless pirates were in the dangerous habit of arming slaves, and slaves enjoyed fighting to enrich their enslavers, the presence of armed and fighting black sailors among pirates suggests they were freemen, not slaves. The black pirate in Sharp's crew, for example, was certainly free. "This fellow," one of Sharp's white pirates remarked, "had been a Slave, whom our Commander had freed, and brought from Jamaica."

Several black pirates weren't only active, but rose to positions of importance, and even authority, within their crews. Caesar, for instance, was given the important task of blowing up the pirates' ship should authorities overtake his crew. Similarly, one Spanish pirate ship's pilot—among the most important positions in the company—was "a Negro Man." Further, as Marcus Rediker points out, "Black crewmen made up part of the pirate vanguard, the most trusted and fearsome men designated to board prospective prizes . . . more than half of Edward Condent's boarding party on the *Dragon*," for instance, "was black." These black pirates are reminiscent of the black soldiers in "the first integrated national institution in the United States," the Continental Army. According to historian David Fischer, some of these men rose to the position of colonel in New England— an impressive feat in 1776. Notably, the Fourteenth Massachusetts Continental, which led the Continental Army's racial integration, hailed largely from Massachusetts fishing towns, such as Marblehead, where seafaring and thus racial integration were more common. But even the Marblehead regiment's integration came more than half a century after pirates'.

Other black pirates' behavior also indicates their free status. A black pirate in Stede Bonnet's crew, for instance, displayed "regular" standing in his company. He verbally accosted a white prisoner, Jonathan Clarke, with the same gusto as other pirates, calling Clarke the "Negroe." As Clarke described it: "I was abaft, and one of the Negroes came and damned me, and asked me what I did there? Why I did not go and work amongst the rest? And told me I should be used as a Negroe."

The experience of mulatto mariner Thomas Gerrard, who this same crew captured, suggests pirates treated black sailors as freemen if they entered the pirates' company voluntarily.

According to Gerrard, when "one of the [pirate] Men came and asked if I would join with them? I told him, No. he said, I was but like a Negro, and they made Slaves of all of that Colour, if I did not join them." In his correspondence with the Council of Trade and Plantations, the governor of Bermuda corroborated the implication of Gerrard's remark. He wrote: "As for the negro men they are grown soe very impudent and insulting of late that we have reason to suspect their riseing, soe that we can have noe dependence on their assistance but to the contrary on occasion should fear their joyning with the pirates." This is a peculiar fear to have if by "joyning with the pirates" blacks were trading one form of slavery for another. But it makes sense if by voluntarily joining the pirates slaves received their freedom.

Finally, although courts sometimes acquitted black crew members aboard pirate ships on the grounds that they were slaves, several viewed black pirates as "regular" pirate crew members on equal footing with the white members of their company. The court presiding over the trial of five black pirates in Blackbeard's company characterized "the said Negroes" as follows: "Being taken on Board a Pyrate vessell and by what appears equally concerned with the rest of the Crew in the Same Acts of Piracy ought to be Try'd in the same Manner; and if any diversity appears in their Circumstances the same may be considered on their Tryal." Evidently no "diversity . . . in their Circumstances" appeared. The court convicted the black pirates and sentenced them to death for their crime. If, as this example suggests, "circumstances" were the same for some black pirates as they were for white ones, these black pirates must have received an equal share of plunder and equally enjoyed the other rights of crew membership.

Eyewitness testimony to one pirate crew's operations, for example, demonstrates not only that free black pirates existed but also that they had the same voting rights as whites. In 1721 a conscripted "surgeon's mate" named Richard Moore sailed as a prisoner in Captain John Taylor's pirate crew. In his deposition following his release Moore records an important vote Taylor's crew took in which "a hundred & twelve white men & forty Blacks voted to go to the West Indias" "to endeavour to get a Pardon." This couldn't have been a situation in which everyone on the pirate ship was allowed to vote, including slaves and other forced men, because "the Surgeons," Moore noted, who like him were conscripts, "had no vote" in the affair. Although Moore's deposition doesn't speak to the issue of black pirates' pay directly, it's almost certain that black pirates who voted received shares equal to every other free crew member. According to Kinkor, for example, Blackbeard-captive Henry Bostock deposed that Blackbeard's black pirates received booty along with white ones. "Rewards and incentives therefore appear to have been based on an individual's ability to function effectively within the pirate crew rather than on skin color."

Concentrated Costs, Dispersed Benefits, and Pirate Slavery

The fact that some, or perhaps even many, blacks sailing on pirate ships were slaves isn't surprising. What's surprising is that *any* blacks sailing on pirate ships were treated as freemen. If anything, we would expect pirates to enslave even the free blacks they captured from merchant vessels. Merchant ship captains couldn't enslave these sailors whose free status the law protected. But pirates, who were full-blown criminals, and thus totally unconstrained by such legal protections, could enslave anybody they wanted—freeman or not. Even if the number of free black pirates was small (which as discussed above there's good reason doubt), how can we account for pirates' extension of freedom to any blacks they could enslave?

Rather easily, it turns out. As in chapter 6, simple cost-benefit reasoning goes a long way. It was often in pirates' economic interest to treat black sailors as freemen, as we'll see.

The benefit of a slave in any productive activity was the additional revenue his "costless" labor earned for his owner. Typically, a slave had only one owner who therefore enjoyed all of the slave's additional revenue. If adding a slave to a sugar plantation, for example, created $1,000 per year in additional revenue for the plantation owner, the plantation owner benefited from the slave in the amount of $1,000.

On pirate ships, however, things were different. As with their ships, pirates jointly owned their slave labor. This was because of pirates' pay system, discussed in chapter 3. This system, recall, pooled the proceeds of the entire crew's labor and divided it into roughly equal shares (except for a few pirate officers who received slightly more). So, if a pirate crew enslaved a black sailor, or anyone else for that matter, the additional piratical revenue his labor created was combined with the revenue created by everyone else's labor and divided among the crew. Of course, booty was only shared among free pirates, which is where the benefit of slavery came in. While a slave's labor was "costless" to the crew in the sense that the crew didn't pay the slave a share of the loot, the slave's labor contributed to greater booty, allowing a larger pool of revenue to be divided among the same number of pirates. Simplifying a bit, in a pirate crew with n free sailors, if by enslaving a black sailor the crew could take a prize worth, say, $1,000 more than it could take without him, each free pirate earned an extra $1,000/n$ from enslaving the black sailor. Note how this situation differs from the plantation owner who enjoyed $1,000 of the additional $1,000 his slave's labor generated. Each free pirate crew member, in contrast, enjoys only $1,000/n$

of the additional $1,000 the slave's labor generates. In this sense, pirates' benefit of slavery was "dispersed."

Adding concrete numbers to this example illustrates how dispersed pirates' benefit of enslaving a black sailor was. As noted in chapter 2, the average pirate ship had about eighty crew members. This figure, however, includes both free and enslaved pirates (assuming there are any of the latter). If, as Kinkor's data suggests, 25 percent of the average pirate crew was black and, furthermore, we assume for the sake of argument that all black pirates were slaves, the remaining crew, among whom booty would be distributed in equal shares, numbered sixty. That means, if, as in the example above, enslaving a black sailor enabled our pirate crew to take a prize worth an additional $1,000, each free pirate earned only ($1,000/60≈) $16.67 extra, or about 1.67 percent of the total additional revenue the slave's labor created. Under pirates' pay system, then, an individual pirate received less than 2 percent of the benefit of a slave that he could potentially enjoy if, like the plantation owner, he was the exclusive owner of the slave's labor. That's quite small.

In contrast, an individual pirate's cost of enslaving a black sailor was largely "concentrated;" each pirate bore the major downside of slavery personally. The costs of enslaving a black sailor were similar to the costs of conscripting a white sailor, discussed in chapter 6. Although some of these costs to an individual pirate were dispersed among the free pirate crew members, the most significant cost of a conscript—the liability he posed in contributing to his crew's capture, and thus to a pirate's execution—was concentrated on each sea bandit individually. Unlike an individual pirate's benefit of slave labor—money and goods—which could be divided and shared, his cost of slave labor—his death—couldn't be. Although, as shown above, under pirates' pay system an individual pirate enjoyed only 1.67 percent of the benefit of a slave he could in principle enjoy, he suffered 100 percent of the cost of a slave he could in principle incur.

Collectively, the cost of a slave who led to his crew's execution was sixty pirates' lives. But from the perspective of an individual, self-interested pirate's cost-benefit calculus, his comrades' fifty-nine lives don't enter the equation. The only death that's costly to him is his own, and that one he always bears fully. The "collective benefit" of a slave, in contrast, *could* in principle be enjoyed exclusively by an individual pirate. If, like the plantation owner, a pirate singly owned a slave's labor, he would reap 100 percent of the benefits associated with the slave. The only reason he doesn't is because of the slave labor ownership arrangement on pirate ships—the result of pirates' pay system—which makes every free pirate an equal "owner" of a slave's labor.

Like white conscripts, slaves could contribute to a pirate crew's capture in multiple ways. One way was through giving minimal effort if authorities accosted their ship, helping their crew to lose in the contest and allowing authorities to overtake their pirate enslavers. Even more important, minority, as well as white, conscripts could revolt against their pirate enslavers and deliver them to the law. We already considered several cases in which forced men did this. But, of course, nonwhite prisoners—slaves—could do so too. For example, an Indian prisoner helped overtake John Phillips's crew. According to one of Phillips's white prisoners, the Indian wasn't merely a participant in the revolt. He was the reason for its success. As the white captive put it, had "it not have been for him our plot would most probably have failed in the execution." Similarly, black prisoners aboard Captain Grinnaway's pirate sloop helped overwhelm their captors. As noted above, if such a revolt proved successful, each free pirate shouldered the full brunt of the resulting cost that mattered to him, which was the end of his piratical employment and often his life. Together with pirate slavery's dispersed benefits, this concentrated cost created an incentive for many pirates to treat black sailors as freemen instead of slaves.

It's interesting to compare the logic of dispersed benefits and concentrated costs associated with enslavement for work purposes on pirate ships with the situation on merchant ships. Since merchant shipping was legitimate, pirates' chief costs of slavery—slaves' contribution to crew member capture and execution—wasn't only not concentrated on merchant ships; it was totally absent. Equally important, rather than facing dispersed benefits of enslaved black sailors as pirate ships did, on merchant vessels the benefits of enslavement were concentrated. As noted above, merchant ships also had black sailors—a few freemen, but primarily slaves. Landed masters or captains sailing the ships black sailors worked on owned the black slaves who manned merchant vessels. Because of this, the full additional earnings associated with the slave accrued to his owner. Instead of being dispersed among many pirates, this benefit was concentrated on the master who therefore had a much stronger incentive to keep his slave a slave. This stronger incentive for the continuing enslavement of blacks sailing on legitimate vessels explains why black slaves on legitimate ships were always slaves, while black slaves who made their way onto pirate ships were sometimes granted their freedom.

Given the dispersed benefit and largely concentrated cost associated with enslaving black sailors, it's not surprising some pirate crews placed black pirates on equal footing with whites instead of enslaving them. But what about the pirates who didn't? As pointed out earlier, some pirates held slaves. Despite the dispersed nature of enslavement's benefits and the concentrated nature of an important part of enslavement's costs, in some cases pirates' benefit of enslaving black sailors must have still exceeded the cost. Why did pirates sometimes find slavery profitable and other times not?

Several factors could contribute to slavery's profitability for pirates. The discussion above focused on black sailors forced to work as slaves on pirate ships. But pirates also desired slaves to sell. In this case the benefit of enslavement wasn't only the additional earnings enabled by "free" slave labor, but also $1/n^{th}$ of the price a slave could fetch when sold. If slave prices were high, this benefit, though dispersed, could be significant. More important, if pirates expected to find a ready market for stolen slaves, the concentrated cost of slaves could be very low. In this case pirates only needed to hold slaves for a short time before unloading them, shrinking slaves' window of opportunity to revolt. Under these circumstances the probability slaves would contribute to pirates' capture, and thus pirates' cost of slavery, was much lower.

Two other factors could also contribute to the profitability of pirate slavery despite the dispersed benefits and concentrated costs discussed above. As discussed in chapter 6, like all ships, pirate ships required certain skilled sailors to function. Compared to unskilled seamen, the skilled variety were difficult to come by. If pirates couldn't find volunteers to fill a needed position, but a captured black sailor could perform this role, the black sailor's indispensability significantly increased the benefit of enslaving him.

Similarly, if pirates captured black slaves who didn't have the sailing or navigational expertise required to sail the ship, this could also affect pirates' cost-benefit calculus of resorting to slavery. Enslaved sailors who revolted against their pirate oppressors posed a considerably lesser threat to their captors if they couldn't bring the ship to authorities. In such cases pirates' cost of enslaving black captives, while still concentrated, was much lower. In turn, pirates had a greater incentive to resort to slavery.

Perhaps the most important factor that could contribute to pirates' incentive to enslave black sailors, however, was the probability they would be brought to justice if slaves wrested control of the ship and delivered it to authorities. Chapter 6 discussed eighteenth-century legal innovations that made pirating riskier than it was previously. The Act for the More Effectual Suppression of Piracy was especially important in this regard. However, parliament didn't make this statue permanent until 1719. Thus it wasn't until 1719 that the machinery of government's antipiracy legislation was firing on all cylinders. Not coincidentally, the few years following parliament's permanent establishment of the 1700 statue correspond with the beginning of the precipitous decline of the Anglo-American pirate population. The year 1719 consequently marked a significant moment in government's war against the pirates.

In light of this legal development, a pirate's probability of government trying and convicting him from 1719 onward increased significantly. Since the concentrated cost of pirate slavery was slaves' potential contribution to bringing pirates to justice, pirates' incentive to hold slaves before 1719 was considerably greater than it was after 1719. This suggests that those pirate crews most likely to have enslaved black sailors were those operating before this date, while those operating after 1719 had a stronger incentive to treat black sailors as freemen, per the concentrated cost reasoning discussed above. As noted earlier, there aren't data on the number of enslaved versus free black sailors on pirate ships to permit us to examine this issue directly. However, the data we do have from table 7.1 on the proportion of black sailors in twenty-three pirate crews operating between 1682 and 1726 allows us to investigate this issue indirectly. And the evidence is consistent with the argument that pirate crews active before 1719 were more likely to carry enslaved black sailors than pirate crews active between 1719 and 1726.

While the average pre-1719 pirate crew in table 7.1 was 46.6 percent black, the average 1719–26 pirate crew was only 34.2

percent black. The 12.4 percentage point difference between the proportion of black sailors in pirate crews before and after parliament made the Act for the More Effectual Suppression of Piracy permanent suggests pirate crews operating in the less stringent legal environment before 1719 may have carried more black slaves than pirate crews operating in the more stringent legal environment established after 1719. What portion of this difference is attributable to black slaves that pre-1719 pirate crews held but post-1719 crews didn't because of the difference in the probability of being brought to justice is uncertain. But in light of the concentrated cost of pirate slavery discussed above, which becomes more binding on pirates' policy toward blacks as the probability of being brought to justice increases, there's good reason to suspect that at least part of this difference is due to black slaves present in earlier pirate crews that weren't present in later ones.

Queer Buccaneers?

A few scholars have suggested that pirates were a community of homosexuals. Historian B. R. Burg's study of pirate sexuality, *Sodomy and the Perception of Evil*, makes this argument most forcefully. Given pirates' progressivism in other areas, such as governance, social welfare, and race relations, it's not hard to also imagine they may have been sexually forward thinking.

Despite this, it's highly doubtful pirates cared one way or another about their fellow rogues' sexual proclivities. As Burg points out, homosexual contact was present on seventeenth- and eighteenth-century marine vessels of all varieties. I think Burg probably overstates the extent of this contact; but there's little doubt homosexuality wasn't confined to landlubbers. Still, there doesn't seem to be any evidence that the pirate community was a predominantly homosexual one, let alone that "homosexual acts . . . were the *only* form of sexual expression engaged in by the members" of the pirate community, as Burg contends.

There *is* evidence, on the other hand, that at least some pirates were *not* gay. Several members of Bartholomew Roberts's crew clearly had a taste for the fairer sex, intending, as they informed a prisoner, "to spend their Money with the Portuguize Negro Women." Other pirates, such as Stede Bonnet, were married . . . to women. According to eighteenth-century rumor, Blackbeard had more than a dozen wives. It's doubtful this is true; but it's equally doubtful Blackbeard would have developed this reputation if he hadn't taken a strong interest in women. Of course, being married wouldn't preclude a pirate from engaging in some side buggery. And it's possible pirates used the façade of heterosexuality to mask hidden homosexual desires. But in the absence of evidence for this, it seems strange to conclude that all pirates were homosexuals.

Two pirates were cross-dressers. Both sailed with the pirate dandy, Captain "Calico" Jack Rackam. These pirates stand out for a reason besides their cross-dressing, however. Both were women. In fact, they're two of only four female Anglo-American pirates we know of in the golden age. One of them, Anne Bonny, was Rackam's lover and sailed with his crew dressed as a man. In an astonishing but confirmed defiance of probability, the other cross-dressing female pirate, Mary Read, was also a member of Rackam's crew. In a peculiar twist, Bonny, taking the pirate lass for a pirate lad, developed a crush on Read only to have her hopes dashed when Read revealed she was actually a woman. As Dorothy Thomas, a prisoner on Rackam's ship, testified at their trial: "the Two Women, Prisoners at the Bar . . . wore Mens Jackets, and long Trouzers, and Handkerchiefs tied about their Heads; and that each of them had a Machet and Pistol in their hands, and cursed and swore at the Men." According

FIGURE 7.1. Cross-dressing pirate co-eds: Anne Bonny and Mary Read. From Captain Charles Johnson, *A General History of the Robberies and Murders of the Most Notorious Pyrates*, 1724.

to two other eyewitnesses, Bonny and Read "were very active on Board, and willing to do any Thing." Apparently the pirate ladies fit right in as pirate gents. Dorothy Thomas was only able to surmise differently "by the largeness of their Breasts."

Even so, Bonny and Read's ample bosom wasn't large enough to halt the wheels of justice. The court sentenced both cross-dressing femmes to death by hanging. But their femininity didn't prove totally worthless either. As Jamaican governor Nicholas Lawes reported to his superiors in England, although "the women, spinsters of Providence Island, were proved to have taken an active part in piracies, wearing men's clothes and armed etc. Being quick with child, their sentence was suspended." Thus were spared the pregnant pirates in history's most infamous co-ed crew.

Entertaining though they are, the cross-dressing practices of Bonny and Read and the details of the almost-lesbian love triangle connecting Bonny, Read, and Rackam don't contain an ounce of evidence of pirate homosexuality. The pirate community was testosterone-driven. As previously discussed, some pirate crews prohibited women from their ships because of the potential for conflict females might introduce. (Though, in fairness, Roberts's crew also prohibited boys). Because of this, Bonny and Read disguised themselves as men. This obviously created some confusion for Bonny, a woman dressed as a man, who developed feelings for Read, who she believed was a man (thus suggesting a heterosexual preference) but was in fact also a cross-dressing woman like herself. But there's no evidence of homosexuality here.

Those protopirates the seventeenth-century buccaneers, which this book has referred to at various points, established an interesting institution called *matelotage*, which some have suggested had homosexual overtones. Under this institution one buccaneer would pair up with another, mutually agreeing to share belongings and creating a contract according to which, in the event either man died in battle, for instance, his share of booty would pass to his *matelot*. If there's something implicitly homosexual about such arrangements, I must confess, it's certainly escaped me. As Exquemelin described it, matelotage agreements sometimes explicitly made provisions for bequeathing property to a dead buccaneer's *wife*: "When a man has finished service, he seeks out a partner and they pool all they possess. They draw up a document, in some cases saying that the partner who lives longer shall have everything, in others that the survivor is bound to give part to the dead man's friends or wife, if he was married."

Like other pirate practices, this one also has a simple economic explanation: risk sharing. Matelotage was as a form of insurance. Buccaneers could diversify the risk of their chosen trade by spreading their potential gains and losses over two people instead of one. Whether they sodomized one another is beside the point. Matelotage created insurance for buccaneers and helped them bear the uncertainties of maritime marauding.

Pirates' relationship to black sailors was peculiar. On the one hand, pirates' attitudes toward blacks don't appear to be different from their lawful contemporaries' attitudes toward them. Pirates took slaves, held slaves, and sold slaves. On the other hand, some pirates displayed significantly more tolerant behavior toward blacks. Upward of a quarter of the average pirate crew may have been black. Many of these sailors were former slaves and at least some of them were treated on equal terms with white sailors in the pirate crews they sailed with. They had equal voting rights in the pirates' democracy and likely received an equal share of the pirates' plunder. This is especially remarkable since, on the surface, pirates had nothing holding them back from enslaving black sailors they captured—bondsmen or free.

The simple logic of the "dispersed benefits and concentrated costs" of slavery on pirate ships may explain pirate tolerance. Since the benefits of enslaving a black sailor on a pirate ship were divided among its many free crew members and a substantial part of the potential cost of enslavement, namely the increased odds of a pirate crew's capture, was borne fully by each free crew member, pirate slavery was sometimes unprofitable. This wasn't always true. But sometimes the invisible hook led pirates to display a racial progressivism in practice that didn't accord with the racial views in their minds.

8 THE SECRETS OF PIRATE MANAGEMENT

Piracy's peak in the eighteenth century lasted little more than a decade. But pirates' swan song in the 1720s isn't a reflection on their ineffectiveness. On the contrary, as previously mentioned, pirates ingeniously extended their presence as the odds mounted against them. And while they lasted, pirates were incredibly successful, sometimes earning in only a few months what it might have taken forty years to earn in legitimate maritime employment. Pirates' demise had little to do with their defects and much to do with a stronger government determined to exterminate them. That pirates lasted as long as they did without a government to maintain peace, or facilitate cooperation, among them is a testament to their effectiveness, not a strike against it. How many other rag-tag bands of miscreants succeeded in causing so much trouble for the world's greatest superpower in so little time? Not many. So, what was the secret to pirates' success? For the answer to that question you'll have to enroll in Professor Blackbeard's Management 101 class. And don't be late. I hear he's got a hell of a temper.

Management 101, Prof. Blackbeard, T and Th,
   1:00–2:15, *Queen Anne's Revenge*

There would be a lengthy waitlist for a management course taught by a pirate captain. And students wouldn't (or at least shouldn't) scurry to enroll in the course only to hear their pirate professor's lectures recounting adventurous tales of his criminal life at sea. They would also hope for a seat in the class because of what they could learn from their pirate professor about successful management. Let's take a look at the course syllabus.

WEEKS 1–2. Follow the Booty

Readings: Adam Smith, *Wealth of Nations*; Bernard Mandeville, *The Fable of the Bees*

Central Lesson: Greed is good.

The idea of allowing the lure of money to drive people's behavior conjures up images of corporate mismanagement—embezzlement, fraud, and others kinds of self-dealing that benefit those at the top and harm pretty much everyone else. In no small part, this is because of the unfortunate misbehavior of a few. But what's overlooked in focusing on this small handful of exceptions is the regular, even routine, profit-driven behavior that results in socially desirable outcomes and makes everyone better off. In the words of *Wall Street*'s Gordon Gekko, a modern-day pirate if there ever was one, "Greed is good."

It's common to associate the "goodness" or "badness" of behavior with the "goodness" or "badness" of the motivations that drive it. But the nobility or ignobility of individuals' motivations often bears no relationship, and in some cases even exhibits an inverse relationship, to the nobility or ignobility of the outcomes these motivations create. Sometimes the basest of intentions can produce the best of outcomes. The milk producer example used in chapter 1 to illustrate Adam Smith's invisible hand principle is one case of this. Your milk producer's motives aren't necessarily "good." He's not trying to help you. He doesn't care about you and doesn't even know you. The milk producer is just a businessman; he's in it for the money. But his ignoble motives don't prevent "good" outcomes. They don't, for instance, prevent you from getting the milk you want at a price you can afford. On the contrary, the milk producer's ignoble motives are precisely the reason you *do* get milk. As Adam Smith put it, "It is not from the benevolence of the butcher, the brewer, or the baker that we expect our dinner, but from their regard to their own interest." The milk producer's greed compels him to serve you. As a result, you get the milk you desire at the best possible price.

The profit motive is the most reliable way to make sure your needs get met. Without the grocer's greed, you'd be scratching for turnips in your backyard. Without your landlord's greed, you'd be living in a tree house somewhere. And without your employer's greed, you wouldn't have a job. The beauty of markets is that they harness individuals' greed and make it service other people's desires. Remove the lure of riches and you remove your best shot at living a materially enriched life.

The important difference between the nobility of individuals' motivations and the actual outcomes their behavior produces sheds important light on how we should go about evaluating pirates. Pirates may have been "bad" men, motivated by ignoble desires, and even willing to use violent means to satisfy these desires. But the outcomes of their profit-motivated behavior were sometimes laudable. For example, profit seeking is what led pirates to avoid blasting their prizes to pieces. It also prevented them from wantonly brutalizing their captives. And it limited their reliance on conscripts. Of course, in each of these cases, piratical greed didn't lead to genuine public "benefits." Pirates' victims would have always been better off if they hadn't faced the threat pirates posed in the first place. But conditional on pirates' presence, pirates' ignoble motives—self-interested greed—softened the harms pirate victims suffered.

Even more significantly, pirate greed is what motivated pirates to pioneer progressive institutions and practices. For example, this greed is responsible for pirates' system of constitutional democracy—a system virtually unknown in the legitimate seventeenth- and eighteenth-century world. It's responsible for pirates' system of social insurance. Pirate greed is also responsible for some sea rogues' superior treatment of blacks. In each of these cases, ignoble pirate motives—indeed, as greedy *criminals*, ignobility in the extreme—generated "enlightened" outcomes consistent with some of the modern world's most heralded values, such as democracy, equality, and social safety.

Pirates didn't embrace "enlightened" values as ends in and of themselves. They embraced money. But their tireless pursuit of the latter gave way to the desirable outcomes associated with the former and did so before their legitimate contemporaries achieved anything like the same. As examined in chapter 3, for instance, piratical institutions reflected the brilliance of Madison's arguments for democratically divided power more than half a century before Madison wrote them down. In this sense pirates were harbingers of our most sacred ideas about social organization. America's Founding Fathers, to borrow the slogan of a popular pirate-inspired rum, "had a little Captain in them." This is why I say pirates deserve more of our respect rather than less of it. In these ways pirates were truly pioneers, or at least provided early testimony of the workability of a society that embraced these values. And in this sense we should be decidedly, and unabashedly, "propirate." "Greed," as Gordon Gekko put it, "is right. Greed works. . . . Greed, in all of its forms . . . has marked the upward surge of mankind." A real pirate couldn't have said it better himself.

WEEKS 3–4. Leave Yer Utopia Buildin' at Madagascar

Readings: Ludwig von Mises, *Socialism*; F. A. Hayek, "The Use of Knowledge in Society," *American Economic Review*

Central Lesson: Let your business drive your thinking about managerial organization, not the other way around.

Pirate ships confronted many of the problems legitimate businesses face in attempting to maximize profits. Foremost among these are preventing firm members with leadership roles from self-dealing and motivating workers to contribute to the firm's goals. As noted above, over the last decade or so in particular, media reports have revealed shady corporate leaders who embezzled their firm's funds, fraudulently represented their firm's financial position, and engaged in other behaviors that benefited themselves at their employees' expense. Conversely, almost all of us can also think of less-than-committed employees we know who steal from the company supply room, conveniently fall sick as deadlines approach, and spend more time in the office "bathroom" than human gastrointestinal limits suggest is possible. Dishonest workers don't receive the media attention dishonest CEOs do, but they're at least as common.

Both sorts of problems—those originating at the point of firm leadership and affecting employees, and those originating at the point of employees and affecting firm leaders (and oftentimes other employees)—negatively affect firms' ability to function. And both sorts of problems have the same source: a failure to properly align management-worker incentives. On a pirate ship, of course, the specific forms these problems took differed from the forms they take in legitimate modern firms. But they posed the same threat to the piratical "firm's" success. Rather than engaging in shady accounting, for instance, pirate captains could self deal by stealing from their crew members, cutting their rations, and abusing their power in other ways. Similarly, instead of spending unnatural amounts of time in the "bathroom," pirate crew members could shirk in their duties by staying back in a fight or hiding loot from their fellow rogues.

As the previous chapters of this book discussed, pirates largely overcame these incentive-alignment problems by organizing their enterprises in enterprising ways. To prevent captain self-dealing, pirates democratically elected their leaders and dispersed power among other members of the crew, such as the quartermaster. Under this managerial setup a captain best served his own interest by serving his crew's interest. If he didn't, his crew could remove him from command. To prevent crew members from shirking, pirate organization made all crew members equal, or nearly equal, "shareholders" in the company's profits. This strengthened the connection between each individual pirate's effort and his individual payoff. To prevent piratical free riding, pirate articles established bonuses for crew members who displayed noteworthy courage and spotted prizes; and in some cases crew members reserved the right to vote on the share a particular pirate received. This allowed pirates to reward hard-working crew members and punish lazy ones. Pirate articles also provided workman's compensation, which reduced private disincentives to take risks that could cause injury. These steps helped align individual crewmembers' incentives, both between "ordinary" pirates and between ordinary pirates and their officers.

Legitimate modern firms take similar steps to overcome the incentive-alignment problems discussed above. Some firms have profit-sharing arrangements, offer their employees stock options to more closely connect employee efforts with the firm's success overall, and allow stockholders, who are often workers, to have a say in the company's leadership. Like the steps pirates took to better align crew member incentives, the measures legitimate modern firms take for this purpose are imperfect. But they must help somewhat or these firms, like pirates, wouldn't adopt them.

Advocates of "workers' democracy" (sometimes called "workers' socialism") take particular delight in the fact that pirate ships carried a great deal of intrafirm decision making by popular vote. Nineteenth-century Christian socialist Charles Kingsley is a good example of this. Kingsley considered a pirate ship a shining example of a "workers' cooperative," which he praised in his poem "The Last Buccaneer." Twenty-first-century proponents of workers' democracy see things similarly. In their view, all firms should be managed by a show of employee hands. Workers should elect managers and CEOs. They should participate in hiring and firing decisions related to other employees. Workers should vote on their company's production activities, employee and CEO wages, among other things. The "evils" of corporate capitalism, these advocates contend, result from many firms' more autocratic managerial structures, which allow corporate leadership to benefit itself at employees' expense. Workers' socialism will solve this and create a more egalitarian and thus "fair" distribution of corporate earnings.

What the advocates of workers' democracy overlook is that profit-seeking drove pirate democracy. In the particular economic context pirates operated in, radical democratic management made sense. As discussed in chapter 2, to maximize profit, pirates required such organization. This, in fact, is why pirates used it. But the sensibility of pirates' democratic managerial organization in the particular context they operated in doesn't mean democratic management makes sense for all firms in all circumstances. Different firms that operate in different economic contexts will find different managerial forms most conducive to making profits.

A number of specific economic factors influence the profitability of various forms of firm management. For very large firms, for example, the decision-making costs of workers' democracy are simply too large to be cost effective. Similarly, for enterprises that require large sums of externally raised capital, it makes sense that external financiers should have a say in the firm's activities, and in particular its leadership, in proportion to the amount of capital they have at stake. Giving everyone, including workers, an equal say in the firm's decision making when a small group of investors is footing the bill for the bulk of the firm's operations would lead to inefficiencies. For instance, workers with much smaller stakes in the firm's capital would bear much smaller losses if they voted for very risky decisions and these risks didn't pan out. In effect, they would be able to foist part of the costs associated with risky decision making onto the firm's primary financiers, who have much more at stake. Because of this, workers would have an incentive to vote for very risky projects—projects that would appear too risky to them if they had to bear the full costs of failure.

The unique nature of piracy prevented such a problem from emerging on pirate ships. Venture capitalists didn't fund pirate "firms." Pirates didn't require capital beyond what they plundered. Each pirate crew member was consequently an equal contributor and part owner of the "firm" in addition to being one of the firm's workers. If pirates had required venture capitalists to finance them, their managerial structure would have looked very different; it would've been less democratic to protect the interests of the firm's major financiers. Privateers, for example, engaged in essentially the same activity as pirates— maritime plunder. However, because they were legal enterprises and couldn't rely on stealing the capital they required as pirates could, they required external financiers to supply the capital they needed to operate. Predictably, privateers used significantly more autocratic management than pirate ships. For instance, privateer financiers appointed privateer captains; crew members didn't elect them. Even though they were engaged in essentially the same activity as pirates, because of the different economic circumstances privateers confronted—namely the fact that they required external financiers to operate—privateer profitability dictated a different managerial organization, one that in some important respects was like merchant ships' managerial organization.

Large modern firms that require lots of capital could get away with piratelike democratic management if their workers fully and equally "financed" their firms as pirates did. But most workers don't have the finances required for this. And many others, quite reasonably, don't wish to bear the risk associated with vesting a substantial portion of their wealth in the firm they also work for. Workers in such firms are better off if specialists with the finances required to supply needed capital, and the capacity to bear the risk associated with doing so, provide the capital their firms need instead. But to attract such financiers, workers can't expect to have an equal say in the firm's decision making. The alternative is for firms to go without externally raised capital, which may permit more democratic management, but will also dramatically reduce the firm's profitability by artificially curtailing production and reduce workers' wages by limiting the amount of capital they have to work with.

For very small firms where would-be employees are willing and able to supply all the capital the firm requires, things may be different. For example, if three friends with bartending experience pool their resources to start a small bar, which they also staff, it may make sense to organize their partnership as a kind of "workers' democracy" where each friend has an equal vote in decisions relating to the business. In this case the decision-making costs of such an arrangement are low; there aren't any external capital suppliers to satisfy, and so on. The different costs and benefits that different types of firms face, which their different economic contexts create, determine the profitability of alternative modes of managerial organization and hence which management mode it makes sense for them to adopt.

In short, there's no such thing as *the* efficient form of managerial organization. What's organizationally efficient for one firm may be totally inappropriate for another. Concluding from the effectiveness of democratic management on pirates ships, or anywhere else for that matter, that democratic management is "the best" kind of management, and that Wal-Mart, for example, should be organized democratically, is like concluding from the effectiveness of "family government" in which the mother or father makes all household decisions dictatorially that dictatorship is "the best" kind of government and that the U.S. government should be organized autocratically. Such a conclusion is, of course, absurd. Family government and the U.S. government cover very different populations and operate in very different contexts. Pirate ships and Wal-Mart also involve very different populations and operate in very different economic contexts. Those who make blanket assertions about the superiority of workers' democracy over all other firm organizational forms propose a one-size-fits-all approach where it doesn't belong and where the particular size they advocate actually fits very few. The desire to make profits drives firms to organize in the most economically efficient manner. This isn't to say firms never make mistakes. But over time the profit motive does a pretty good job of leading them down the correct managerial paths. What we should take away from pirates' "workers' democracy," if one insists on calling it that, isn't the universal desirability of democratic management, but rather the universal desirability of allowing profits to drive firms' organizational forms.

WEEKS 5–6. Smite Me Blind and Speechless but Don't
Regulate Me Crew

Readings: Geoffrey Brennan and James M. Buchanan,
The Reason of Rules: Constitutional Political Economy;
G. Warren Nutter, "Strangulation by Regulation," in
Political Economy and Freedom.

Central Lesson: Regulations are important, but using
government to impose them can backfire.

Class Reminder Next week is spring break. Enjoy your
vacation and don't forget to practice reloading your
blunderbuss. You'll be tested on this when we return.
See you on the beach.

As discussed in chapter 3, rules and regulations are necessary
for any society to function. Whether government supplies
these rules or private governance does instead, for greed to service cooperation rather than undermine it, individuals' require
some kind of regulatory regime to direct self-interest toward
activities that enhance the former and away from activities that
lead to the latter. Since pirates were outlaws, they operated outside the scope of government regulations. To prevent their
criminal enterprise from imploding, they regulated themselves
instead. Pirate regulations, which were privately and voluntarily
adopted, were successful because they were private and voluntary. Pirates had a better idea about the kinds of regulations
their ships needed than outsiders did. They knew, for instance,
that it was important for them to restrict smoking in the hold
but unimportant to ban smoking altogether. Pirates had what
economists call "local knowledge" of their particular circumstances and how various rules were likely to affect life aboard
their ships.

Legitimate modern firms also have more "local knowledge"
about what kinds of regulations they require to facilitate worker

cooperation, and what kinds of regulations are unnecessary and might even stifle workers' ability to cooperate, than outsiders do. Modern governments aren't terribly interested in this, however, and often act as if they had better local knowledge about what regulations various firms need than firms do themselves. Government's regulatory impositions may very well have noble motivations. But as the discussion above pointed out, motivations and actual outcomes can be worlds apart. Just as self-interested motives can generate socially desirable outcomes, "benevolent" motives can generate socially undesirable outcomes. Thus as important as appreciating the potential "benefits of vice" is appreciating the potential "harms of virtue."

Often times, when people deliberately aim to help others, they actually hurt them rather than helping them. Consider, for instance, the Americans with Disabilities Act (ADA). The U.S. government created the ADA in 1990 to prevent employers from discriminating against disabled workers. The ADA seeks to do this by prohibiting "wrongful termination" of disabled employees, along with introducing a number of other mandates. Under the ADA a disabled worker who believes his employer has fired him or otherwise discriminated against him because of his disability can sue his employer. This legislation's intent is to increase disabled Americans' employment. That's certainly a noble goal. But this legislation's outcome has been just the opposite of its intention. The ADA's actual effect has been ignoble indeed. In a 2001 study of the ADA's effects on disabled individuals' employment, MIT economists Daron Acemoglu and Joshua Angrist found the ADA significantly *reduced* the number of disabled citizens American employers hired. In economist lingo, the ADA creates "perverse, unintended consequences." The ADA rules raise the cost of hiring disabled workers. If such a worker proves less diligent or productive, for example, even for reasons totally unrelated, to his disability, the ADA makes it more difficult to fire him. So, employers simply avoid hiring disabled workers in the first place.

Allowing the profit motive to drive the regulations firms adopt isn't perfect. But it tends to produce better outcomes, and fewer "regulatory backfires," like in the ADA example above, than government-imposed regulations. Because they were profit driven, pirates, recall, had an incentive to create rules and regulations that created a more desirable workplace. For instance, to attract willing sailors, pirate "firms" needed to create rules that ensured officers wouldn't cheat them out of their shares or abuse them in other ways. Because they're also profit motivated, legitimate modern businesses confront similar pressures to create desirable workplaces for their employees, lest they lose them to competitors that do. This includes voluntarily adopting workplace rules and regulations that facilitate cooperation and provide for workers' safety. Since firms have local knowledge about what regulations make sense in their particular case and what ones don't, the rules they introduce are more likely to be effective and less likely to generate the undesirable, unintended consequences government regulation can produce.

WEEKS 7–8. An Open Mind Is a Full Treasure Chest

Readings: Gary S. Becker, *The Economics of Discrimination*; Thomas Sowell, *Race and Economics*

Central Lesson: Don't let your prejudices get in the way of a better payday.

As discussed in chapter 7, to maximize the profitability of their enterprise, pirates sometimes had to put aside their thinking about black and white to focus on seizing silver and gold. This lesson is doubly important for legitimate modern firms to appreciate. Pirates' "competitors" were other ships operated by men as racist as they were. Further, the minority sailors pirate ships dealt with were often escaped slaves with very little bargaining power to "shop around" for a better deal than the one offered by the ship they sailed on. Thus, although profit seeking in the presence of the "concentrated costs and dispersed benefits" of slavery led some pirates to display racial tolerance despite their racist beliefs, competitive pressures didn't have any influence on pirates' racial policies.

For modern legitimate firms, however, simple competitive pressures can have a substantial influence on their bottom lines. Whether an employer is prejudiced against blacks, women, disabled workers, or pirates, he can indulge his prejudice only at his profit's peril. Chapter 7 discussed why this is so. Refusing to hire a worker because an employer doesn't like him—for whatever reason—will backfire if the worker adds more value to the firm than he's asking for in compensation. If a prejudiced employer does this, his more profit-driven rival will hire the worker instead, leading the prejudiced employer to lose and his rival to gain. Thus, even more so than for pirates, for legitimate modern firms, an open mind is paramount to profit maximization.

Weeks 9–10. Look Sharp to the Law and Devil Damn Ye if Ye Don't

Readings: F. A. Hayek, *The Constitution of Liberty*; James M. Buchanan, Robert D. Tollison, and Gordon Tullock, *Toward a Theory of the Rent-Seeking Society*

Central Lesson: Be on the lookout for legal changes that might affect your bottom line.

To protect themselves against the rising cost of their illicit trade that new antipiracy legislation created, pirates needed to be aware of the changing legal environment they confronted and develop ways to try and circumvent these changes. Pirates did their best; they staged "shows" of impressments and used "ads of force" to adduce evidence of their innocence if their crews were caught. These strategies were partly effective; but they weren't enough to survive a British government determined to squelch sea dogs' very existence.

Legitimate modern firms also face an uphill battle when it comes to changing laws that make it more difficult for them to survive. The tremendous growth of government over the last 280 years has created continuously sprawling legislation that affects every firm that operates today. More than ever, this makes economic survival dependent on knowledge of and adaptation to a changing legal environment. One way firms have adapted to the expanding reach of legislation is through what economists call "rent seeking." Some firms have cleverly figured out how to make the far-reaching regulatory environment they confront work to their advantage.

Firms of all stripes invest astonishing sums every year to "capture" the legislative process on which their continued livelihood depends. For example, since the legislative process has the power to protect domestic steel producers against foreign steel producers by imposing tariffs on foreign steel, domestic steel producers spend money lobbying legislators to use the law to protect them this way. If, for instance, the value of a potential tariff to domestic steel producers is $5 million—that is, the tariff will allow domestic steel producers to earn $5 million more than if they were subjected to competitive pressures from more efficient foreign steel producers—in principle, they'll be willing to spend up to $5 million to capture legislators' support for a law that protects them through such a tariff.

The incredible growth of government in the twentieth century has given it the power to make or break any firm or industry it desires by granting special privileges or imposing new costs on firms, or their competitors, through the legislative process. As a result, firms engage in unprecedented rent seeking to capture government's power to create laws that help them and harm their competitors. Economists David Laband and John Sophocleus estimated that private parties in the United States invested nearly $7.4 billion in political "capturing" activities in 1985 alone. In 2007 they spent more than $2.8 billion just on lobbying.

Although rent seeking makes good sense for firms in the face of an active government, its effects on the overall economy aren't so desirable. The resources firms spend trying to capture the legislative process are resources they don't use to produce goods and services—wealth—that benefit society. In the example above, for instance, the $5 million domestic steel producers spend capturing the political process is $5 million they could have spent producing steel, which is wasted on socially unproductive rent-seeking activities instead. Thus rent seeking makes society poorer instead of richer. Further, the privileges the legislative process bestows on successful rent-seeking firms tend to prevent other firms from competing with them on a level playing field. This reduces the competitive pressures that make markets work and also makes society poorer.

Unfortunately, rent-seeking activity isn't likely to disappear any time soon. Nor should it. As long as government has the power to privilege some producers at the expense of others, it pays firms to rent seek. Businesses that want to thrive must pay close attention to prospective changes in the legal environment to effectively maneuver in the face of such changes.

WEEKS 11–12. Trademark Yer Terror

Readings: Instead of readings, your assignment for this
lesson is to come to class with the most terrifying
image you can concoct. The student with most
terrifying image will receive 5 extra credit points.
The student with the least terrifying image will be
marooned.

Central Lesson: Nothing beats a brand name.

Branding is critical to any successful business, as it was for piracy. Chapter 5 discussed how pirates used the same basic
methods to develop their brand name that legitimate modern
firms do: word of mouth and advertising. Unwittingly, pirate
victims and eighteenth-century newspapers acted as pirate pub-
licists, broadcasting and institutionalizing pirates' fearsome
reputation as violent madmen.

Legitimate modern firms spend enormous sums hiring
branding experts to develop logos and slogans for them and to
help them develop and project the images they desire to be
known for. Despite this, very few have achieved the instant
brand-name recognition pirates achieved without fancy specialists. Pirates' skull-and-bones symbolism against a black background may be even more widely recognized than the golden
arches. Their "logo" is so powerful that it's been appropriated
by innumerable contemporary firms selling everything from
tater-tots to T-shirts.

What brought this symbolism to life was pirates' dedication
to the message it conveyed—slaughter for resistors, mercy for
those who peacefully submit—and an equal dedication to appearing heartless and insane. As the *Princess Bride*'s Dread Pirate Roberts quipped, "Once word leaks out that a pirate has
gone soft, people begin to disobey him and it's nothing but
work, work, work all the time." So, pirates made sure they never

appeared soft, brutally torturing captives who hid or destroyed valuables and behaving like madmen even if captives didn't.

If imitation truly is the greatest form of flattery, pirates should be blushing in their watery graves. The incredible range of pirate-inspired products available today—from Captain Morgan Rum, to *Pirates of the Caribbean* movies, to Ralph Lauren's Rugby line of apparel—is a contemporary testament to seventeenth- and eighteenth-century pirates' effectiveness in brand naming themselves. It's their brand name's strength that's made pirates so memorable. And it's their band name's lasting success that gives pirates power over the "pieces of eight" in our pocketbooks to this day.

EPILOGUE
OMNIPRESENT ECONOMICS

Pirates provide at least one other lasting lesson: the ubiquity of economics. The rational choice framework, introduced in chapter 1, truly is a universal way of understanding human behavior. Every person who has goals and takes steps to attain those goals is susceptible to economic analysis. That pretty much covers everyone—from politicians, to lovers, to thieves. The power of economics isn't just that it *can* be applied so widely. It's that *only* with economics can we make sense of a great deal of otherwise unintelligible individual behavior. Without economics, pirates, for example, are a veritable ball of contradictions. They're sadistic pacifists; womanizing homosexuals; treasure-lusting socialists; and madmen who outwitted the authorities. They're stealthy outlaws who loudly announced their presence with flags of skulls and bones. They're libertarians who conscripted nearly all their members, democrats with dictatorial captains, and lawless anarchists who lived by a strict code of rules. They're torturous terrorists who command honest men's adoration.

Economics and, I'd argue, only economics, can disentangle this mess of piratical paradoxes. This, in fact, has been one of the major purposes of this book. History is critical. But history alone cannot accomplish this task. The "raw material" contained in the historical record needs to be "filtered" through a theoretical framework that makes sense of its often puzzling elements.

The rational choice framework, the theoretical apparatus of economics, is uniquely suited to this purpose because of its emphasis on purposive, self-interested behavior. In chapter 1 I stated that once pirates had been run through the "economic filter," you'd understand why they were closer to a Fortune 500 company than to the savage band of children in William Golding's *Lord of the Flies*. If I've succeeded in my task, the reasons for this should now be clear.

It should be equally clear that the distinctive economic context pirates operated in is responsible for pirates' distinctive practices. Pirates, like everyone else, were creatures of incentives. They responded rationally to the costs and benefits they confronted, seeking to decrease the former and increase the latter associated with "piratical production." For example, pirates faced potential costs in the form of resistant victims who hid or destroyed booty. Pirates reduced these costs by developing a brand name for ruthlessness and insanity, allowing them to benefit more from their sea roving. Similarly, in the early eighteenth century the legal costs of pirating increased because of more stringent and effective laws against piracy. Pirates used "shows" of force and "ads of force" to reduce these costs. Or, think about the Jolly Roger. Pirates faced costs in the form of quarries that violently resisted their ships' attacks. To reduce these costs and thus increase the benefit of maritime marauding, pirates developed their infamous black ensign of skull and bones. I could continue, but I think you get the point. Pirates didn't use democracy because they were "more democratic" than merchant owners. They didn't torture prisoners because they were naturally sadistic. And they didn't treat some black sailors as equals because they were less bigoted than their contemporaries. Pirates just acted to maximize profits in the particular, and rather unusual, economic context they confronted. The strangeness of these circumstances, not of pirates themselves, is what accounts for the strangeness of pirate practices.

At the same time, I hope you don't feel pirates have lost any of the adventure and mystique that makes them so attractive to us in the first place. If I've tackled my task appropriately, just the opposite should be true. I hope you have a newfound sense of respect, awe, and even wonder about seventeenth- and eighteenth-century pirates. As I mentioned earlier, I certainly think they deserve this. There's no reason to fear subjecting sea dogs to analytic scrutiny. Even if such analysis did take some of the mystery out of pirates, there remains a considerable body of pirate lore I doubt even economics could penetrate. After finishing Blackbeard in 1718, for example, Lieutenant Maynard beheaded the notorious pirate, keeping the bearded monstrosity as a trophy and tossing his body overboard. Legend has it Blackbeard's decapitated corpse swam three laps around the ship before sinking to the ocean's floor. Of course, this legend is no more than a silly myth. Everyone knows it was only two laps.

YOU CAN'T KEEP A SEA DOG DOWN: THE FALL AND RISE OF PIRACY

As the seventeenth century drew to a close, the Red Sea Men were busy marauding in the Indian Ocean to the English government's growing consternation. Government responded to this situation at the beginning of the eighteenth century by emboldening its efforts to exterminate the watery rascals. Central to this endeavor was the Act for the More Effectual Suppression of Piracy, introduced in 1700, made permanent in 1719, and later bolstered through follow-up legislation. England didn't have much chance to test drive its new antipiracy law, however. In 1702 it plunged headlong into the War of the Spanish Succession. During the war England directly or indirectly provided employment for many would-be pirates as privateers, temporarily rendering the pirate problem moot. But the reprieve was short-lived. Within a few years of war's end the pirate population swelled once again. The critical difference was that, now, effective antipiracy legislation was in place. The law couldn't work by itself, however. Authorities needed to capture pirates so they could be tried, or otherwise cajole sea dogs into surrendering their swashbuckling lifestyle.

England's decision in 1717 to send former privateer captain Woodes Rogers to put the pirates' largest and most important land base in the Bahamas under government rule was one important step in this direction. As Colin Woodard points out, when Rogers returned to England in 1721 after completing his governorship, he did so having accomplished an important feat: the "pirates' republic" at New Providence was extinguished and, although a considerable number of sea bandits remained at large, they were scattered and forced to continue without a home base to retreat to.

Madagascar, that old pirate haunt from the late seventeenth century, ceased to operate as a substitute land base around the same time Rogers left New Providence for England. At the request of the East India Company, which had suffered from the pirate problem since the days of the Red Sea Men, in 1721 the British government sent Commodore Thomas Mathews with four navy ships into eastern waters to eradicate pirates located in and around Madagascar. Mathews, it turned out, didn't have to do much. When Madagascar-based pirate captains John Taylor and Oliver La Bouche got wind of his naval squadron's plans, they fled for the coast of Africa. Shortly thereafter, piracy in the eastern seas died.

Britain capitalized on the upper hand it was gaining over pirates in the early 1720s by improving the naval resources it devoted to hunting sea bandits. In 1721 government began replacing unwilling and ineffective naval commanders charged with protecting colonial waters with more willing and effective ones. It also stationed more ships in the colonies to deal with pirates. But as Peter Earle points out, Britain's seaborne fight against sea dogs floundered in its first years. This largely resulted from inhibiting rules government imposed on its pirate-hunting naval ships. One regulation, for instance, prohibited naval vessels from reprovisioning in the West Indies. This had the unhelpful effect of preventing ships from patrolling pirate-infested waters for too long since they had to return to England when their food or drink ran out. Another regulation prohibited ships from careening. As a result, navy vessels already disadvantaged relative to pirate vessels in terms of maneuverability were now disadvantaged when it came to speed too. On top of these regulations, navy ships sent to hunt or protect against pirates rarely carried a full complement of sailors.

Why the inhibiting navy policies? To keep costs down, of course. Provisions were pricier in the West Indies than they were at home; careening was expensive; and so were full complements of men. The considerable cost of hunting pirates is an important part of the reason Britain didn't manage to extinguish sea bandits until it did. For a long time, it simply wasn't prepared to drop the kind of coin required to wage a serious antipiracy campaign at sea.

Political rulers, like everyone else, exist in a world of scarcity and thus must make choices that involve trade-offs. If you want a new a car, you might have to curtail your nights out on the town until you've saved enough to purchase one. Your resources are scarce so you must choose: more drinks but less car, or more car but less drinks? Either way you choose involves sacrificing some bit of one thing you'd like for some additional bit of something else you'd like too. Similarly, if, say, government wants to repay creditors who financed the last war, it may need to send fewer ships out to hunt pirates, or impose rules that reduce existing pirate hunters' effectiveness but save money. Resources Britain devoted to its antipiracy campaign couldn't be devoted to other important purposes, like financing wars.

Even after the War of the Spanish Succession was over, Britain had competing demands on its naval resources. When Queen Anne died in 1714 the threat of Jacobite rebellion—perhaps even civil war—loomed large. Jacobites plotted a foiled rebellion in England in 1714; but in 1715 actual rebellion struck in Scotland. The Jacobite uprising justified King George's fear that Stuart loyalists would try to remove him from the throne and emphasized the perceived importance of ensuring that the navy was available to defeat future attempted encroachments on his government. This often meant keeping naval vessels close to home.

The threat of Jacobite rebellions wasn't the only competing claim on naval resources, however. In 1718 Britain deployed naval resources to oppose Spain's attempts to reclaim Sicily—a possession Spain lost in the previous war. Shortly thereafter the War of the Quadruple Alliance officially broke out, demanding British naval resources again. From the time the War of the Spanish Succession ended in 1714 until 1721, British merchant ships engaged in Baltic trade also competed for the navy's attention. While the Northern War raged between Russia and Sweden, British commercial vessels sailing in Baltic waterways required protection. So there were many competing claims on naval resources when piracy reemerged after 1714. And compared to these needs, squelching piracy wasn't a priority.

In the early 1720s the dwindling importance of these competing uses for naval resources and the fact that in 1720 the pirate population reached an all-time high improved government's incentive to step up its naval war against pirates. Prohibitions against reprovisioning in the West Indies and careening were revoked; more men were allowed to sail on pirate-hunting navy ships; and the number and quality of naval vessels devoted to antipiracy were improved. In short, the rising benefit and declining cost of fighting pirates at sea encouraged Britain to devote more resources to this purpose.

Together with improved antipiracy legislation, the beefed-up seaborne assault on pirates proved effective. In 1722 Britain's antipiracy crusade hit its stride when HMS *Swallow*, captained by one Chaloner Ogle, killed piracy's most successful captain, Bart Roberts, and captured his remaining crew. One hundred sixty-six men from Roberts's crew stood trial at Cape Coast Castle in

Ghana. Second perhaps only to Woodes Rogers's mission to New Providence, Ogle's monumental capture was a watershed moment in pirate history and marked the most important victory in bringing sea bandits who remained at large after 1721 to justice.

Several notorious pirates discussed in this book, including George Lowther and Edward Low, continued to ply their trade after Roberts's death. But they didn't escape government's tightening grip for long. Over the next year, privateer captain Walter Moore picked off Lowther's men while they were careening off the coast of Venezuela. Lowther himself actually escaped Moore's clutch. His Houdini stunt didn't extend his life much, though. Lowther never made it off the island where Moore attacked his crew and in the end committed suicide.

Low's pirates didn't fare any better. In 1723 Captain Solgard of HMS *Greyhound* attacked Low and his consort Charles Harris near New England. Low gave Solgard the slip and resumed pirating until 1725 when the French government caught up with him. Harris met a similar fate only sooner. Thanks to Solgard's efforts, he and thirty-five others stood trial in Newport, Rhode Island, in the summer of 1723. The court convicted twenty-eight of them. On July 19, twenty-six pirates hanged at Bulls Point "within the Flux and Reflux of the Sea."

Marcus Rediker dates the end of piracy's golden age to 1726. This would make pirate captains William Fly and Philip Lyne, both of whom were hanged that year, among the last surviving sea scoundrels of note in of great age of piracy. A few pirates outlasted Fly and Lyne. Pirate John Brie lived to plunder another day; he wasn't executed until 1727. Similarly, authorities didn't manage to bring John Upton to justice until 1729. Oliver La Bouche didn't die until 1730 when he was hanged in Réunion. But these men were the exception. The pirate population dwindled from a height of about two thousand sea dogs in 1720 to half that by 1723, and only a few hundred by 1726.

Pirates' source of revenue didn't dry up in these years. Commercial vessels may have had better protection from pirates than they did previously; but merchant shipping was as plentiful as it had been. In this sense the benefit side of piracy remained largely as before. However, the cost side of piracy changed considerably. Because of government's crackdown, the cost of piracy rose sharply over these years, leading to fewer pirates. As David Cordingly points out, between 1716 and 1726 some four hundred pirates were hanged—an average of forty sea dogs per year. Eighty-two of these executions came in 1723 alone, a strong indication government's bolstered antipiracy efforts, in full swing by the early 1720s, were having the desired effect. It seems that rising costs rather than falling benefits drove eighteenth-century pirates' extinction.

Historians of piracy tend to emphasize the abrupt end to piracy's golden age. It's true; pirates went from their peak power to virtual extinction in only half a decade. But for all its abruptness, piracy's decline wasn't particularly climactic. The final battle between Chaloner Ogle and Bartholomew Roberts was appropriately dramatic; it took place amidst a great thunderstorm. A few other pirates' last stands were also as impressive as one would expect from men who "declared War against all the World." Blackbeard's final battle is the best example of this; but his memorable brawl took place in 1718 before the sun was setting on piracy's golden age. In contrast, the very last act of this period had no grand finale, no epic clash between the combined forces of remaining pirates and the British navy. William Fly, for example, was the victim of his own shortsightedness and poor planning. He pressed too many sailors, who revolted and turned him in. Piracy ended as the world does in T.S. Eliot's *Hollow Men*, "not with a bang, but a whimper."

After the pirates of the golden age disappeared there were others. The nineteenth century endured the scourge of the pirates of the South China Sea. Unlike their Anglo-American counterparts, these Chinese pirates weren't a few thousands, but many tens of thousands—perhaps as many as 150,000—strong.

There are also contemporary pirates. Over the last decade or so in particular there's been a resurgence of sea banditry off the horn of Africa and in the Straits of Malacca. Like seventeenth- and eighteenth-century pirates, the modern variety chooses to plunder ships in waters where government enforcement is weak, such as those around Somalia and Indonesia, and commercial vessels are abundant. Besides this, however, modern pirates share little in common with their predecessors. Seventeenth- and eighteenth-century pirates lived together for protracted periods of time at sea. Although they retired to land between expeditions, they spent much of their time together prowling the ocean in search of prey. Because of this, their ships formed miniature "floating societies" that, like all societies, required social rules and governance institutions to function.

In contrast, most modern pirates spend very little time together on their ships. There are three main modes of modern piracy. The first and most common mode is little more than maritime muggery. Pirate "crews" of two to six hop in small boats; pull alongside ships, usually in territorial waters close to the coast; and threaten their prey at gunpoint to give up their watches, jewelry, and whatever money they may be carrying. These sea bandits are part timers. After mugging some passersby they return to their villages on the coast where they live among nonpirates and resume their day jobs.

A second and less-common mode of modern piracy is somewhat different. Crews are still small—between five and fifteen men—and spend little time together at sea. But professional land-based criminals hire them to steal boats they convert into "phantom ships" and resell. Land-based criminals pay these modern pirates lump sums and contract them on a case-by-case basis. Like the maritime muggers, pirates-for-hire rely predominantly on hijacking methods to steal ships, though for larger vessels they've been known to plant "insiders"—sailors who pretend to be legitimate sailors seeking employment—who take the target from the inside.

The third mode of modern piracy may also be "contracted out" by land-based criminals. Here, typically tiny but well-armed crews hijack commercial vessels and take their passengers hostage. They then ransom the ship, its cargo, and the passengers. Not exactly the stuff of Captain Blackbeard or even of William Fly; but it pays well. The pirates who hijacked a German ship in the Gulf of Aden in July 2008, for example, extorted $750,000 from a shipping agency that paid the ransom on behalf of the vessel's owners.

Since modern pirates tend to sail in very small groups and don't live, sleep, and interact together on their ships for months, weeks, or even days on end, they don't constitute a society and consequently face few, if any, of the problems their forefathers did. Because of this, most modern sea dogs don't exhibit any discernible organizational structure. Their in-and-out M.O., coupled with the fact that their crews tend to be tiny, means they don't require elaborate rules for creating order. Most modern pirates don't even require captains in the usual sense. There is, of course, someone who steers the motorboat and acts as a leader among the six or so pirates; but he isn't a captain in the way eighteenth-century pirate captains were.

For a few modern pirates things are different. They sail in larger crews, spend more time together at sea, and consequently come closer to forming modern pirate societies. As this book has emphasized, predictably, this in turn has led social institutions to emerge among them. For instance, the Somali pirates that captured the French ship *Le Ponant* in April 2008 divided their booty along similar lines as their eighteenth-century predecessors. This same crew adopted a social insurance system reminiscent of that of their forefathers: if a pirate died on the job, his family received $15,000. These modern pirates even created a partial "pirate code," a written manual with rules regulating how crew members could treat prisoners.

Still, even these contemporary sea scoundrels are poor substitutes for their predecessors. They aren't harbingers of our most sacred ideas about social organization; they haven't pioneered progressive practices; they don't even fly flags with skulls and bones. Sadly, modern pirates simply aren't as interesting as their golden age predecessors. Then again, this comparison is probably unfair: Blackbeard, Calico Jack, and the rest set a high bar indeed.

WHERE THIS BOOK FOUND
ITS BURIED TREASURE
A NOTE ON SOURCES

To say pirates weren't as diligent note takers as we'd like would be putting it mildly. Historian Philip Gosse chalks this up to pirates' "diffidence . . . in recording their own deeds." But there are more obvious reasons why so few pirates put quill to parchment. Literacy limitations are one. According to historian Peter Earle, two-thirds of ordinary fore-mastmen on merchant ships could at least sign their names. Since pirates drew their members from the merchant sailor population, it stands to reason many pirates could do this as well. But it's doubtful they could write full-fledged accounts of their experiences. Then there's the troublesome fact that pirates were criminals and so sought to fly (sail?) below the radar as much as possible. Publishing a chronicle of one's murders and grand thefts might raise some suspicion. Despite this, we have several "pirate memoirs," all written by buccaneers, no doubt because of their quasi-legitimacy. William Dampier, for example, kept a journal of some of his exploits. So did John Cox, Basil Ringrose, William Dick, Bartholomew Sharp, and Lionel Wafer. As I discuss below, Alexander Exquemelin's buccaneer chronicle is the most important and famous "pirate memoir." However, pirates from the period between 1716 and 1726, the sea bandits this book is most concerned with, left no such journals.

Fortunately, a number of other documents exist that can illuminate the economics of pirates. There are two undisputed "kings" of the primary source historical record relating to piracy. The first is Captain Charles Johnson's *A General History of the Pyrates*, published in two volumes, the first in 1724 and the second in 1728. The second is Alexander O. Exquemelin's *Buccaneers of America*, first published in Dutch in 1678 and translated into English in 1684. Since my discussion relies heavily on both sources, a few more words about them are in order.

Typical for a pirate, our knowledge of Exquemelin's life is sketchy. At the age of about twenty he began work as an indentured servant for the French West Indian Company only to leave three years later and join the buccaneers at Tortuga. Exquemelin sailed with his buccaneering brethren for the next decade in the important position of surgeon. According to Jack Beeching, an expert on Exquemelin, our buccaneer temporarily retired from sea roving to Europe in 1674, but appears again sailing with the buccaneers before their extinction in 1697. Shortly after returning to Europe, Exquemelin wrote his book providing a detailed firsthand account of the buccaneers' raids, system of rules, and social organization. It was a smashing success, even in Exquemelin's time, and remains "the principal source of our knowledge about the buccaneers."

In the early twentieth century it was popular to argue that Exquemelin was actually the seventeenth-century Dutch romance novelist Hendrick Barentzoon Smeeks. However, in 1934 new research put this ill-founded theory to bed. As Beeching points out, "in 1934, M. Vriejman found the names of both Exquemelin and Smeeken [sic] on the books of the Dutch Surgeons' Guild, as having passed their qualifying examinations. Exquemelin, therefore, on his return from the West Indies, went to Amsterdam to qualify professionally, and must have been living there while the history that bears his name was written and published. The 'pseudonym' theory will not hold water." Today, Exquemelin is universally acknowledged as Exquemelin.

The story with Captain Charles Johnson is similar. Almost nothing is known for certain about Johnson, whose book was also a best seller. Some suspect he was a maritime worker, others, a journalist, still others, a pirate. According to David Cordingly, "What is certain is that Captain Johnson must have attended several pirate trials in London and that he interviewed pirates and seamen who had voyaged with them." Whatever the cause, much of Johnson's book is consistent with the other primary source materials in the pirate historical record.

Around the time scholarly circles exonerated Exquemelin as the genuine author of *The Buccaneers of America*, doubts surfaced about Johnson's identity. In 1932 John Robert Moore declared that Captain Johnson was none other than Daniel Defoe, author of *Robinson Crusoe*. Moore based his claim on what he felt was a strong stylistic similarity between Defoe's books and Johnson's *General History of the Pyrates*, as well as Defoe's well-known infatuation with sea robbers.

This view went largely unchallenged until 1988 when, according to Cordingly, "two academics, P. N. Furbank and W. R. Owens, demolished Moore's theory in their book *The Canonisation of Daniel Defoe*. They showed that there was not a single piece of documentary evidence to link Defoe with the *General History of the Pirates*, and pointed out that there were too many discrepancies between the stories in the book and the other works on pirates attributed to Defoe. So convincing are their arguments that there seems no alternative but to abandon the attractive theory that Defoe wrote the *General History of the Pirates* and to return the authorship of the work to the mysterious Captain Johnson." Today, many, though not all, historians of piracy agree with Cordingly's assessment.

Although Johnson's true identity remains a mystery, no one doubts he "had extensive first-hand knowledge of piracy." And, as Marcus Rediker points out, "Johnson is widely regarded as a highly reliable source for factual information" on pirates. Johnson's book contains several errors and apocryphal accounts, such as the fictitious Captain Mission and his pirate colony called Libertalia. However, its detail and general accuracy have preserved its status as "the prime source for the lives of many pirates of what is often called the Golden Age of Piracy."

I can mention the remaining historical sources this book relies on more briefly. A few pirate prisoners whose captors ultimately released them, such as William Snelgrave and Philip Ashton, published longer works describing their harrowing captivities. I make ample use of these sources, especially Snelgrave, which contain valuable information about pirate life and organization. Joel H. Baer has recently edited a superb four-volume collection that contains numerous rare and hard-to-find pieces of primary source pirate history, which I also use extensively. These volumes contain, among other things, published accounts of pirate trials, which include fascinating testimony from pirate victims and pirates themselves, contemporary newspaper accounts relating to piracy, and various pirates' "dying speeches" before the gallows at their executions. J. Franklin Jameson has also edited an excellent, though far less comprehensive, collection of related seventeenth- and eighteenth-century documents covering pirates and privateers. These include the depositions and examinations of pirates, pirate victims, and others who had contact with sea dogs. In addition to these sources I rely on records in the *Calendar of State Papers, Colonial North America and West Indies* series, which contain correspondence from colonial governors and others relating to piracy, the Public Record Office's Colonial Office Papers, and the High Court of Admiralty Papers. These sources are veritable treasure troves of pirate-related documents from government officials, pirate victims, and so forth. I also draw on the published "final sermons" of various men of religion, such as Reverend Cotton Mather, and their conversations with pirates in the days leading up to their executions.

Finally, I rely heavily on and am deeply indebted to a voluminous and superb literature by modern historians of piracy. Several of these authors have already been mentioned, including Marcus Rediker, Joel Baer, David Cordingly, Philip Gosse, Hugh Rankin, Patrick Pringle, Angus Konstam, Kenneth Kinkor, and Jan Rogozinski. The historical material presented in this book isn't original to me. Many others have discussed it for many years. This literature covers all aspects of piracy, including those discussed here, although the "economic angle," which I'm concerned with, is either absent or only hinted at.

NOTES

Chapter 1. The Invisible Hook

1   *a Crime so odious*   *The Tryals of Major Stede Bonnet, and other Pirates . . .* (London: Benj. Cowse, 1719), 8, reprinted in Joel H. Baer, ed., *British Piracy in the Golden Age: History and Interpretation, 1660–1730*, vol. 2 of 4 vols. (London: Pickering and Chatto, 2007).

1   *Sea-monsters; Hell-Hounds; Robbers, Opposers*   Cotton Mather, *Instructions to the Living, from the Condition of the Dead . . .* (Boston: Nicholas Boon, 1717), reprinted in Baer, *British Piracy in the Golden Age*, vol. 4; Captain Charles Johnson, *A General History of the Pyrates . . .* , ed. Manuel Schonhorn (Mineola, NY: Dover, 1999 [1726–28]), 607 (hereafter cited as *GHP*); *A Full and Exact Account, of the Tryal of all the Pyrates, Lately Taken by Captain Ogle . . .* (London: J. Roberts, 1723), 5, reprinted in Baer, *British Piracy in the Golden Age*, vol. 3.

1   *Devils incarnate*   John Barnard, *Ashton's Memorial . . .* (Boston: Printed for Samuel Gerrish, 1715), 62.

1   *Children of the Wicked One*   Cotton Mather, *The Lord-High-Admiral of All the Seas, Adored . . .* (Boston: S. Kneeland, 1723), 20.

1   *Danger lurked in their very Smiles*   Johnson, *GHP*, 334.

1   *a sort of People; Subvert and Extinguish*   *Boston News-Letter*, February 9–February 16, 1719, reprinted in Baer, *British Piracy in the Golden Age*, vol. 1; *The Trials of Eight Persons Indited for Piracy &c . . .* (Boston: John Edwards, 1718), 2, reprinted in Baer, *British Piracy in the Golden Age*, vol. 2.

1   *declared War against*   Johnson, *GHP,* 319.

1   *These men, whom we term*   Ibid., 527.

2   *Adam Smith's* Wealth of Nations   Adam Smith, *An Inquiry into the Nature and Causes of the Wealth of Nations,* 2 vols., ed. R. H. Campbell and A. S. Skinner (Indianapolis, IN: Liberty Fund, 1976 [1776]).

7   *Pirates prey upon all Mankind*   *Tryals of Major Stede Bonnet,* 8. See also, *Trials of Eight Persons,* 7.

7   *Privateers weren't pirates since they had state backing*   Things were more complicated than this, however. First, opposing nations often saw privateers as pirates. Second, privateers sometimes abused their licenses, raiding beyond the scope of their commissions. In this capacity, privateers acted without state support as criminals—as pirates.

8   *Buccaneering ... was a peculiar blend*   Jennifer G. Marx, "The Brethren of the Coast," in *Pirates: Terror on the High Seas—From the Caribbean to the South China Sea,* ed. David Cordingly (Atlanta: Turner, 1996), 38.

8   *the aims and means of [buccaneering]*   David J. Starkey, "Pirates and Markets," in *Bandits at Sea: A Pirates Reader,* ed. C. R. Pennell (New York: New York University Press, 2001), 109.

8   *banditti of all nations*   Governor Sir N. Lawes to the Council of Trade and Plantations, January 31, 1719, Item 34, vol. 31 (1719–20), 12–21, *Calendar of State Papers, Colonial Series, America and West Indies, 1574–1739,* CD-ROM, consultant eds. Karen Ordahl Kupperman, John C. Appleby, and Mandy Banton (London: Routledge, published in association with the Public Record Office, 2000) (hereafter cited as CSPC). See also, Captain Candler to Mr. Secretary Burchett, CSPC, Item 639 i, vol. 29 (1716–17), 339–40; Governor Hamilton to the Council of Trade and Plantations, CSPC, October 3, 1716, Item 350, vol. 29 (1716–17), 183–84. Pirates also exhibited some diversity in social standing. Although most pirates were uneducated and from the lower classes of society, a few, such as Stede Bonnet, the "Gentleman Pirate," were from higher stations in life. At his trial, Bonnet

was described in his prepirate life as "a Gentleman, a Man of Honour, a Man of Fortune, and one that has had a liberal Education." See *Tryals of Major Stede Bonnet*, 9.

9 *Nationalities of 700 Caribbean pirates* Angus Konstam, *The History of Pirates* (Guilford, CT: Lyons, 2002), 9.

9 *Where other pirates hailed from* Jennifer G. Marx, "The Golden Age of Piracy" in Cordingly, *Pirates: Terror on the High Seas*, 103.

9 *Bermudan governor's estimate of pirate population* Lt. Governor Bennett to the Council of Trade and Plantations, CSPC, July 30, 1717, Item 677, vol. 29 (1716–17), 360–61.

9 *Official's estimate of pirate population in 1718* Mr. Gale to Col. Thomas Pitt, Jr., CSPC, November 4, 1718, Item 31 i, vol. 31 (1719–20), 10.

9 *Dummer's estimate of pirate population* Jeremiah Dummer to the Council of Trade and Plantations, CSPC, February 25, 1720, Item 578, vol. 31 (1719–20), 365–68.

9 *Johnson on pirate population in the Indian Ocean* Johnson, *GHP*, 132. That same year, the *Boston News-Letter* reported on a letter from the governor of the Bahamas that estimated "the Number of the Pirates" at "upwards of 1500." See *Boston News-Letter*, October 9–October 16, 1721. For a contemporary's estimate of the pirate populate in the late seventeenth century, see Captain Thomas Warren, of HMS *Windsor*, to the East India Company, CSPC, November 28, 1697, Item 115 i, vol. 16 (1697–98), 68–71.

9 *Estimate of pirate population in any one year between 1716 and 1722* See, for instance, Konstam, *History of Pirates*, 6; Marx, "The Golden Age of Piracy," 102, 111; Patrick Pringle, *Jolly Roger: The Story of the Great Age of Piracy* (New York: Norton, 1953), 185; Johnson, *GHP*, 132; Marcus Rediker, *Between the Devil and the Deep-Blue Sea: Merchant Seamen, Pirates and the Anglo-American Maritime World, 1700–1750* (Cambridge: Cambridge University Press, 1987), 256.

9 *Average number of Royal Navy sailors in any one year between 1716 and 1726* Rediker, *Between the Devil and the Deep Blue Sea*, 256.

9   *1680 population in North American colonies and US population in 1790*   Jonathan R.T. Hughes and Louis P. Cain, *American Economic History*, 4th ed. (New York: HarperCollins, 1994) 20, 28.

9   *Pirates' New Providence land base*   As one contemporary described it, New Providence was "the usual Retreat and general Receptacle for Pirates" before Rogers brought it under control. See *Boston News-Letter*, December 16–December 23, 1717.

9   *Average pirate crew size*   Rediker, *Between the Devil and the Deep Blue Sea*, 256.

9   *Several larger pirate crews*   See, for instance, William Snelgrave, *A New Account of Some Parts of Guinea and the Slave-Trade* (London: Cass, 1972 [1734]), 199; Examination of John Brown, May 6, 1717, Suffolk Court Files, No. 11945, Paper 5, reprinted in J. Franklin Jameson, ed., *Privateering and Piracy in the Colonial Period: Illustrative Documents* (New York: Macmillan, 1923), 295; Deposition of Theophilus Turner June 8, 1699, Colonial Office Papers (hereafter cited as CO) 5: 714, No. 70 VI, reprinted in Jameson, *Privateering and Piracy in the Colonial Period*, 201; Examination of John Dann, August 3, 1696, CO 323: 2, No. 25, reprinted in Jameson, *Privateering and Piracy in the Colonial Period*, 169; Deposition of Adam Baldridge, May 5, 1699, CO 5: 1042, No. 30 II, reprinted in Jameson, *Privateering and Piracy in the Colonial Period*, 180; Johnson, *GHP*, 442; David Cordingly, *Under the Black Flag: The Romance and the Reality of Life among the Pirates* (New York: Random House, 1996), 165; Deposition of John Brown, CSCP, March 12, 1718/19, Item 797 i, vol. 30 (1717–18), 410–11.

9   *200 brisk Men*   *Boston News-Letter*, April 29–May 6, 1717, reprinted in Baer, *British Piracy in the Golden Age*, vol. 1.

10   *Crew size on* Queen Anne's Revenge   Deposition of Henry Bostock, CSPC, December 19, 1717, Item 298 iii, vol. 30 (1717–18), 150–51.

10   *Average crew size on 200-ton merchant ship*   Rediker, *Between the Devil and the Deep Blue Sea*, 107.

10   *Size of Roberts's squadron*   Cordingly, *Under the Black Flag*, 111.

10 *Size of Morgan's fleet* Alexander O. Exquemelin, *The Buccaneers of America*, trans. Alexis Brown (Mineola, NY: Dover, 1969), 171.

10 *had a force of at least twenty vessels* Ibid., 69. See also, 85, 105, 93.

10 *Size of Dampier's expedition* William Dampier, *Buccaneer Explorer: William Dampier's Voyages*, ed. Gerald Norris (Woodbridge, UK: Boydell Press, 2005 [1697–1707]), 62.

10 *cheerfully joined their Brethren* Snelgrave, *A New Account of Some Parts of Guinea*, 198.

10 *Pirate age data* Marcus Rediker, *Villains of All Nations: Atlantic Pirates in the Golden Age* (Boston: Beacon Press, 2004), 49.

11 *Pirates motivated by non-material concerns* See, for instance, Kenneth J. Kinkor, "Black Men under the Black Flag," in *Bandits at Sea*; B. R. Burg, *Sodomy and the Perception of Evil: English Sea Rovers in the Seventeenth-Century Caribbean* (New York: New York University Press, 1983); Marcus Rediker, "Liberty beneath the Jolly Roger: The Lives of Anne Bonny and Mary Read, Pirates," in *Iron Men, Wooden Women: Gender and Seafaring in the Atlantic World, 1700–1920*, ed. Margaret S. Creighton and Lisa Norling (Baltimore: Johns Hopkins University Press, 1996).

11 *Number of British navy sailors during and after War of the Spanish Succession* Rediker, *Villains of All Nations*, 23.

12 *Average able seaman's wage* Ralph Davis, *The Rise of the English Shipping Industry in the Seventeenth and Eighteenth Centuries* (London: Macmillan, 1962), 136–37. For the conversion to modern U.S. dollars, I used the year 1720 and the currency converter (first from 1720 pounds to 2007 pounds using the retail price index, and then 2007 pounds to 2007 USD) available at http://www.measuringworth.com hosted by EH.net.

12 *Privateers in Time of War* Johnson, *GHP*, 4.

12 *The Privateering Stroke* Cotton Mather, *Faithful Warnings to Prevent Fearful Judgments* ... (Boston: Timothy Green, 1704), 37.

13   *Since the calling in*   Governor Sir N. Lawes to the Council of Trade and Plantations, CSPC, August 24, 1720, Item 213, vol. 32 (1720–21), 126–29.

13   *for want of encouragement*   Ibid., December 6, 1719, Item 479, vol. 31 (1719–20), 275–81.

13   *At a time when Anglo-American*   Jennifer G. Marx, "The Pirate Round," in *Pirates: Terror on the High Seas,* 141.

13   *Every's crew's prize*   *Flying Post,* October 17–October 20, 1696, reprinted in Baer, *British Piracy in the Golden Age,* vol. 1. For other examples of impressive late-seventeenth-century pirate hauls, see Copies of Extracts from Letters Received by the East India Company, CSPC, January 15, 1696–97, Item 115 i, vol. 16 (1697–98), 68–71; and Deposition of Samuel Burgess, CSPC, May 3, 1698, Item 473 ii, vol. 16 (1697–98), 227–28.

13   *which yielded them 500 l; White's crew's earnings*   Johnson, *GHP,* 480, 485.

13   *Condent's crew's prize; Taylor and La Bouche's crew's prize*   Marx, "The Pirate Round," 161, 163.

14   *Evans's crew's earnings*   Johnson, *GHP,* 340.

14   *they had got Riches*   Information of Richard Moore, 1/55, fol. 98, 1724, High Court of Admiralty Papers (hereafter cited as HCA).

14   *In an honest service*   Johnson, *GHP,* 244. Throughout this book I've kept text that's italicized in original sources italicized in my discussion. This is why several long italicized quotes appear here and later. Unless otherwise noted, all italicized text in quotations is italicized in the original source.

14   *Unpleasant working conditions attended low pay on merchant ships*   Peter Earle's excellent book, *Sailors: English Merchant Seamen 1650–1775* (London: Methuen, 1998), considers the merchant sailor's life more fully. As he points out, the merchant seaman's life was not a singularly brutal and miserable one, and it's not my intention to suggest otherwise. N.A.M. Rodger's, *The Wooden World: An Anatomy of the Georgian Navy* (New York:

W. W. Norton, 1996), makes a similar point about life in the Royal Navy. However, as I discuss here and in the next chapter, there was ample latitude for officer mistreatment on merchant ships, which more than a few officers took advantage of. Compared to the ability of captains on pirate ships to prey on their crew members, this was especially significant and so constituted an important element of some sailors' decision to go pirate. For an excellent and more in-depth discussion of sailor mistreatment aboard merchant ships, see Rediker, *Between the Devil and the Deep Blue Sea*.

15   *unlimited power, bad views*   William Betagh, *A Voyage Round the World* ... (London: For T. Combes, J. Lacy, and J. Clake 1728), 41.

15   *were att short allowance*   Babb v. Chalkley, HCA, 24/127, 1701; quoted in Rediker, *Between the Devil and the Deep Blue Sea*, 247.

15   *Docked wages and paid in debased currency; voyages without consent*   Richard B. Morris, *Government and Labor in Early America* (New York: Harper and Row, 1965), 237; Adam Gifford, Jr., "The Economic Organization of 17th- through mid-19th Century Whaling and Shipping," *Journal of Economic Behavior and Organization* 20(2) (1993): 137–50, quote at 144.

15   *Hit sailors in head with hard objects*   Jones v. Newcomin, HCA, 24/138, 1735; quoted in Rediker, *Between the Devil and the Deep Blue Sea*, 216.

16   *above a hundred Blows*   Information of Benjamin Bush, HCA, 1/55, fol. 92, 1724.

16   *without any provocation*   Deposition of William Bennett, HCA, 1/55, 1729/1730.

16   *seditious fellow ... I gave him*   Nathaniel Uring, *The Voyages and Travels of Captain Nathaniel Uring* (London: Cassell and Company, 1928 [1726]), 176–77.

16   *Interference with captain punishment mutinous*   Morris, *Government and Labor in Early America*, 264–65.

16   *to fetch a Pail of Water*   Information of Richard Mandewell, HCA, 1/55, fol. 22, 1722.

16   *they had better be dead*   *The Tryals of Captain Jack Rackam, and other Pirates* . . . (Jamaica, 1721), reprinted in Baer, *British Piracy in the Golden Age*, vol. 3.

17   *had Lawful provocation*   Broughton v. *Atkins*, Massachusetts Vice Admiralty Records, Box II, f. 25, 1727; quoted in Morris, *Government and Labor in Early America*, 264.

17   *Sailor population in mid-18th century*   Gifford, "The Economic Organization of 17th- through mid-19th Century Whaling and Shipping," 147.

18   *it is frequently the misfortune*   Quoted in Morris, *Government and Labor in Early America*, 271.

18   *The too great severity*   *Piracy Destroy'd: or, A Short Discourse Shewing Rise, Growth and Causes of Piracy of Late; with a Sure Method how to put a Speedy Stop to that Growing Evil* (London: John Nutt, 1701), 4, 12, reprinted in Baer, *British Piracy in the Golden Age*, vol. 3.

18   *a Supercargo Son of a B—h*   *A Full and Exact Account, of the Tryal of all the Pyrates, Lately Taken by Captain Ogle*, 45.

18   *I could wish that Masters*   Quoted in Johnson, *GHP*, 351.

18   *Our Captain and his Mate*   Cotton Mather, *A Vial Poured Out Upon the Sea* . . . (Boston: T. Fleet, 1726), 21.

18   *He would advise the Masters*   Ibid., 48. See also, Benjamin Colman, *It is a Fearful Thing to Fall into the Hands of the Living God* . . . (Boston: John Phillips and Thomas Hancock, 1726), 39, reprinted in Baer, *British Piracy in the Golden Age*, vol. 4; *Boston News-Letter*, July 7–July 14, 1726.

19   *Sailors attracted to piracy between 1716 and 1726*   Rediker, *Villains of All Nations*, 30.

Chapter 2. Vote for Blackbeard

23   *who by his Counsel*   Johnson, *GHP*, 195.

24   *War against the whole; The Guns are then fired*   See, for instance, the postelection ceremonies of captains Davis and North. Johnson, *GHP*, 167–68, 525.

24 *Buccaneers' pre-English Bill of Rights democratic checks* See, for instance, Philip Ayres, *The Voyages and Adventures of Capt. Barth. Sharp and others, in the South Sea* ... (London: R.H. and S.T., 1684), 2, 17, 80, reprinted in Baer, *British Piracy in the Golden Age*, vol. 1.

25 *New England's representative democracy* George Brown Tindall and David Emory Shi, *America: A Narrative History* (New York: W.W. Norton, 1997), 34.

25 *Puritan church organization and New England democracy* See, for instance, James F. Cooper, Jr., *Tenacious of their Liberties: The Congregationalists in Colonial Massachusetts* (Oxford: Oxford University Press, 1999).

25 *Restricted suffrage in New England and Athens* On Athens, see Mogens Herman Hansen, *The Athenian Democracy in the Age of Demosthenes* (Oxford: Blackwell, 1991). On Massachusetts Bay Colony, see Robert Emmet Wall, Jr., "The Massachusetts Bay Colony Franchise in 1647," *William and Mary Quarterly* 27 (1970): 136–44.

26 *democracy that ... bordered on anarchy* Hugh F. Rankin, *The Golden Age of Piracy* (Williamsburg: Colonial Williamsburg, 1969), 28.

26 *they acknowledged no countrymen* Copies of Extracts from Letters Received by the East India Company, CSPC, Item 115 i, vol. 16 (1697–98), 68–71.

26 *have no Country, but by the nature* Tryals of Thirty-Six Persons for Piracy ... (Boston: Samuel Kneeland, 1723), reprinted in Baer, *British Piracy in the Golden Age*, vol. 3.

26 *denied common humanity* Trials of Eight Persons, 6.

26 *that abominable Society* Johnson, *GHP*, 114.

27 *how shatter'd and weak* Ibid., 194.

27 *But what is government itself* Alexander Hamilton, James Madison, and John Jay, *The Federalist Papers*, ed. Clinton Rossiter (New York: Menton, 1961 [1788]), 322.

28　*Dysfunctional governments in Sub-Saharan Africa*　On the plight of underdeveloped countries and their failure to overcome Madison's paradox, see Christopher J. Coyne and Peter T. Leeson, "The Plight of Underdeveloped Countries," *Cato Journal* 24 (2004): 235–45; and Peter T. Leeson, "Escaping Poverty: Foreign Aid, Private Property, and Economic Development," *Journal of Private Enterprise* 23 (2008): 39–64.

28　*Ruler predation shapes citizens' incentive to cooperate*　See Martin C. McGuire and Mancur Olson, Jr., "The Economics of Autocracy and Majority Rule: The Invisible Hand and the Use of Force," *Journal of Economic Literature* 34 (1996): 72–96.

29　*A dependence on the people is, no doubt*　Hamilton, Madison, and Jay, *Federalist Papers*, 322 (emphasis added).

29　*The Rank of Captain*　Johnson, *GHP*, 214. Captain Spriggs, given two votes by his crew, is the only exception I can find to the "one pirate, one vote" rule. Even here, however, as one released prisoner described it, Spriggs was still "over-power'd by Votes" from the remaining crew. See *British Journal*, August 22, 1724, reprinted in Baer, *British Piracy in the Golden Age*, vol. 1. The only members of the pirate crew who might not be allowed to vote were boys and forced men. See *The Arraignment, Tryal, and Condemnation, of Capt. John Quelch* ... (London: Ben. Bragg, 1704), 18, reprinted in Baer, *British Piracy in the Golden Age*, vol. 2; *Trials of Eight Persons*, 24.

29　*it was not of any great Signification*　Johnson, *GHP*, 194.

30　*doing every Thing*　Ibid., 525.

30　*13 captains in a single voyage*　*An Account of the Conduct and Proceedings of the Late John Gow* ... (New York: Burt Franklin, [1725] 1970), xi–xii.

30　*refused to take and plunder*　*Trials of Eight Persons*, 23.

30　*falls on one superior for Knowledge*　Johnson, *GHP*, 214.

30　*Behaviour was obliged*　Ibid., 139.

30　*was turned out of Command*　Information of Richard Moore, HCA, 1/55, fol. 96, 1724.

30   *at last forced him*   Snelgrave, *A New Account of Some Parts of Guinea*, 198.

30   *a great difference falling out*   Boston *News-Letter*, February 4– February 11, 1725, reprinted in Baer, *British Piracy in the Golden Age*, vol. 1.

32   *they only permit[ed] him*   Johnson, *GHP*, 213.

32   *La Bouche deposed and flogged*   Jan Rogozinski, *Honor among Thieves: Captain Kidd, Henry Every, and the Pirate Democracy in the Indian Ocean* (Mechanicsburg, PA: Stackpole Books, 2000), 177.

32   *severall of his men have deserted*   The President and Council of the Leeward Islands to Secretary Vernon, May 18, 1699, CO, 152: 3, No. 21, reprinted in Jameson, *Privateering and Piracy in the Colonial Period*, 195–96.

32   *should a Captain be so sawcy*   Johnson, *GHP*, 194–95.

32   *The Captain is very severe*   Quoted in Rogozinski, *Honor among Thieves*, 139. See also, Deposition of Benjamin Franks October 20, 1697, CO, 323: 2, No. 124, reprinted in Jameson, *Privateering and Piracy in the Colonial Period*, 194. The captain referred to here is the privateer-turned-pirate, Captain Kidd, who was ultimately executed for his crimes. Notably, Kidd's privateer (like others) was financed by absentee owners.

33   *Every man had as much say*   Quoted in Robert C. Ritchie, *Captain Kidd and the War against the Pirates* (Cambridge: Harvard University Press, 1986), 124.

33   *Lodging, etc., similar for captains and crewmembers*   According to Johnson, on Captain Howell Davis's pirate ship, however, several of the crew's more senior pirates "had assumed the Title of Lords, and as such took upon them to advise or counsel their Captain upon any important Occasion; and likewise held certain Privileges, which the common Pyrates were debarr'd from, as walking the Quarter-Deck, using the great Cabin, going ashore at Pleasure, and treating with foreign Powers, that is, with the Captains of Ships they made Prize of." See *GHP*, 193. If the

division between "Lords" and "Commoners" remained under Davis's successor, Bart Roberts, it couldn't have meant much since Roberts's articles, discussed in chapter 3, guaranteed all pirates voting rights, "equal Title" to food and drink, and made no distinction between "Lords" and "Commoners" when it came to pay.

33 *every Man, as the Humour*   Johnson, *GHP*, 213–14.

33 *any body might come and eat*   *A Full and Exact Account, of the Tryal of all the Pyrates, Lately Taken by Captain Ogle*, 26.

33 *the Captain himself not being allowed*   Snelgrave, *A New Account of Some Parts of Guinea*, 217.

33 *even their Captain, or any other Officer*   Clement Downing, *A Compendious History of the Indian Wars* (London: Printed for T. Cooper, 1737), 108.

33 *The captain is allowed no better fare*   Exquemelin, *Buccaneers of America*, 70–71.

33 *at Meals the Quarter-Master*   *British Journal*, August 22, 1724, reprinted in Baer, *British Piracy in the Golden Age*, vol. 1. See also, Downing, *A Compendious History of the Indian Wars*, 108.

33 *the People [pirates overtook]*   Snelgrave, *A New Account of Some Parts of Guinea*, 203.

34 *but experience has taught mankind*   Hamilton, Madison, and Jay, *Federalist Papers*, 322.

34 *Most of them having suffered*   Arthur L. Hayward, ed., *Lives of the Most Remarkable Criminals . . .*, vol. 1 (London: Reeves and Turner, 1874 [1735]), 42.

35 *For the Punishment of small Offences*   Johnson, *GHP*, 213.

35 *went by that Name*   *Tryals of Major Stede Bonnet*, 38. See also, Snelgrave, *A New Account of Some Parts of Guinea*, 199–200; *British Journal*, August 22, 1724, reprinted in Baer, *British Piracy in the Golden Age*, vol. 1.

36 *the Captain can undertake nothing*   Johnson, *GHP*, 423.

36   *by their own Laws; The Captain's Power is uncontroulable*   Ibid., 139, 214.

36   *Elected captains* and *quartermasters*   In one pirate crew, the crew aboard John Phillips's *Revenge*, Phillips appointed the quartermaster rather than the crew electing him. Notably, this led to considerable conflict and was eventually the undoing of the pirate company. The crew's carpenter, Fern, became miffed when Phillips didn't appoint him quartermaster and tried to desert his crew on several occasions. Phillips shot him for the offence. Fern's replacement was the conscripted carpenter Edward Cheeseman, discussed in chapter 6, who delivered his crew to the authorities.

36   *Vane's crew deposed him, elected quartermaster*   *Tryals of Captain Jack Rackam.* See also, Johnson, GHP, 479.

36   *Ambition must be made*   Hamilton, Madison, and Jay, *Federalist Papers*, 322.

37   *The Pirate Captains having taken*   Snelgrave, *A New Account of Some Parts of Guinea*, 257.

37   *Groups of merchants owned merchant ships*   Ownership groups were sizeable because of the need to diversify the risk of merchant shipping. Each merchant purchased a small share in multiple ships rather than being the sole owner of one.

37   *Merchant ship owners were absentee owners*   Because most merchant ships were owned by groups of investors, even in cases when a merchant captained his vessel himself there remained absentee owners, his coinvestors.

38   *Merchant ship owners specialized in commercial activities*   Absentee ownership was further assured by the fact that the members of merchant vessel ownership groups engaged in commercial activities besides their concern in a particular merchant ship. These other commercial activities often required merchants to be on land to tend to their affairs rather than at sea.

38   *Merchant ships could be gone for months*   Although merchant ships engaged in coastal trade were at sea for shorter periods,

merchant ships engaged in long-distance trade could be gone for periods of nine months or more.

38   *Merchant ship autocracy solution to principal-agent problem*   In addition to using autocratic captains to cope with this principal-agent problem, merchant ships also held back a portion (or sometimes all) of sailors' wages until a voyage was complete.

39   *Like sailors, merchant ship captains earned fixed wages*   A few merchant ships engaged in part-time fishing used a share system of payment similar to the one privateers, whalers, and pirates used. The overwhelming majority of merchant ships used a fixed wage system. In vessels engaged in coastal shipping, sailors were paid lump-sum wages. In vessels engaged in long-distance shipping, sailors were paid monthly wages.

39   *Merchant ship captains became stakeholders*   The owner-sailor, principal-agent problem couldn't have been overcome by converting every crew member's fixed wage to a profit-sharing scheme. Even under profit sharing, sailors would still have an incentive to consume cargo, liberal provisions, etc., and then blame the loss on the uncertainties of the sea, such as pirates or wreck. Although this opportunism would reduce each sailor's share of the voyage's net proceeds, since the cost of such behavior is borne partially by the absentee owners, sailors have an incentive to act opportunistically. Further, converting sailor wages to shares wouldn't have deterred the crew from the most costly kind of opportunism—absconding with the ship and its freight. Because the benefit of such theft would exceed the crew's fraction of a successful voyage's proceeds, which are shared with the absentee owners under a profit-sharing scheme, absent an authority to monitor and control their behavior, crews would still have an incentive to steal the ships they sailed on. This is why both privateers and whaling ships, for instance, which used a piratelike profit-sharing system, but also had absentee owners, still required and used autocratic captains. On the efficiency of the fixed wage system for the merchant marine and efficiency of the share system for privateers and whalers, which also applies to pirates, see Gifford, "The Economic Organization of 17th- through mid-19th Century Whaling and Shipping."

39   *Owners appointed captains with familial connections*   Davis, *Rise of the English Shipping Industry*, 128.

39   *Familial connections reduced captain opportunism*   A third device owners used for this purpose, though of declining importance over time, was that of the supercargo—an agent hired by the ship's owners who sailed on the ship and managed commercial aspects of the voyage, such as buying and selling cargo at port, and sometimes deciding what ports the ship should stop at, when the captain could not be trusted in these capacities. See Davis, *Rise of the English Shipping Industry*.

40   *Merchant sailor opportunism rare*   For a discussion of how merchant sailors facilitated mutiny in the face of the collective action problems of rebellion, see Peter T. Leeson, "Rational Choice, Round Robin, and Rebellion: An Institutional Solution to the Problems of Revolution," Unpublished paper, 2008.

41   *Pirates stole their ships*   There is at least one eighteenth-century pirate, however, Stede Bonnet, "who, it seems, at his own Cost and Charges fitted from thence a large Sloop called the *Revenge* with *ten* Guns, and about eighty Men." See *Tryals of Major Stede Bonnet*, iii.

41   *sea-going stock company*   Pringle, *Jolly Roger*, 106.

Chapter 3. An-*arrgh*-chy

45   *profess'd Enemys to all Order*   "General Officers of the Army" Petition to the King on Behalf of Woodes Rogers, CO, 23/12, 1726.

46   *Society ... cannot subsist among*   Adam Smith, *The Theory of Moral Sentiments*, ed. D. D. Raphael and A. L. Macfie (Indianapolis, IN: Liberty Fund, 1976 [1759]), 86.

46   *devices ... to control the abuses*   Hamilton, Madison, and Jay, *Federalist Papers*, 322.

47   *If men were angels*   Ibid., 322.

51   *Anarchy doesn't mean the absence of rules and order*   On the private emergence of institutions of social cooperation, see, for

instance, Bruce L. Benson, "The Spontaneous Evolution of Commercial Law," *Southern Economic Journal* 55: 644–61; David Friedman, "Private Creation and Enforcement of Law: A Historical Case," *Journal of Legal Studies* 8 (1979): 399–415. Peter T. Leeson, "Trading with Bandits," *Journal of Law and Economics* 50 (2007): 303–21; Peter T. Leeson, "Social Distance and Self-Enforcing Exchange," *Journal of Legal Studies* 36 (2008): 161–88; Peter T. Leeson, "Efficient Anarchy," *Public Choice* 130 (2007): 41–53; Peter T. Leeson, "Better Off Stateless: Somalia before and after Government Collapse," *Journal of Comparative Economics* 35 (2007): 689–710; Peter T. Leeson, "The Laws of Lawlessness," *Journal of Legal Studies* 38 (2009); David B. Skarbek, "Putting the 'Con' into Constitutions: The Economics of Prison Gangs," *Journal of Law, Economics and Organization* 26 (2010).

53   *External costs fall on people who didn't fully produce them*   As Nobel Prize-winning economist Ronald Coase pointed out, the people who live near the factory did partly produce it, however. The external cost they bear is partly the result of the factory's actions, but also partly the result of their own actions in living near the factory. In this sense all externalities are "jointly produced." See R. H. Coase, "The Problem of Social Cost," *Journal of Law and Economics* 3 (1960): 1–44.

58   *The buccaneers resolve by common vote*   Exquemelin, *Buccaneers of America*, 71–72.

60   *for the better Conservation*   Johnson, *GHP*, 210.

60   *Constitutions similar across crews*   Rediker, *Between the Devil and the Deep Blue Sea*, 261.

60   *the Laws of this Company*   Johnson, *GHP*, 213.

60   *Percentage of pirates traceable back to three captains*   Rediker, *Between the Devil and the Deep Blue Sea*, 267.

60   *All [pirates] swore to 'em*   Johnson, *GHP*, 342.

60   *When ever any enter*   Downing, *A Compendious History of the Indian Wars*, 107.

61   *to prevent Disputes and Ranglings*   Johnson, *GHP*, 342.

61   *Pirates free to search for better terms*   The status of forced men on pirate ships varied. Some were compelled to sign the ship's articles. Others weren't compelled to do so but didn't have a vote in the company's affairs until they signed. See Rediker, *Villains of All Nations*, 79–81.

61   *offering himself as an Ally*   Johnson, *GHP*, 319.

61   *a Spirit of Discord*   Ibid., 175.

61   *Tiebout competition*   See Charles M. Tiebout, "A Pure Theory of Local Expenditures," *Journal of Political Economy* 64 (1956): 416–24.

62   *Pirates' incentive to create favorable rules*   This isn't to say pirates never coerced anyone to join them; they certainly did. However, as discussed in depth in chapter 6, most pirates were volunteers. Furthermore, at the stage at which pirate articles were forged— before launching an expedition—the deciding pirates were volunteers. Thus, exit, and therefore Tiebout competition, was operational at this stage.

62   *wickedly united*   Johnson, *GHP*, 253.

62   *Every Man has a Vote*   Ibid., 211–12.

64   *to Strike or Abuse one another*   *Boston News-Letter*, August 1– August 8, 1723, reprinted in Baer, *British Piracy in the Golden Age*, vol. 1. Captain George Lowther's crew's articles, as reported by Johnson (*GHP*, 307–8), are nearly identical to those the *Boston News-Letter* and the *Tryals of Thirty-Six Persons for Piracy* attribute to Edward Low's company. Since Lowther and Low sailed in consort for a time, it's possible, especially in light of the similarities between pirate crews' articles more generally, that the closeness results from this. Alternatively, Johnson, the *Boston News-Letter*, or the *Tryals of Thirty-Six Persons for Piracy* may have mistakenly attributed the articles to Low when they belonged to Lowther or vice versa.

64   *any Man ... [to] steal any Thing*   Johnson, *GHP*, 342–43.

64   *Nature, we see, teaches*   Ibid., 527.

64   *Punishment among them for something*   *A Full and Exact Account, of the Tryal of all the Pyrates, Lately Taken by Captain Ogle*, 48.

64   *Coupled marooning with ostracism*   See, for instance, Exquemelin, *Buccaneers of America*, 72.

65   *If the Robbery was only betwixt*   Johnson, GHP, 211.

65   *Random searches for holding back loot*   Exquemelin, *Buccaneers of America*, 205–6.

65   *Their Money was kept*   *Trials of Eight Persons*, 25. See also, Marx, "The Brethren of the Coast," 44.

65   *Moses's Law; If at any Time we meet*   Johnson, GHP, 342, 343. See also, *A Full and Exact Account, of the Tryal of all the Pyrates, Lately Taken by Captain Ogle*, 19.

65   *shall suffer what Punishment*   See, for instance, Low's articles in the *Boston News-Letter*, August 1–August 8, 1723.

65   *all the Pyrates Affairs*   *A Full and Exact Account, of the Tryal of all the Pyrates, Lately Taken by Captain Ogle*, 27.

66   *If any one commits an Offence*   *British Journal*, August 22, 1724, reprinted in Baer, *British Piracy in the Golden Age*, vol. 1.

66   *acts as a Sort of civil Magistrate*   Johnson, GHP, 213.

66   *The Quarter-Master of the Ship*   Ibid., 212. See also, 339.

66   *They had no discipline*   Pringle, *Jolly Roger*, 272.

67   *which kept Peace amongst*   *Weekly Journal*, May 23, 1724, reprinted in Baer, *British Piracy in the Golden Age*, vol. 1.

67   *Pack of Sea Banditti*   Ibid., June 6, 1724, reprinted in Baer, *British Piracy in the Golden Age*, vol. 1.

67   *Sold or auctioned troublesome booty*   See, for instance, Rogozinski, *Honor among Thieves*, 169; Snelgrave, *A New Account of Some Parts of Guinea*; *A Full and Exact Account, of the Tryal of all the Pyrates, Lately Taken by Captain Ogle*, 158.

68   *The Captain is to have two full shares*   *Boston News-Letter*, August 1–August 8, 1723.

68   *the Captain shall have one full share*   Johnson, *GHP*, 342.

68   *Merchant ship pay scale steeper than pirates'*   Davis, *Rise of the English Shipping Industry*, 138.

70   *That Man that shall not keep*   Johnson, *GHP*, 342–43.

70   *give a Check to their Debauches*   Ibid., 211.

70   *this being a good political Rule*   Snelgrave, *A New Account of Some Parts of Guinea*, 256–257. See also, Johnson, *GHP*, 212.

70   *That man that shall snap*   Johnson, *GHP*, 342–43.

71   *If . . . any Man should lose a Limb*   Ibid., 211–12.

72   *He that shall have the Misfortune*   Ibid., 308.

72   *Those who behaved courageously*   Exquemelin, *Buccaneers of America*, 156.

72   *He that sees a sail first*   *Boston News-Letter*, August 1–August 8, 1723. See also, *A Full and Exact Account, of the Tryal of all the Pyrates, Lately Taken by Captain Ogle*, 66.

72   *It must be observed*   Johnson, *GHP*, 191.

72   *In Case any Doubt*   Ibid., 213.

74   *Buchanan and Tullock's costs of creating governance*   James M. Buchanan and Gordon Tullock, *The Calculus of Consent: Logical Foundations of Constitutional Democracy* (Ann Arbor: University of Michigan Press, 1962).

78   *If quartermaster abused power, entire crew may react*   On the co-ordinating role of constitutions for preventing ruler predation, see Barry R. Weingast, "The Economic Role of Political Institutions: Market-Preserving Federalism and Economic Development," *Journal of Law, Economics and Organization* 11 (1995): 1–31.

78   *Burgess marooned for predation*   Rogozinski, *Honor among Thieves*, 177.

79   *loaded him with Irons*   *An Account of the Conduct and Proceedings of the Late John Gow*, 23.

79   *as great robbers*   Barnaby Slush, *The Royal Navy: Or a Sea Cook Turn'd Projector* (London: Bragg, 1709), viii; quoted in Rediker, *Between the Devil and the Deep Blue Sea*, 287.

80   *Puritan church covenants*   On Puritan church government, see Cooper, *Tenacious of their Liberties.*

80   *it was every one's Interest*   Johnson, *GHP*, 210.

80   *As society cannot subsist unless the laws of justice*   Smith, *Theory of Moral Sentiments*, 87.

81   *their greatest Security lay*   Johnson, *GHP*, 210.

81   *Pirate ships more orderly than many legitimate vessels and colonies*   Rogozinski, *Honor among Thieves*, 179. Chinese pirates, who also relied on private governance mechanisms aboard their ships, enjoyed similar order. Referring to these pirates, for example, historian Philip Gosse notes that "the discipline of the crew was little short of exemplary." See Philip Gosse, *The History of Piracy* (New York: Tudor, 1932), 273.

81   *At sea, they perform*   Jacobus de Bucquoy, *Zestien Jarrige Reis naas de Inidien gedan door de Jacob de Bucquoy.* (Harlem: Bosch, 1744), 116; translated and quoted in Rogozinski, *Honor among Thieves*, viii.

Chapter 4 Skull & Bones

83   *Going about like roaring Lions*   Johnson, *GHP*, 118.

83   *go on the Account*   Ibid., 487.

84   *Description of navigation and pirate tactics*   My discussion of navigation and pirate tactics here is based largely on Angus Konstam, *Blackbeard: America's Most Notorious Pirate* (Hoboken, NJ: John Wiley, 2006).

84   *How the backstaff worked*   Other eighteenth-century maritime navigational tools, such as the "astrolabe," worked in essentially the same way.

84   *Determining longitude and speed*   Konstam, *Blackbeard*, 165. See also, Kriss E. Lane, *Pillaging the Empire: Piracy in the America's 1500–1750* (Armonk, NY: M.E. Sharpe, 1998), 59.

86   *twenty-four guns, with two wooden ones*   Edward Barlow, *Barlow's Journal . . .*, ed. Basil Lubbock (London: Hurst and Blackett, 1934), 327; quoted in Davis, *Rise of the English Shipping Industry*, 346.

86   *Pirates used chicken coops and cargo to disguise ship*   Konstam, *Blackbeard*, 174.

87   *this wasn't always practical*   Ibid., 174.

87   *Take of Powder 102*   Quoted in Charles Grey, *Pirates of the Eastern Seas* (London: Kennikat Press, 197), 45.

88   *Pirate armaments, their uses, and capabilities*   Konstam, *Blackbeard*, 178–79.

90   *Their whole policy*   Pringle, *Jolly Roger*, 113.

91   *A Sable Flag*   Quoted in Grey, *Pirates of the Eastern Seas*, 17.

91   *large black Flag*   *Trials of Eight Persons*, 24.

91   *Black Flags and Deaths Heads*   *Boston News-Letter*, June 9–June 16, 1718, reprinted in Baer, *British Piracy in the Golden Age*, vol. 1. See also, *Tryals of Major Stede Bonnet*, v, 16.

91   *when they fight under Jolly Roger*   *British Journal*, August 22, 1724, reprinted in Baer, *British Piracy in the Golden Age*, vol. 1.

91   *let fly her Jack; had the Figure of a Skeleton*   Johnson, *GHP*, 68, 245.

92   *Jolly Roger, for so they call*   *British Journal*, August 22, 1724, reprinted in Baer, *British Piracy in the Golden Age*, vol. 1. See also, *Boston Gazette*, March 21–March 28, 1726, reprinted in Baer, *British Piracy in the Golden Age*, vol. 1; *New England Courant*, July 22, 1723, reprinted in George Francis Dow and John Henry Edmonds, *The Pirates of the New England Coast, 1630–1730* (New York: Dover, 1996), 308. Spriggs's flag is similar to this description of Captain John Phillips's "own dark Flag, in the

middle of which an Anatomy, and at one side of it a Dart in the Heart, with drops of Blood proceeding from it; on the other side an Hour-glass, the sight dismal." See *Boston News-Letter*, May 28–June 4, 1724.

92 *a white Ensign with the figure* Governor Hamilton to the Council of Trade and Plantations, CSPC, January 6, 1718, Item 298, vol. 30 (1717–18), 146–53.

92 *English Colours flying* *Boston News-Letter*, August 15–August 22, 1720, reprinted in Baer, *British Piracy in the Golden Age*, vol. 1.

92 *The Colours they fought under* *A Full and Exact Account, of the Tryal of all the Pyrates, Lately Taken by Captain Ogle*, 5.

92 *Roberts was so enraged* Johnson, *GHP*, 221.

92 *a black Silk Flag flying* Ibid., 234. See also, 352.

93 *to terrify Merchant-Men* Snelgrave, *A New Account of Some Parts of Guinea*, 199.

93 *Meaning of pirate flag symbols* Konstam, *History of Pirates*, 100.

94 *Peacock signaling* Amotz Zahavi, "Mate Selection—A Selection for a Handicap," *Journal of Theoretical Biology* 53 (1975): 205–14.

96 *that the Spaniards ... man and his vessell* Lt. Governor Spotswood to the Council of Trade and Plantations, CSPC, May 31, 1717, Item 595, vol. 29 (1716–17), 316–21.

97 *Repeated complaints against coast guards* See, for instance, *Boston Gazette*, July 6–July 13, 1724, reprinted in Baer, *British Piracy in the Golden Age*, vol. 1; Governor Sir N. Lawes to the Council of Trade and Plantations, CSPC, June 12, 1721, Item 523, vol. 32 (1720–21), 334–35; Governor Sir N. Lawes to the Council of Trade and Plantations, CSPC, May 18, 1722, Item 142, vol. 33 (1722–23), 69–70; Captain Beverley, of Virginia, to the Governor of Jamaica, CSPC, Item 10 ii, vol. 30 (1717–18), 6–7; Captain Brathwaite to Governor Hart, CSPC, February 14, 1723, Item 496 i, vol. 33 (1722–23), 240; Deposition of John Jones, CSPC, September 15, 1724, Item 258 iv, vol. 34

(1724–25), 142–43; Governor Hart to the Council of Trade and Plantations, CSPC, July 12, 1724, Item 260, vol. 34 (1724–25), 143–57; Anonymous Paper on the Sugar Trade, CSPC, July 22, 1724, Item 276, vol. 34 (1724–25), 168–70; Deposition of John Kenney, CSPC, December 10, 1716, Item 425 i, vol. 29 (1716–17), 230–31; Governor Sir N. Lawes to the Council of Trade and Plantations, CSPC, January 31, 1719, Item 34, vol. 31 (1719–20), 12–21; Governor Sir N. Lawes to the Council of Trade and Plantations, CSPC, November 13, 1720, Item 288, vol. 32 (1720–21), 193–95; Lt. Governor Spotswood to the Council of Trade and Plantations, CSPC, May 31, 1721, Item 513, vol. 32 (1720–21), 326–29; Lt. Governor Hope to the Council of Trade and Plantations, CSPC, August 21, 1724, Item 338, vol. 34 (1724–25), 207–8; Deposition of Richard Thompson, CSPC, April 22, 1725, Item 574 v, vol. 34 (1724–25), 359–60; Governor Phenney to the Duke of Newcastle, CSPC, April 16, 1725, Item 574, vol. 34 (1724–25), 359–61; Lt. Governor Pulleine to the Council of Trade and Plantations, CSPC, April 22, 1714, Item 651, vol. 27 (1712–14), 332–34; Sir N. Lawes to the Council of Trade and Plantations, CSPC, August 29, 1717, Item 54, vol. 30 (1717–18), 17–18; Governor Hart to the Council of Trade and Plantations, CSPC, April 9, 1723, Item 496, vol. 33 (1722–23), 238–41; Council of Trade and Plantations to the Duke of Newcastle, CSPC, July 24, 1724, Item 291, vol. 34 (1724–25), 172–85; Governor Sir N. Lawes to the Council of Trade and Plantations, CSPC, July 9, 1722, Item 215, vol. 33 (1722–23), 106–8; Petition of the Merchants of London, CSPC, May 20, 1726, Item 152, vol. 35 (1726–27), 74–75.

97 *Government-sanctioned cruisers limited in viciousness* English privateers, for example, were instructed "that no Person or Persons taken or surprised by you in any Ship or Vessel as aforesaid, though known to be of the Enemies side, be in cold Blood killed, maimed, or by Torture or Cruelty in humanly treated contrary to the Common Usage or Just Permission of War." See *Arraignment, Tryal, and Condemnation, of Capt. John Quelch*, 21. Similar instructions were most likely also issued to Spanish and French privateers and coast guard vessels.

97 *Government-sanctioned cruisers couldn't slaughter crew after quarter requested* If they did and their victims' government captured them, they could be tried and hanged as pirates. See, for instance, Captain Thomas Southey, *Chronological History of the West Indies,* 3 vols. (London: Printed for Longman, Rees, Orme, Brown, and Greene, 1827), 2: 225. Alternatively, in principle at least, their own government might punish them.

98 *No Quarter should be given* Snelgrave, *A New Account of Some Parts of Guinea,* 206.

98 *asking them if they would stand* *Boston News-Letter,* June 9–June 16, 1718.

98 *black Flag with a Death's Head* *White-hall Evening Post,* October 18–October 21, 1718, reprinted in Baer, *British Piracy in the Golden Age,* vol. 1.

99 *to surrender on penalty* Quoted in Pringle, *Jolly Roger,* 124.

99 *Everybody knew what these images* Konstam, *History of Pirates,* 100.

99 *had [a victim's] Ears cut off* Johnson, *GHP,* 335.

99 *and because at first they shewed* Ibid., 324.

99 *mentaining an obstinate defence* News from Barbadoes, Antigua and Jamaica–Sent April 25, 1721 from Governor Bennett to the Council of Trade and Plantations, CSPC, February 18, 1721, Item 463 iii, vol. 32 (1720–21), 294–96.

99 *after a desperate resistance* Johnson, *GHP,* 118.

99 *England was inclined to favour* Ibid., 121.

100 *Captain England having sided* Ibid., 122. For other examples of pirates' policy of harsh punishment for resistance, see, for instance, Extracts from Letters Received by the East India Company, February 17, 1698, Item 235, vol. 16 (1697–98), 112–14.

100 *observe strictly that Maxim* Snelgrave, *A New Account of Some Parts of Guinea,* 219.

100 *Good Quarters to be given* *Boston News-Letter,* August 1–August 8, 1723.

100 *that have made Resistance* Ibid., June 16–June 23, 1718. See also Cordingly who notes that "in the great majority of cases merchant ships surrendered without a fight when attacked by pirates." *Under the Black Flag*, 121.

100 *deliberately publicized* Pringle, *Jolly Roger*, 113.

100 *Supposing him to be one* Johnson, *GHP*, 226.

101 *Fearing the Consequence* Ibid., 312.

101 *He threaten'd all with present Death* Ibid., 323.

101 *sail'd away down the Coast* Ibid., 371.

102 *under a Black Flag, flagrantly* *A Full and Exact Account, of the Tryal of all the Pyrates, Lately Taken by Captain Ogle*, 5.

102 *who is now cruising among* Governor Hart to Mr. Popple, CSPC, November 30, 1726, Item 360, vol. 35 (1726–27), 179–80.

103 *When he finds any vessel* Ibid.

103 *To intimidate . . . frequently hoisted* Petition of the Merchants of London, CSPC, May 20, 1726, Item 152, vol. 35 (1726–27), 74–75.

104 *as dangerous as it now is* Anonymous Paper on the Sugar Trade, CSPC, July 22, 1724, Item 276, vol. 34 (1724–25), 168–70.

Chapter 5. Walk the Plank

107 *No record of 17th- or 18th-century pirates making captives walk the plank* There is, however, one nineteenth-century case of pirates forcing an individual to "walk the plank." See Cordingly, *Under the Black Flag*, 131.

107 *to whom it was a sport* John Barnard, *Ashton's Memorial: An History of the Strange Adventures, and Signal Deliverances of, Philip Ashton* . . . (Boston: Printed for Samuel Gerrish, 1715), 7.

107 *It is impossible to particularly recount* Johnson, *GHP*, 216.

108 *Like their Patron* Ibid., 334.

108 *I scorn to do any one a Mischief* Ibid., 587.

109   *Crewmembers hid valuables from pirates*   Such valuables included, for instance, the "Rings and Buckles" the cook on one of Roberts's prizes stashed away. See *A Full and Exact Account, of the Tryal of all the Pyrates, Lately Taken by Captain Ogle*, 14. Hiding places varied. When merchant ship captain Radford tried to hide "350 Ounces of Silver" from pirate Paul Williams, for instance, he "buried [it] in his [ship's] Ballast." See *Boston News-Letter*, June 24–July 1, 1717.

109   *hung eleven thousand moydores*   Governor Hart to the Council of Trade and Plantations, CSPC, March 25, 1724, Item 102, vol. 34 (1724–25), 71–73.

110   *all their Papers were perused*   Johnson, *GHP*, 88.

110   *Barbarous and Inhumane Wretches*   *An Account of the Behaviour, Dying Speeches, and Execution of Mr. John Murphey . . .* (London: Printed for T. Crownfield, 1696), reprinted in Baer, *British Piracy in the Golden Age*, vol. 4.

112   *making their Hellish Inventions*   *The Tryals of Sixteen Persons for Piracy, &c . . .* (Boston: Joseph Edwards, 1726), 14, reprinted in Baer, *British Piracy in the Golden Age*, vol. 3.

112   *Lowe cutt off*   Governor Hart to the Council of Trade and Plantations, CSPC, March 25, 1724, Item 102, vol. 34 (1724–25), 71–73.

112   *They cut and whiped*   *American Weekly Mercury* June 13, 1723, quoted in Dow and Edmonds, *Pirates of the New England Coast*, 206.

112   *bound [one captive's] hands*   Deposition of Edward North, CSPC, May 22, 1718, Item 551 ii, vol. 30 (1717–18), 263.

113   *threatened to sink*   Deposition of Robert Leonard, CSPC, February 24, 1718/19, Item 797 vi, vol. 30 (1717–18), 412.

113   *placing lighted matches*   Deposition of John Wickstead, CSPC, Item 754 iv, vol. 33 (1722–23), 365.

113   *threatened to shoot*   Information of John Stephenson, HCA, 1/55, fol. 6, 1721.

113 *barbarously used ... Mac Clenan* *Boston News-Letter*, August 11–August 18, 1718.

113 *they strappado'd him* Exquemelin, *Buccaneers of America*, 200. See also, John Style to 'the Principal Secretary of State, Whitehall,' CSPC, January 4, 1670, Item 138, vol. 7 (1669–74), 49–51.

113 *they tied long cords* Exquemelin, *Buccaneers of America*, 150.

114 *being possessed of a devil's fury* Ibid., 107.

114 *squeezed their [prisoners'] joints* Quoted in Grey, *Pirates of the Eastern Seas*, 318.

114 *The Manner of a Sweat* *British Journal*, August 8, 1724, reprinted in Baer, *British Piracy in the Golden Age*, vol. 1.

114 *was by some set bare* John Style to 'the Principal Secretary of State, Whitehall,' CSPC, January 4, 1670, Item 138, vol. 7 (1669–74), 49–51.

115 *learned from some* Barnard, *Ashton's Memorial*, 7.

115 *the Quarter-master came forward* *A Full and Exact Account, of the Tryal of all the Pyrates, Lately Taken by Captain Ogle*, 14.

116 *In the Commonwealth of Pyrates* Johnson, *GHP*, 85. See also, 121.

116 *good Policy ... to prevent her* Ibid., 298.

116 *bloody, merciless ruffian; diabolical disposition; dread to fall into* Increase Moseley, *A Narration of the Captivity of John Fillmore and His Escape from the Pirates* (Bennington, VT: Haswell and Russell, 1790), reprinted in John Richard Stephens, ed., *Captured by Pirates: 22 Firsthand Accounts of Murder and Mayhem on the High Seas* (Cambria, CA: Fern Canyon, 1996), 355, 358, 354.

117 *Something about [the pirates'] temper* Baer, *British Piracy in the Golden Age*, vol. 1, 282.

117 *The Pyrates gave us an account* *American Weekly Mercury*, June 13, 1723, quoted in Dow and Edmonds, *Pirates of the New England Coast*, 206.

118 *They have no Thoughts of ever* British Journal, August 22, 1724, reprinted in Baer, *British Piracy in the Golden Age*, vol. 1.

118 *often saying they would not go* Boston News-Letter, August 15–August 22, 1720, reprinted in Baer, *British Piracy in the Golden Age*, vol. 1.

118 *a merry Life and a short one* Johnson, GHP, 244.

118 *as to his part, he hoped he should* Snelgrave, *A New Account of Some Parts of Guinea*, 210.

119 *Teach called for a Glass* Boston News-Letter, February 23–March 2, 1719, reprinted in Baer, *British Piracy in the Golden Age*, vol. 1.

119 *with madness and rage* Ibid., August 15–August 22, 1720, reprinted in Baer, *British Piracy in the Golden Age*, vol. 1. See also, *Tryals of Thirty-Six Persons for Piracy*.

119 *every Thing that please them not* British Journal, August 8, 1724, reprinted in Baer, *British Piracy in the Golden Age*, vol. 1.

120 *in Possession of the Devil; laughing at the very* An Account of the Behaviour and Last Dying Speeches of the Six Pirates . . . (Boston: Printed for Nicholas Boone, 1704), reprinted in Baer, *British Piracy in the Golden Age*, vol. 4; Colman, *It is a Fearful Thing to Fall into the Hands of the Living God*, 22.

120 *In ravaging the Vessel* Boston News-Letter, August 4–August 11, 1718; reprinted in Baer, *British Piracy in the Golden Age*, vol. 1.

120 *sometimes to prevent giving Intelligence* Johnson, GHP, 134.

120 *answer'd, it was for fun* A Full and Exact Account, of the Tryal of all the Pyrates, Lately Taken by Captain Ogle, 71.

120 *declared themselves to live* Trials of Eight Persons, 6.

120 *notorious pyrate better known* Petition of the Council and Assembly of the Settlements in South Carolina to the King, CSPC, February 3, 1720, Item 541, vol. 31 (1719–20), 332–43.

120 *his Beard . . . did not little* Johnson, GHP, 84.

121 *Captain Teach, assumed the Cognomen* Ibid., 84–85.

121 *There is no doubt that Blackbeard* Robert E. Lee, *Blackbeard the Pirate: A Reappraisal of His Life and Times* (Winston-Salem: John F. Blair, 1974), 22.

121 *He is a middle-sized man* CSPC, May 9, 1700, Item 400 ii, vol. 18 (1700), 236.

123 *Blackbeard never had to kill anyone* Konstam, *Blackbeard*, 157.

123 *murther'd the French Governor* Weekly Journal, July 29, 1721, reprinted in Baer, *British Piracy in the Golden Age*, vol. 1.

123 *irreconcilable Aversion; let none of that Country* Johnson, *GHP*, 326, 328.

124 *taking out his Heart* Boston News-Letter, June 20–June 27, 1723, reprinted in Baer, *British Piracy in the Golden Age*, vol. 1.

124 *Spriggs's reason for revenge same as Low's* Dow and Edmonds, *Pirates of the New England Coast*, 282.

124 *burn his Ship because she belonged* Boston News-Letter, June 9–June 16, 1718, reprinted in Baer, *British Piracy in the Golden Age*, vol. 1. See also, *Tryals of Major Stede Bonnet*, 45.

124 *if the Prisoners [in Boston] suffered* Suffolk Court Files, fragment 99, Trial of Thomas Davis, October 28, 1717, contained in Jameson, *Privateering and Piracy in the Colonial Period*, 308.

124 *manned partly with English* Johnson, *GHP*, 335.

125 *The Pirates seem much enraged* Boston News-Letter, August 15–August 22, 1720, reprinted in Baer, *British Piracy in the Golden Age*, vol. 1.

125 *They us'd . . . barbarously, because* Johnson, *GHP*, 217.

125 *when any Ship belonging* Ibid., 215.

125 *They beat the Bermudians* Deposition of Samuel Cooper, CSPC, May 24, 1718, Item 551 i, vol. 30 (1717–18), 263. See also, Deposition of Nathaniel Catling, CSPC, May 17, 1718, Item 551 v, vol. 30 (1717–18), 263–64.

125 *expected to be joined* Lt. Governor Spotswood to the Council of Trade and Plantations, CSPC, May 31, 1721, Item 513, vol. 32 (1720–21), 326–29.

125 *barbarous wretches can be moved* Col. Spotswood to the Council of Trade and Plantations, CSPC, June 16, 1724, Item 210, vol. 34 (1724–25), 112–20.

126 *endeavour'd my destruction* Lt. Governor Hope to the Duke of Newcastle, CSPC, February 2, 1725, Item 491, vol. 34 (1724–25), 320–21.

126 *fear'd that this very execution* Lt. Governor Hope to the Council of Trade and Plantations, CSPC, January 14, 1724, Item 13, vol. 34 (1724–25), 9–17. See also, Rediker, *Villains of all Nations*, 96.

126 *they pretend one reason* William Snelgrave to Humphrey Morice, August 1, 1719, Humphrey Morice Papers from the Bank of England, Slave Trade Papers and Journals (Marlboro, Wiltshire, England: Adam Mathew Publications), quoted in Rediker, *Villains of All Nations*, 89.

128 *examin[e] the Men concerning* Johnson, GHP, 338.

128 *whole Salt Fleet* Ibid., 582.

128 *Ah, Captain Skinner!* Ibid., 115. See also, *Boston News-Letter*, June 20–June 27, 1723; reprinted in Baer, *British Piracy in the Golden Age*, vol. 1.

129 *could not spare using* A Full and Exact Account, of the Tryal of all the Pyrates, Lately Taken by Captain Ogle, 44.

129 *endeavoured to beat; Safe provided none* Snelgrave, *A New Account of Some Parts of Guinea*, 207, 208.

129 *did intreat earnestly* British Journal, August 8, 1724, reprinted in Baer, *British Piracy in the Golden Age*, vol. 1.

129 *he was an honest Fellow* Boston News-Letter, November 14–November 21, 1720, reprinted in Baer, *British Piracy in the Golden Age*, vol. 1.

129   *belonging to Carolina*   Johnson, *GHP*, 597.

130   *They gave the ship taken*   *Trials of Eight Persons*, 23.

130   *it is a common practice*   Alexander Spotswood, *The Official Letters of Alexander Spotswood*, 2 vols. (Richmond: Virginia Historical Society, 1882–85) (May 20, 1720), vol. 2, 340.

130   *took what they wanted*   CSPC, May 31, 1720, Item 33 i, vol. 32 (1720–21), 18–19.

130   *ma[k]e a Reparation*   *An Account of the Conduct and Proceedings of the Late John Gow*, 23.

130   *The far greater hazard*   Morris, *Government and Labor in Early America*, 271.

131   *Fury of unreasonable; gave you the Liveliest*   Barnard, *Ashton's Memorial*, 64, 62.

132   *Instigated by the Devil; the Folly and Madness*   *Tryals of Five Persons for Piracy and Robbery* (Boston: S. Gerrish, 1726), 5, reprinted in Baer, *British Piracy in the Golden Age*, vol. 3; Johnson, *GHP*, 219.

132   *a Dish of Candles*   *British Journal*, August 8, 1724. See also, *Boston News-Letter*, February 4–February 11, 1725, both reprinted in Baer, *British Piracy in the Golden Age*, vol. 1.

133   *being a greazy Fellow*   Johnson, *GHP*, 323. See also, *Weekly Journal*, August 31, 1723, and *Boston News-Letter*, February 4–February 11, 1725, reprinted in Baer, *British Piracy in the Golden Age*, vol. 1; *Tryals of Thirty-Six Persons*.

133   *threaten'd to hang*   Johnson, *GHP*, 324.

Chapter 6. Pressing Pegleg

135   *pirates had no difficulty*   Cordingly, *Under the Black Flag*, 122. See also, Rankin, *The Golden Age of Piracy*, 34.

135   *the People were generally glad*   Snelgrave, *A New Account of Some Parts of Guinea*, 203.

136   *might hazard, and, in Time*   Johnson, *GHP*, 248.

136   *to over-throw the pyratical*   Ibid., 346. See also, *American Weekly Mercury*, July 7–July 14, 1725, reprinted in Baer, *British Piracy in the Golden Age*, vol. 1.

136   *Forced men overwhelmed William Fly*   See *Boston News-Letter*, June 30–July 7, 1726.

136   *a Man and a Woman*   *Daily Courant*, August 31, 1720, reprinted in Baer, *British Piracy in the Golden Age*, vol. 1.

137   *on the Grand Comanos*   *Boston News-Letter*, April 4–April 11, 1723.

137   *surrender'd himself to the Government*   *An Account of the Conduct and Proceedings of the Late John Gow*, 32.

137   *Forced men less willing to give their all*   In some cases it appears pirates allowed forced men to receive shares like everyone else. However, even if a coerced sailor received a share of the plunder, this payment was obviously less than he was willing to take the job for. If it weren't, he wouldn't need to be compelled. So, any forced sailor was always earning less than he was willing to pirate for and therefore had less incentive to "give his all" as a pirate.

137   *was for giving Chase*   Johnson, *GHP*, 601.

137   *as a Reason against*   *An Account of the Conduct and Proceedings of the Late John Gow*, 24.

137   *Low tried persuasion to recruit Ashton*   Pirate captain John Phillips similarly attempted persuasion before force to recruit a captive he desired. As the captive put it, "To induce me to join them they used more arguments of a persuasive than a compulsory nature." See Moseley, *A Narration of the Captivity of John Fillmore*.

137   *according to the Pirates usual custom; asked the Old Question*   Barnard, *Ashton's Memorial*, 2, 3–4.

138   *I fear they will soon multiply*   Lt. Governor Bennett to the Council of Trade and Plantations, CSPC, May 31, 1718, Item 551, vol. 30 (1717–18), 260–64.

138 *strength increases daily*   Spotswood, *Official Letters*, May 30, 1717, vol. 2, 249.

139 *This was dun . . . without*   Deposition of Jeremiah Tay, July 6, 1694, Suffolk Court Files, No. 3033, Paper 6, reprinted in Jameson, *Privateering and Piracy in the Colonial Period*, 150.

139 *it was the Custome among*   Trial Records of Thomas Davis, October 28, 1717, Suffolk Court Files, fragment 99, reprinted in Jameson, *Privateering and Piracy in the Colonial Period*, 308. See also, Trial Records of Simon van Vorst October 1717, Suffolk Court Files, No. 10923, reprinted in Jameson, *Privateering and Piracy in the Colonial Period*, 304; Johnson, *GHP*, 170.

139 *more would have enter'd; the Pyrates despised*   A Full and Exact Account, of the Tryal of all the Pyrates, Lately Taken by Captain Ogle, 50, 51.

139 *that he might have none*   Barnard, *Ashton's Memorial*, 3.

139 *none but Sailors*   A Full and Exact Account, of the Tryal of all the Pyrates, Lately Taken by Captain Ogle, 13.

139 *which Country Folks*   Ibid., 37.

140 *forced on board all Carpenters*   Johnson, *GHP*, 489.

140 *a Light Pair of Heels*   Ibid., 168.

141 *because he could play*   Tryals of Thirty-Six Persons.

141 *Doubtless 'tis possible*   An Account of the Conduct and Proceedings of the Late John Gow, 14.

141 *were at first forc'd*   British Journal, August 22, 1724, reprinted in Baer, *British Piracy in the Golden Age*, vol. 1.

141 *forced at first . . . since had done*   A Full and Exact Account, of the Tryal of all the Pyrates, Lately Taken by Captain Ogle, 40.

141 *drubb'd . . . Williams that he might*   Johnson, *GHP*, 601.

142 *In the Beginning*   Ibid., 194.

142 *begg'd of Roberts*   A Full and Exact Account, of the Tryal of all the Pyrates, Lately Taken by Captain Ogle, 28.

142 *that they were forc'd men*   Johnson, *GHP*, 260.

142 *would, have shot them*   Ibid., 260.

143 *Anti-piracy legislation*   My discussion of antipiracy law is based largely on Joel Baer's excellent account of antipiracy legislation in *British Piracy in the Golden Age* and *Pirates of the British Isles* (Stroud, UK: Tempus, 2005).

143 *Offenses at Sea Act*   "Offenses at Sea Act," 28 Hen. VI, c. 15.

143 *1684 ruling on colonial jurisdiction*   Baer, *Pirates of the British Isles*, 25.

144 *An Act for the More Effectual Suppression of Piracy*   "An Act for the More Effectual Suppression of Piracy," 11–12 Will. III, c.7.

145 *1700 Act made permanent in 1719*   "Perpetuation of Acts, etc.," 6 Geo. I, c.19.

145 *Quotations from An Act for the More Effectual Suppression of Piracy*   "An ACT made at *Westminster* in the Kingdom of *Great Britain* in the Eleventh and Twelfth Years of the Reign of King *William* III," reprinted in Baer, *British Piracy in the Golden Age*, vol. 3.

146 *for every Commander*   *Boston News-Letter*, December 2–December 9, 1717. See also, *Boston News-Letter*, February 9–February 16, 1719, both reprinted in Baer, *British Piracy in the Golden Age*, vol. 1.

146 *like Dogs to their Vomits*   *Tryals of Major Stede Bonnet*, 11.

146 *reduc'd above a thousand*   Woodes Rogers's Petition to the King, CO, 23/12, 1727.

147 *submitted to His Majesty's Act*   "General Officers of the Army" Petition to the King on Behalf of Woodes Rogers, CO, 23/12, 1726.

147 *Rogers's estimate of pirates who return to trade*   Cyrus H. Karraker, *Piracy Was a Business* (Rindge, NH: Richard R. Smith, 1953), 181.

147 *any wise trade with any pirate* "An Act for the More Effectual Suppressing of Piracy," 8 Geo. I, c. 24.

147 *the neglect of the Commanders* Governor Sir. N. Lawes to the Council of Trade and Plantations, CSPC, June 21, 1718, Item 566, vol. 30 (1717–18), 270–72.

148 *People are easily led* Spotswood, *Official Letters*, May 26, 1719, vol. 2, 319. See also, Governor the Earl of Bellomont to the Council of Trade and Plantations, CSPC, Oct 24, 1699, Item 890, vol. 17 (1699), 486–494; Governor the Earl of Bellomont to Council of Trade and Plantations, CSCP, May 18, 1698, Item 473, vol. 16 (1697–98), 224–29; Information of Henry Watson, CSPC, Aug 25, 1698, Item 770, vol. 16 (1697–98), 403.

148 *willing to be forced* Johnson, *GHP*, 65.

148 *given to Reading* *A Full and Exact Account, of the Tryal of all the Pyrates, Lately Taken by Captain Ogle*, 61. Though, in fairness to this fellow, this character evidence was presented to support the claim he was forced.

149 *the plea of Force* Johnson, *GHP*, 248.

149 *The court acquitted* Cordingly, *Under the Black Flag*, 233.

149 *The three Circumstances* Johnson, *GHP*, 249–50.

149 *there must go an Intention* Ibid., 449.

150 *forced on Board ... desired one* *A Full and Exact Account, of the Tryal of all the Pyrates, Lately Taken by Captain Ogle*, 14.

150 *Sailors willing to place ads for fellow seamen* See, for example, *Boston News-Letter*, April 7–April 14, 1718; *Boston News-Letter*, August 22–August 29, 1720; *Boston News-Letter*, August 7–August 14, 1721; *New-England Courant*, May 13–May 20, 1723; *Boston Gazette*, September 30–October 7, 1723; *Boston Gazette*, May 10–May 17, 1725; *Boston News-Letter*, November 25–December 2, 1725; *Boston Gazette*, December [?], 1725; *Boston News-Letter*, August 1–August 8, 1723, all reprinted in Baer, *British Piracy in the Golden Age*, vol. 1.

150 *gave all his Wages*   A Full and Exact Account, of the Tryal of all the Pyrates, Lately Taken by Captain Ogle, 21.

150 *the Quarter-Master of the Pirate*   Boston News-Letter, July 2–July 9, 1722, reprinted in Baer, *British Piracy in the Golden Age*, vol. 1.

150 *ordered ... to declare upon*   Ibid., October 10–October 18, 1723.

151 *Their request was granted*   Pringle, *Jolly Roger*, 115.

151 *whether they were willing*   A Full and Exact Account, of the Tryal of all the Pyrates, Lately Taken by Captain Ogle, 50.

151 *the pretended constraint*   Johnson, GHP, 248.

152 *this ruse often worked*   Pringle, *Jolly Roger*, 115.

152 *was a forced Man ... lamented his Wife*   A Full and Exact Account, of the Tryal of all the Pyrates, Lately Taken by Captain Ogle, 27.

152 *I was a Prisoner, Sir*   Johnson, GHP, 261. See also, 271, 274, 652–53.

152 *several times [he] wished*   A Full and Exact Account, of the Tryal of all the Pyrates, Lately Taken by Captain Ogle, 12.

153 *Plea of constraint*   Tryals of Thirty-Six Persons.

153 *That the said Bellamy's; at that time [Bellamy's crew]; be hanged up*   Trials of Eight Persons, 12, 11, 14.

153 *that Hackney Defense*   Tryals of Sixteen Persons, 14.

153 *said he was a forced Man*   Tryals of Thirty-Six Persons.

153 *Swetser's defense was an ad of force*   For Swetser's ad, see *Boston News-Letter*, June 11–June 18, 1722.

Chapter 7. Equal Pay for Equal Prey

156 *Blacks without political and other rights until even later*   While, officially, the Fifteenth Amendment (1870) granted blacks the right to vote, various state practices, particularly in the South, effectively denied black citizens voting rights until the 1965 Voting

Rights Act, which empowered the Justice Department to monitor the treatment of black voters.

157 *the impression is that* W. Jeffrey Bolster, *Black Jacks: African American Seamen in the Age of Sail* (Cambridge: Harvard University Press, 1997), 13.

157 *a resolute Fellow* Johnson, *GHP*, 82.

157 *Percentage of blacks in pirate crews* Kinkor, "Black Men under the Black Flag," 200.

159 *The pirates shared the same prejudices* Cordingly, *Under the Black Flag*, 16.

161 *Some black pirates carried arms and fought* Kinkor, "Black Men under the Black Flag," 201.

161 *Black pirates fought alongside Blackbeard* *Boston News-Letter*, February 23–March 2, 1719, reprinted in Baer, *British Piracy in the Golden Age*, vol. 1. See also, *Arraignment, Tryal, and Condemnation, of Capt. John Quelch*, 8.

161 *Negro, who had his Leg* Ayres, *Voyages and Adventures of Capt. Barth. Sharp*, 70. Consistent with pirates' opportunistic racial tolerance discussed above, however, this same crew, one of its members remarked, "ke[pt] . . . Negroes to do our drudgery," 79.

161 *This fellow . . . had been a Slave* Ibid., 71.

162 *a Negro Man* *Boston News-Letter*, September 5–September 12, 1728.

162 *Black crewmen made up* Rediker, *Villains of All Nations*, 54.

162 *the first integrated national* David Hackett Fischer, *Washington's Crossing* (New York: Oxford University Press, 2004), 21–22.

162 *Negroe . . . I was abaft* *Tryals of Major Stede Bonnet*, 29.

163 *one of the [pirate] Men* Ibid., 30.

163 *as for the negro men they are grown* Lt. Governor Bennett to the Council of Trade and Plantations, CSPC, May 31, 1718, Item 551, vol. 30 (1717–18), 260–64.

163 *the said Negroes . . . being taken*   Quoted in Kinkor, "Black Men under the Black Flag," 203.

164 *a hundred & twelve white men*   Information of Richard Moore, HCA, 1/55, fol. 96, 1724.

164 *Rewards and incentives therefore appear*   Kinkor, "Black Men under the Black Flag," 200.

165 *Dispersed costs of pirate conscripts*   One of these costs, recall from chapter 6, was pirate conscripts or slaves deliberately "giving little" in battle. This cost of slave labor encouraged pirates to rely on voluntary, free labor instead. In a similar vein, warships in classical antiquity were typically rowed by free men although slaves were available for this purpose. Disgruntled and disarmed galley slaves would have been liabilities to those relying on their labor. For a discussion of galley slavery and its introduction by Mediterranean states at the end of the fifteenth century, see David Friedman, "Making Sense of English Law Enforcement in the Eighteenth Century," *University of Chicago Law School Roundtable* (spring/summer 1995).

167 *Indian prisoner helped overtake Phillips's crew*   *Boston Gazette*, April 27–May 4, 1724, reprinted in Baer, *British Piracy in the Golden Age*, vol. 1.

167 *it not have been for him our plot*   Moseley, *A Narration of the Captivity of John Fillmore*, 365.

167 *Black prisoners helped overtake Grinnaway's crew*   *Boston News-Letter*, August 4–August 11, 1718, reprinted in Baer, *British Piracy in the Golden Age*, vol. 1. For an example of black and white prisoners attempting to escape their pirate captors together, see *A Full and Exact Account, of the Tryal of all the Pyrates, Lately Taken by Captain Ogle*, 56.

171 *Scholars suggested pirates community of homosexuals*   In addition to those mentioned below, see also, for instance, Nigel Cawthorne, *A History of Pirates: Blood and Thunder on the High Seas* (London: Arcturus, 2003); Clinton V. Black, *Pirates of the West Indies* (Cambridge: Cambridge University Press, 1989); David Mitchell, *Pirates* (New York: Dial Press, 1976).

171 *Burg's argument about pirate sexuality* For additional discussion of pirates and homosexuality, see also, Hans Turley, *Rum, Sodomy, and the Lash: Pirate Sexuality, and Masculine Identity* (New York: New York University Press, 1999).

171 *Homosexuality not confined to landlubbers* On the extremely low incidence of homosexual activity in the Royal Navy, for instance, see David Cordingly, *Seafaring Women: Adventures of Pirate Queens, Female Stowaways, and Sailors' Wives* (New York: Random House, 2007), 145.

172 *to spend their Money* Boston News-Letter, August 15–August 22, 1720, reprinted in Baer, *British Piracy in the Golden Age*, vol. 1.

172 *Bonny and Read two of only four female pirates* The other two female pirates of the golden age, not discussed here, are Mary Harley and Mary Crickett.

172 *the Two Women, Prisoners* Tryals of Captain Jack Rackam.

173 *The women, Spinsters* Governor Sir N. Lawes to the Council of Trade and Plantations, CSPC, June 12, 1721, Item 523 i, vol. 32 (1720–21), 334–35.

174 *Bonny and Read disguised because of rules prohibiting women* Though, it seems both women dropped the charade and dressed as women after some point when they were among their fellow crew members. Only when actively pirating did they revert to men's dress.

174 *When a man has finished* Exquemelin, *Buccaneers of America*, 55.

Chapter 8. The Secrets of Pirate Management

178 *It is not from the benevolence* Smith, *Wealth of Nations*, 26–27.

179 *had a little Captain* I owe this turn of phrase to *The Atlantic*, which first wrote that my research on pirates "suggests that the American system of checks and balances appears to have a little Captain Morgan in it." See *The Atlantic*, "Democrats of the Caribbean," October 2007, 39.

179 *Greed ... is right.* Michael Douglas as Gordon Gekko, *Wall Street*, 1987.

182 *Kingsley considered pirate ship shining example of a workers' cooperative* Mitchell, *Pirates*, 9. On the ostensible socialism of pirate society, see also, Karraker, *Piracy Was a Business*, 55.

184 *Privateers required different managerial organization* For a discussion of how particular similarities and differences in the economic contexts privateers and pirates faced resulted in corresponding similarities and differences in their internal organization, see Peter T. Leeson, "An-*arrgh*-chy: The Law and Economic of Pirate Organization," *Journal of Political Economy* 115 (2007): 1049–94.

186 *Pirates had local knowledge* On the importance of local knowledge for economic decision making and government's dearth of such knowledge, see F. A. Hayek, "The Use of Knowledge in Society," *American Economic Review* 35 (1945): 519–30.

187 *Study of ADA's effect on employment* Daron Acemoglu and Joshua D. Angrist, "Consequences of Employment Protection? The Case of the Americans with Disabilities Act," *Journal of Political Economy* 109 (2001): 915–57.

190 *Firms invest to capture legislative process* On rent seeking and its destructive consequences, see Gordon Tullock, *Government Failure: A Primer in Public Choice* (Washington, D.C.: Cato Institute, 2002).

191 *Study of spending on political capture in 1985* David N. Laband and John P. Sophocleus, "An Estimate of Resource Expenditure on Transfer Activity in the United States," *Quarterly Journal of Economics* 107 (1992): 959–83. According to Laband and Sophocleus, these expenditures constitute "estimated investments (in 1985) by private parties to influence direct and indirect public sector transfers" and include spending on lobbyists, on political action committees, and individual contributions to political campaigns (966).

191 *Sum spent on lobbying in 2007* OpenSecrets.org. http://www .opensecrets.org/lobby/index.php. Accessed June 10, 2008.

192 *once word leads out* Cary Elwes as Dread Pirate Roberts, *The Princess Bride*, 1987.

Epilogue. Omnipresent Economics

194 *All human behavior susceptible to economic analysis* One of the first economists to point to the universal applicability of economics was the great Austrian economist, Ludwig von Mises. See Ludwig von Mises, *Human Action: A Treatise on Economics* (New Haven: Yale University Press, 1949).

Postscript. You Can't Keep a Sea Dog Down

197 *Rogers's effect on pirate base at New Providence* Colin Woodard, *The Republic of Pirates* (New York: Harcourt, 2007).

198 *Ineffective naval commanders replaced in 1721* Pringle, *Jolly Roger*, 263.

198 *Regulations inhibit pirate-hunting navy ships* Peter Earle, *The Pirate Wars* (New York: St. Martin's Press, 2003), 185–86.

199 *Jacobite threat and government response* N.A.M Rodger, *The Command of the Ocean: A Naval History of Britain, 1649–1815* (New York: W.W. Norton, 2004), 226–29.

200 *Government repeals inhibiting regulations* Earle, *Pirate Wars*, 187–88.

201 *Lowther's suicide* Johnson, *GHP*, 317.

201 *French government takes Low in 1725* Rediker, *Villains of All Nations*, 172.

201 *within the Flux* *Tryals of Thirty-Six Persons for Piracy.*

201 *Declining pirate population, 1720, 1723, 1726* Cordingly, *Under the Black Flag*, 203.

202 *Number of pirates hanged, 1716–1726 and 1723* Ibid., 227.

202 *Battle between Ogle and Roberts in thunderstorm* Ibid., 215.

202 *not with a bang* T. S. Eliot, *Poems: 1909–1925* (London: Faber and Gwyer, 1925).

203 *South China Sea pirate population* See Dian H. Murray, "Chinese Pirates," in *Pirates: Terror on the High Seas*, 222; Konstam, *History of Pirates*, 174.

203 *Recent resurgence of piracy* For discussions of modern piracy, on which this account is largely based, see John S. Burnett, *Dangerous Waters: Modern Piracy and Terror on the High Seas* (New York: Plume, 2002); Jack A. Gottschalk and Brian P. Flanagan, *Jolly Roger with an Uzi: The Rise and Threat of Modern Piracy* (Annapolis, MD: U.S. Naval Institute Press, 2000); William Langewiesche, *The Outlaw Sea: A World of Freedom, Chaos, and Crime* (New York: North Point, 2004). See also, Roger Middleton, *Piracy in Somalia* (London: Chatham House/Royal Institute of International Affairs, 2008).

204 *Ransom for ship hijacked in Gulf of Aden* Abdiqani Hassan, "Somali Pirates Free German Ship after Ransom," Thomson Reuters, July 9, 2008.

204 *A few modern pirate crews closer to societies* On the larger size of some modern pirate crews, see, for instance, Mary Harper, "Life in Somalia's Pirate Town," BBC News, September 18, 2008.

204 *Somali pirates' booty division and social insurance* "Somalie–Pas de répit chez les pirates," Le Devoir.com, September 20–21, 2008. See also, Jonathon Gatehouse, "Blackbeard Lives," *Maclean's Magazine*, October 8, 2008.

205 *Modern pirate code* Thierry Leveque, "Somali Pirates Tell French Police of 'Sea Militia,'" Thomson Reuters, April 17, 2008. Some Somali pirates have even taken to describing themselves as "gentlemen who work in the ocean," echoing eighteenth-century sea dogs who sometimes called themselves "gentlemen of fortune." See Paul Salopek, "Off the Lawless Coast of Somalia, Questions of Who is Pirating Who," *Chicago Tribune*, October 10, 2008.

Where This Book Found Its Buried Treasure: A Note on Sources

207 *diffidence ... in recording* Gosse, *History of Piracy*, foreword.

207 *Proportion of foremastmen who could sign name* Earle, *Sailors*, 20.

207 *Description of Exquemelin's life* See Jack Beeching's introduction to Exquemelin's, *Buccaneers of America*, 18–19.

208   *the principle source*   Beeching, *Buccaneers of America*, 20.

208   *in 1934, M. Vriejman*   Ibid., 19.

209   *What is certain; Johnson's book consistent with other records*   Cordingly, *Seafaring Women*, 80; Cordingly, *Under the Black Flag*, xix.

209   *two academics, P.N. Furbank*   Cordingly, *Under the Black Flag*, xx.

209   *Many, but not all, historians agree with Cordingly on authorship of GHP*   See, for instance, Cordingly, *Under the Black Flag*; Rediker, *Villains of All Nations*; Woodard, *Republic of Pirates*; Dow and Edmonds, *Pirates of the New England Coast*. For the opposing view, see Rogozinski, *Honor among Thieves*.

210   *had extensive first-hand knowledge*   Angus Konstam, *Scourge of the Seas: Buccaneers, Pirates, and Privateers* (New York: Osprey, 2007), 12.

210   *Johnson is widely regarded*   Rediker, *Villains of All Nations*, 180.

210   *the prime source*   Cordingly, *Under the Black Flag*, xx.

210   *Baer's superb four-volume collection*   Baer, *British Piracy in the Golden Age*.

210   *Contemporary newspaper accounts*   In addition to the newspaper accounts Baer reprints, I draw on newspaper accounts I've collected as well.

210   *Jameson's collection*   Jameson, *Privateering and Piracy in the Colonial Period*.

INDEX

at Sea Act, 143–44; pardons and, 146–47; pirate code and, 52–81 (*see also* pirate code); pirate justice and, 126–32; predatory captains and, 16–17; property forfeiture and, 145; Second Reform Act and, 24; separation of powers and, 24–26, 34–37; trial by jury and, 145; unanimity and, 60–61, 74–79
legitimacy: Jolly Roger and, 102–6; torture and, 117–18, 131; trademark practices and, 192–93
lesbians, 172–74
Leviathan (Hobbes), 46
Lewis, William, 129–30
Libbey, Joseph, 153
lips, 112
literacy, 207
lobbying, 191, 252n191/9
local knowledge, 186–87, 252n186/16
L'Ollonais, François, 113–14
longitude, 84, 233n84/21
Lord of the Flies (Golding), 6, 195
Low, Edward, 201; articles of agreement of, 100; conscription and, 137–39, 141, 153, 244n137n31; cruelty of, 99; democracy and, 30; hatred of New England, 123–24; Jolly Roger and, 100–101; pay scales and, 68; pirate code and, 60–61, 64, 72, 229n64/4; torture and, 109, 112, 123–25, 132–33
Lowther, George, 60–61, 90, 113, 201, 229n64/4
Lyne, Philip, 201

Macrae, James, 99–100
Madagascar, 8, 13, 198
Madeira, 133
Madison, James, 3, 27–28, 34, 46, 47, 179, 221n25/32, 222n28/20
madness, 119–21, 132, 240n119/17
management: Americans with Disabilities Act (ADA) and, 187–88; Blackbeard approach to, 176–93; CEO issues and, 180, 182; dishonesty and, 180–81; free riding and, 181; government regulation dangers and, 186–88; greed and, 177–79; incentive-alignment problems and, 180–85; large firms, 184; legal changes and, 189–91; local knowledge and, 186–87, 252n186/16; open-mindedness and, 188–89; organizational motivations and, 180–85; prejudicial barriers and, 188–89; profitability factors and, 183–85; small firms, 184–85; trademark practices and, 192–93; workers' democracy and, 182–85
Mandeville, Bernard, 177
man-o'-wars, 11, 82, 102, 123–24
markets: Council of Trade and Plantations and, 9, 125, 147; interlopers and, 96, 99; invisible hook and, 1–6; Treaty of Tordesillas and, 8; Treaty of Utrecht and, 96
marooning, 62–65, 78, 100
Martinique, 92, 123
Massachusetts, 162
Massachusetts Bay Colony, 25
massacres, 98–99
matelotage, 174–75
Mather, Cotton, 12, 211
Mathews, Thomas, 198
Mauritius, 33
Maynard, Robert, 119, 123, 196
media: ads of force and, 149–54, 190, 195, 247n150/6; pirate press and, 21, 134, 153; torture and, 113, 117–20, 124. *See also* specific newspaper
Mercedes-Benz, 111
merchant ships, 12, 202, 207; autocracy and, 39–41; democracy and, 33; fines for not fighting, 147; Guarda Costa and, 96–98, 102, 104; organization of, 15; pirate democracy and, 37–38, 225n37/21,33, 225n38/2,20; pirate justice and, 126–31; predatory captains and, 15–21, 40–41; principal-agent problem and, 38–44; punishments

210, 238n210/26; economic motivations for, 11–14 (*see also* economics); ethnic demographics of, 8–9;
fleets of, 10; Golden Age of, 96,
197–203, 210; to go on the account
and, 83; historical paradoxes of,
194–96; homosexuality and, 171–
75; increased costs of, 202; invisible
hook and, 1–6, 177–78; Jolly Roger
and, 82–106; journals of, 207–8;
land-based colleagues of, 203–4;
land bases of, 9–10; legal issues
and, 13–14 (*see also* legal issues);
literacy of, 207; "Lord" title and, 23,
223n33/8; madness and, 119–21,
132, 240n119/17; management
techniques of, 176–93; maritime
backgrounds of, 10–11; modern,
203–5, 254n203/5; as outlaws, 6–8;
pardons and, 146–47; pay scales
and, 68–69 (*see also* wages); peaceful nature of, 88–94; popular image
of, 11, 107; population demographics of, 9, 127, 201–2; Prize Act and,
11–12; rational choice theory and,
5–6; retirement and, 14; ruses to
gain close proximity to prey, 86–87;
self-interest of, 2–6 (*see also* self-
interest); signaling and, 94–106; as
social revolutionaries, 11; stinkpots
and, 87–88; time of war and, 12;
torture and, 107–133; treasure and,
11–14 (*see also* treasure); unemployment and, 12–13; various
names for, 1, 6–7
pirate society, 19; age demographics for,
10–11; autocracy and, 39–41; black
pirates and, 156–71; British law and,
26; crew size and, 9–10; Declaration
of Independence and, 22; democracy
and, 23–44 (*see also* democracy);
egalitarianism of, 68–70; floating
societies and, 203; homosexuality
and, 171–75, 250n171/17,18,32;
incentive-alignment problems and,
180–85; ownership structure of, 20;

reputation of, 45–46; romantic por-
trayal of, 11; state capitalism and,
11; tolerance and, 21–22; unanimity and, 60–61, 74–79; violence
of, 45
Pirates of the Caribbean (Disney film series), xiii, 193. *See also* Sparrow,
Captain Jack
Plato, 67
Political Economy and Freedom, 186
polity: conflict prevention and, 52–53,
57, 63–70, 81; crew size and, 9–10;
democracy and, 23–44. *See also* pirate code
Ponant, Le (ship), 204
pooling equilibrium, 95, 102–5
Portuguese, 9, 124
Prince, Lawrence, 130
Princess Bride (film), 192
principal-agent problem, 38–44,
226n38/28
Pringle, Patrick, 41, 66, 152, 211
privateers, 6; government backing of, 7;
loss of commissions and, 12; Prize
Act and, 11–12; time of war and,
12; unemployment and, 12–13;
wages and, 12–13; War of the Spanish Succession and, 11
private property rights, 53–55
Prize Act, 11–12
profits. *See* wages
property forfeiture, 145
public goods, 56–57, 71–74
Public Record Office, 210
Puerto Rico, 103
punishments: amputations, 151, 196;
cat-o'-nine tails, 39; common
knowledge and, 78; conflict prevention and, 52–53, 57, 63–70, 81;
dying speeches and, 210; fines, 48;
flogging, 32, 35, 39, 112, 113, 128,
223n32/7; governance and, 48–49;
imprisonment, 48; keel-hauling, 64;
marooning, 62–65, 78, 100; Moses's
Law and, 65; pirate code and, 63–
70; predatory captains and, 15–19;